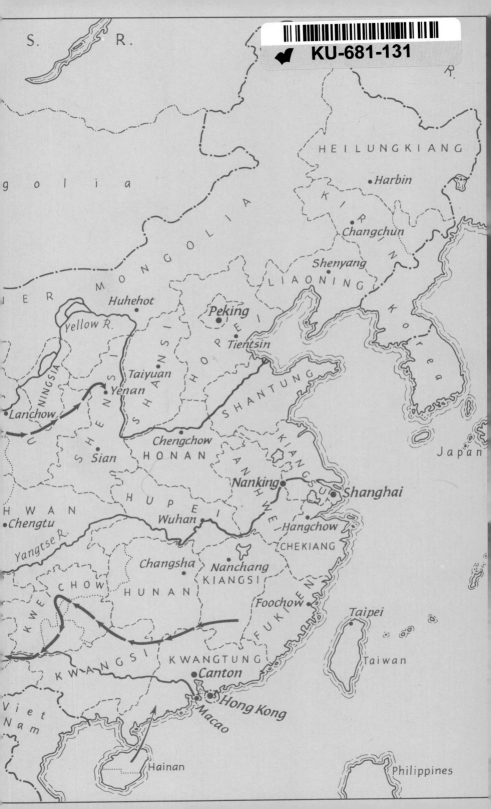

PETER WORSLEY

INSIDE CHINA

Allen Lane

ALLEN LANE
PENGUIN BOOKS LTD
17 GROSVENOR GARDENS, LONDON SW1

ISBN 0 7139 0796 7

Printed in Great Britain
by Ebenezer Baylis and Son Ltd
The Trinity Press
Worcester, and London

Designed by Gerald Cinamon

To Shelagh and Bill, who care –
and worry –
about these things too

9   Acknowledgements

11 Introduction

1

27 1. Capitalist Asia

55 2. Across the Bridge

85 3. Stability and Revolt

2

125 4. The Heart of the Matter: the Communes

171 5. The Cities

193 6. Conclusion

251 Appendix: Prices of Some Everyday Goods

261 Suggestions for Further Reading

265 Index

ACKNOWLEDGEMENTS

My thanks are due to Ronald Frankenberg and John Gittings for reading through the manuscript, to Teodor Shanin, Ruth First, Paul Kelemen, and my daughters, Deborah and Julia, for reading parts of it, and to John Gardner, who helped me with his sinological expertise. Anselm Strauss and Huw Beynon also read the MS for me. The conventional remark that they are not to be taken as endorsing what is said here, while true, is coupled with a hope that I have taken their perspicacious criticisms into account. Apart from myself, the person who has suffered most from the consequences of trying to write a book at high pressure in the midst of an already busy existence has been Marjorie Gray. I apologize to her for having shredded up so many of her beautifully-typed drafts with a pair of scissors, a desecration she has borne with a patience worthy of Griselda herself, and thank her, too, for her shrewd, critical, and most un-Griselda-like comments. Switching to the part of Hawkeye, she read the proofs equally efficiently.

Passages from the following books or articles are reproduced in the text:

Robert Conquest, *The Great Terror*, Macmillan, 1968 (p. 479), Penguin, 1971.

W. J. Hail, *Tseng Kuo-Fan and the Taiping Rebellion*, Yale University Press, 1927 (p. 297).

Régis Debray, *Revolution in the Revolution?*, Penguin, 1968 (pp. 41–3, 51).

Basil Davidson, *The Liberation of Guiné*, Penguin, 1969 (p. 55).

Jan Myrdal and Gun Kessle, *China: The Revolution Continued*, Pelican, 1973 (pp. 103–4).

David and Isobel Crook, *The First Years of Yangyi Commune*, Routledge and Kegan Paul, 1966 (pp. 28–9).

Maria Antonietta Macchiochi, *Daily Life in Revolutionary China*, Monthly Review Press, 1972 (pp. 26–7, 306).

Robin Jenkins, *Exploitation*, Paladin, 1971 (p. 18).

Reinhard Bendix, *Nation Building and Citizenship*, Anchor Books, 1964 (p. 1).

Hans-Jürgen Krahl, 'Class Struggle in Czechoslovakia', *New Left Review*, 53, 1968 (p. 6).

Talcott Parsons, *Essays in Sociological Theory*, Free Press, 1964 (p. 333).

Jack Belden, *China Shakes the World*, Penguin, 1970 (pp. 248–9).

José Yglesias, *In the Fist of the Revolution*, Penguin, 1970 (p. 307).

C. Bettelheim, J. Charrière, and H. Marchisio, *La Construction de la Socialisme en Chine*, Maspéro, Petite Collection, No. 22, 1972.

The section on Hong Kong owes much to the books listed below:

I. C. Jarvie and J. Agassi (eds.), *Hong Kong: a Society in Transition*, Routledge and Kegan Paul, 1969; especially the Introduction, Chapter V, 'Hong Kong under Japanese Occupation' by Henry J. Lethbridge, pp. 77–127; Chapter VIII, by Judith Agassi, 'Housing the Needy', pp. 247–56; and Chapter IX, by L. F. Goodstadt, 'Urban Housing in Hong Kong 1945–63' (pp. 257–98).

Keith Hopkins (ed.), *Hong Kong: The Industrial Colony*, Oxford University Press, Hong Kong, 1971; especially the author's Preface; Chapter IV, by Nicholas C. Owen, 'Economic Policy in Hong Kong', pp. 142–206; Chapter V, by Joe England, 'Industrial Relations in Hong Kong', pp. 207–59; and Chapter VII, by Keith Hopkins, 'Housing the Poor', pp. 271–335.

Hong Kong: Britain's Last Colonial Stronghold, Association for Radical East Asian Studies, vol. 2, No. 1, 1972 (6 Endsleigh Street, London, WC1).

Peter Worsley
Manchester, October 1973

INTRODUCTION

In 1972, a quarter of a century and two generations after Liberation, the Western world discovered China. A new star had risen in the East, not a Christian one this time, but a Communist one, first sighted through Western instruments by Edgar Snow in the nineteen-thirties, but for long periods since obscured. The star that symbolized the birth of Christ carried with it dreams, hopes and aspirations: the promise of a new ideal world. Christianity also called on men to change their behaviour on this earth, to live Christian lives in the here-and-now. But though life on earth was to be informed by Christian values, the real and ultimate reward for the true believer and the liver of a devout life was to be union with Christ, not on the earth, but after his passage through this vale of tears. The new world of the red star, on the other hand, is firmly located on the Chinese earth, and the people who have brought it into our field of vision have been peasants, not princely wise men.

Speaking about China round the country to very different kinds of groups, I have encountered a profound, almost sub-terranean sense of the great import of what has happened in

China. People want to find out because they feel that China
represents two things: the revival of hope in the possibility of
change, including very radical and revolutionary change, and a
fascinated interest in the detailed lineaments of the Chinese
model itself. Normally, in a country like Britain, parochialism
and torpor, disillusion and non-involvement, are the routine
conditions of political life: most people only become involved
when they are sucked along, as if by some power exerted from
the moon, by the ebbs and flows of the electoral tides, a
rhythm which asserts itself where even quite major events do
not. Thus, the single most important post-war event affecting
the lives of everyone – entry into the European Community –
was preceded not by the advertised 'Great Debate', but by a
resounding tinkle. Entry into the E.E.C. was not approved of
by two-thirds of the population, who nevertheless made hardly
any effort to discuss the issue, let alone to translate that
negative lack of enthusiasm into anything remotely resembling
positive opposition.

This kind of inertness stands at the other pole from the
personal commitment, the mass mobilization, and the root-and-
branch politicization of Chinese society. But it would clearly be
far too facile to characterize people in Britain as politically
inert, particularly after the miners' strike of 1972. They are only
inert in relation to certain styles of politics and certain kinds of
issues. In terms of electoral politics, for example, the best-
known study of 'affluent' workers (who might reasonably have
been expected to turn Conservative) showed that 80 per cent of
them were actually Labour voters, and that they were solidly
involved in trade union activities at the local branch level, even
if they were uninterested in the affairs of the union at national
level, except insofar as wage-negotiations were concerned. And
whilst parochialism and chauvinism are still very much alive,
and Enoch Powell could command no less than two-thirds of
the vote at the 1972 Conservative Party Conference, he was
outpaced by a Conservative Leader who dealt the death-
blow to Britain's traditional nationalism.

Lack of enthusiasm for the issues and positions of conventional politics, or even for what is new in Europe, does not
mean that all interest in change is dead. What is striking,
indeed, in the new wave of enthusiasm for China is that it is
not, as is usual and understandable, a response mainly among
the young; older people are equally interested. Nor is it an
interest confined to the Left. Even people of impeccably

reactionary credentials seem fascinated by the spectacle of a society which embodies all they are opposed to. I have not the slightest doubt that, were they ever to be confronted, on their own doorstep, with the reality rather than the image, they would reach for their guns. At present, however, it is a remote curiosity that may be comfortably indulged. There is another level of interest, too: one of admiration for the Chinese achievement on the part of people long-saturated with a mixture of the Protestant work-ethic and a more modern, technocratic and science-based ethos of industrial and 'business-like' efficiency. At an almost invisible level, there is, I suspect, a deeper, residual, unextinguished, sneaking, but very repressed and virtually lost hankering human feeling that the cardinal communist virtues – equality and fraternity – *are* virtues after all, and virtues that we lack. At the lowest level of all, interest in China is simply a guilty *frisson* engendered by contact with what is taboo, or a form of cultural voyeurism analogous to older, and equally racist, fascination with the weird, the exotic, and the bizarre customs of savages.

The mix, in this new-found enthusiasm, is indeed mixed. But it is the middle ground that is the most receptive: those critically-minded, politically and socially conscious people who are usually to be found in local cause-groups, often left of centre or liberal (though sneeringly dismissed by the hard Left as 'liberals', *tout court*), and usually highly educated, middle class, professional and young. The Left proper is a different kettle of fish. Firstly, the men who staff the classical 'Labour movement' evince little interest. Their international perspectives are similar to their domestic ones. Most of them are not too concerned about 'foreign affairs'. Those who are will doggedly take up the defence of their opposite numbers, their fellow underdogs, in the shape of the peasants of Vietnam, but they are less consumed with a burning interest in the positive socialist alternative that has actually been built up in China. When they do hear about it, they are deeply interested, but Labour Party and trade union leaderships do nothing to draw their attention to China, and pro-Russian 'hard-liners' from the Communist Party work hard to restrict exposure to dangerous Maoist heresies. The ex-Communists (and it has been said that the 'ex-Communist Party' is the biggest party in Britain), like the activistic Left in the shape of the Marxist sects dedicated to establishing the nuclei of future revolutionary parties, are, in some ways, the most interesting of all in their reaction to

China, for they are often the most hostile. For these are people who have no need to listen since they already know. They know that I saw the wrong things, or that what I saw was only an elaborate façade, a led-by-the-nose procession through a carefully contrived and selected presentation of reality, designed for political innocents, but no more real than the villages which Potemkin tarted up for Catherine the Great and filled with jolly, bucolic and prosperous peasants. Now I would not discount for a minute the possibility that I was shown either what the Chinese wanted me to see or that I saw only what I wanted to see. (In fact, as I discuss below, I went with more than my quota of suspicions, reservations and doubts, and some hostilities, the greater proportion of which I found to be sad misconceptions.) As one who came into political existence at the time of Stalingrad, when the Russians, instead of collapsing or taking the opportunity of the Nazi invasion to revolt, proceeded to defend their country with their cardboard tanks, it was not difficult to distrust either the factual reliability or the interpretations of the enemies of the U.S.S.R. It was therefore seductively easy to reject virtually anything emanating from such sources and to be taken in, too, by cunning deceptions. In 1944, for example, Henry Wallace, then Vice-President of the United States, visited a labour-camp at Kolyma in the Arctic, with Owen Lattimore, who described it as 'a combination of the Hudson Bay Company and the T.V.A.' (Robert Conquest, *The Great Terror*.) A later writer was to describe it as *Gulag Archipelago*.

Some people reacted to this kind of cosmic deception, and to shame at their own gullibility, by withdrawal and by a misanthropic rejection not so much of hope as of striving, and a loss of all confidence in the possibility of what I still like to call 'progress'. For my part, I resolved to steer clear of 'gods' of any kind, secular or otherwise, and to keep my eyes specially peeled for missionaries. I am suspicious, too, of all claims to possess 'the truth', and of assumptions that having the right ideas necessarily ensures that governments, groups or individuals who hold them will try or be able to put them into effect. Being sensitive to the likelihood of being duped, and conscious of my personal proclivities to react and express myself forcefully rather than in nuances, I nevertheless confess that I have since found it infuriating to be told that I did not see what I did see, or that if I did see it I had the wrong glasses on and have not interpreted it correctly, often by people who had not merely not visited China, but have never read a single book about that country. I have more often, though, been saddened rather than infuriated by the responses of friends otherwise generous and humane in their personal relations and reactions, who have nevertheless become so cynical about human capacity to create new structural societal arrangements – even less to change 'human nature' – that they deny flatly what they hear about China or interpret it within the Procrustean categories to which they have become habituated. I have had a distinguished scholar assure me that it could not be true that prostitution was wiped out within a few years of Liberation, since this was counter to 'all we know' about human nature. Such wisdom was abundantly proffered to me before I went, too. I was informed by eminent experts in Hong Kong that I would find the private plots flourishing like bay trees in China, since 'economic rationality' had begun to reassert itself once more, following the recession of the 'madness' of the Cultural Revolution. Sheer lack of imagination prevents other people from grasping the Chinese fact.

Right-wing disbelief and hostility or unreadiness to think or listen one can comprehend. It is part and parcel of a more or less coherent lengthy process of ideological socialization (which we generally think of as something that only occurs in societies where the State or the Party overtly sets out to bring this about). It results in self-images, self-interest and class-interests entirely antithetical to those which pervade Chinese society. But the Left-wing case is different. It is not so much that they are consciously or unconsciously defending vested interests, material or immaterial, certainly not those of property and status, or of Establishment modes of thought. Their problem is not that they defend what they have got; it is that they have lost that which was once their greatest pride, for they are descendants of the generation for whom God first failed – not the God who died in the nineteenth century, but the twentieth century hope of all revolutionaries – the U.S.S.R. The original generation who directly experienced this modern equivalent of Satan's Fall, experienced it, naturally, much more vividly than the contemporary anti-Soviet Left. The young, however, have never lost their innocence or faith; they absorbed the idea that the U.S.S.R. is lost beyond redemption with their mother's milk, and see that country now as having moved from 'socialism in one country' to 'coexistence' with capitalism, and from ambiguous, vacillating or neutral postures vis-à-vis revolution in the rest of the world to conscious collaboration to contain it. The internal source of this external degeneration is the emergence, within the U.S.S.R., of a new kind of class system variously labelled (using categories they find ready-made) 'State capitalism', a 'degenerated workers' State', etc., etc., according to whatever particular variety of Marxism the sect espouses. But why should they condemn a China which has carried through not just one, but two Communist revolutions in less than a quarter of a century? There are two reasons: firstly, that the society evolved in China does not accord with their utopian model of a perfected Communist society. Secondly, they hold that the structural defects of the system of 'democratic centralism' are such – particularly the domination of civil society by the Party – that it is bound to degenerate just as the Soviet Union did. It is this notion of 'bound to' that is crucial in this mode of thought, for it implies a determinism which parallels quite non-Marxist deterministic theories of revolution.

What links all of them is a 'natural history' conception of revolutions as necessarily passing through a sequence of stages of development, or, with Crane Brinton, as having a common 'anatomy'. Trotsky, on the other hand, still the fountain-head for Marxist critics of the U.S.S.R., did not regard the degeneration of the Soviet Union as something which inevitably happens to *any* revolution. For him, it was due to quite specific circumstances peculiar to the historical situation in Russia at the time when the first Communist State emerged: a situation of post-war dislocation on a catastrophic scale, of later civil war and famine, of massive destruction, consequent shortages and competition for scarce goods, and the physical death of the majority of the politically-conscious workers. To keep order and to regulate demand, the bureaucracy did not hesitate to use any methods it found to work, including both the use of random and focused violence as a normal 'administrative' procedure, and the systematic rewarding of those who conformed. Yet in the imagery Trotsky uses to label the successive phases of this process, the deterministic language of natural history again asserts itself, not so much drawn from the realms of biology or geology, as from the experience of the French Revolution, a revolution which took place more than 125 years earlier in quite different historical and cultural conditions. The phases are nevertheless depicted as being similar in both revolutions. The revolution comes to power. It polarizes into radical and moderate wings. The radicals push through the Terror against the class enemy, initially, but then against the moderates, who in their turn react by using their own weapons against them. Having eaten its children, the Revolution undergoes a 'Thermidorean' reaction (named after the French revolutionary month of Thermidor, when Napoleon took power by using a 'whiff of grapeshot'). Further change then ceases; the Revolution is stabilized and consolidated. Like most such schemas, this one is very loose, since, for instance, Stalin's 'Thermidor' did not involve using the Army, but gaining control of the Party and then using the secret police and the camps.

Because the structure of the Chinese Communist Party is still based on Leninist 'democratic centralism', and because the relationship of Party to Government and civil society is also Leninist, many Marxists thought that the Chinese Party would go the way of the Soviet one, and Chinese respect for Stalin did little to disabuse them of this notion. Instead, the Chinese launched a second revolution, directed precisely against the existing tendency, which the critics had correctly pointed to, for Government and Party to become separated agencies, separated out from the rest of society as privileged, powerful, and specialized élites at the top of a stratified society. The critics, in this respect, were more perceptive and honest than those supporters of everything the Chinese do, who failed to mention these tendencies before the Cultural Revolution made it 'legitimate' to do so. As far as the postulated inevitable emergence of internal stratification is concerned, however, the critics have been, in the end, sadly wrong. Hence, rather desperately, they point instead to some aspects of Chinese foreign policy, particularly Chinese support for the government of Sri Lanka (Ceylon) in its suppression of the rebellion in that country in 1971 and Chinese support for Pakistan in the Bangla Desh war. These they see as first signs of a Chinese degeneration into a non-revolutionary Power, more concerned with maintaining itself in the face of a hostile world than with spreading and supporting world revolution. Anything positive that one has to report about China, then, evokes a characteristic grimace that I have learned to anticipate: a look of bored *déjà vu* (the drooping eyelid), world-weary and cynical, accompanied by a glare of hostility (the curled lip). Deep in their hearts, I believe, some of these people basically *want* the Chinese Revolution to fail, for they are purists of a religious rather than a this-worldly kind who seek a Utopia not to be found on this earth and a revolutionary perfection not to be found amongst mortal men. For them, the *rapprochement* with Nixon is the first formal step towards a Chinese latter-day version of Soviet co-existence. The only Marxist microsects which do not subscribe in any degree to this type of thinking are the self-styled 'Maoist' groups, who (despite their protestations to the contrary) mechanically attempt to transfer to the industrialized capitalist world not only political strategies and tactics, but even styles of language rooted deeply in Chinese historical experience and Chinese cultural history, in a way that seems to have embarrassed even Chou En-Lai.

Such debates within the conventicles of the Far Left might seem unimportant were it not that in historical hindsight the doings of such tiny groups have often proved to have been pregnant foreshadowing of major historical movements. Thus the early disputes amongst a handful of founders of the First International, among them Karl Marx; the obscure proceedings of a group of black anti-colonialists in Manchester in 1945, among them Nkrumah and Kenyatta; the sectarian animosities in Russian *émigré* political circles in pre-1914 Switzerland, among them Lenin and Trotsky; or the discussions of the handful of men in Shanghai in 1922, among them Mao Tse-Tung, were barely noticed when they occurred, except by security police. I relish, in particular, the apocryphal story of the gentleman seated in a café in Switzerland in the era of World War I, who scornfully dismissed the Russian revolutionaries at a nearby table with the remark: 'And who can possibly believe that these people will ever amount to anything? Take that fellow Bronstein, there, for example!' He was talking about Trotsky.

Nevertheless, I find it hard to believe that the wave of the future is represented by sects which seem as incapable of coming to terms with Chinese experience as they are of grasping the historical and cultural specificities of their own society.

Rather, it is the much more theoretically sophisticated, but more politically and humanly responsive centre-left who have responded to China. Not that the appeal of China to them is necessarily political in the narrow sense of the word. They are interested in China because it seems to them to represent *possibility*: a fundamental transformation of the entire range of human social relationships in a society that, starting from

scratch, has tackled health, housing, education, industrialization and agricultural modernization in radically new ways.
Indeed, some of them expect too much from China. The
experience of a semi-colonialized peasant country emerging
from a hundred years of turmoil – during the dying decades of
the last imperial dynasty; the birth of the Republic; the ghastly
inter-war decades of warlordism; the repression launched by
Chiang Kai-Shek; the Japanese invasion; through World
War II and the final campaigns leading to Liberation; not to
mention the stormy post-Liberation years during which a new
kind of modern society has been built – is an experience
scarcely easily transferred to the industrialized West, even if
the principles underlying this transformation certainly are.

*

Books on China are now beginning to appear at a fair rate.
Anyone who adds to their number, especially a non-specialist,
must justify doing so to more people than himself. The obvious
justification lies on the 'demand' side: people are avid to know
about China. On the 'supply' side, accounts based on direct
experience of that country are few and far between. A number
of reports of visits such as I made, usually short and usually by
several hands, do exist, though none of any substance by
visitors from Britain. I wanted to attempt something different
from any of these often excellent accounts: to communicate
what I felt and experienced in a way that, far from pretending
to a spurious 'objectivity', would be personal, but which
would make my personal biases explicit rather than hidden.
Moreover, I find too many existing reports uncritical, while the
'outside' writings of the China-watchers are, in general, so
distorted by political animosity as to diminish their value
as assemblages of factual material. What follows, then, com-
bines direct reporting with prior and subsequent reflection.
What has happened in China is so important to me that I am
impelled to tell the story as I see it. In particular, I hope that
people will think about China anthropologically, i.e., against a
background of their own society, seeing the one against the
other. For China is not simply a strange and exotic phenomenon out of Asia: it requires us to answer some fundamental questions about our own way of life and about quite
basic assumptions and institutions. It challenges what is often
taken to be self-evidently natural or superior. As Alvin
Gouldner has recently observed, 'comparative' perspectives

only lead us to ask how societies *differ* at a given point in time. They do not ask the question the older evolutionists used to ask: whether there is a 'logic' in history such that, over time, one form of society will replace another.

If the direct relevance of the Chinese model for developed countries is not immediately apparent, China obviously constitutes a more directly-imitable model for underdeveloped societies. The rise of this great country, too, alters the world balance of forces. These changes in the underdeveloped world, will, in their turn, have direct and indirect effects even on the developed countries – in the most dramatic possible form if other underdeveloped countries were to go communist. To speak of the industrialized world must also involve the Soviet Union and its dependencies, since the strengthening of China on the international scene must sharpen the Soviet dilemma of opting for association with existing and future underdeveloped communist countries, or closer alignment with industrialized, but capitalist powers.

Apart from these over-arching political issues, the Chinese attempt to transform human values and personal relationships at the level of everyday life, to challenge assumptions that certain modes of behaviour are 'naturally' entailed under conditions of industrial or city life (in particular, that developed societies are inevitably stratified societies and that some form of class system, even if not capitalist, is inevitable; that the subsidiary position of women, too, is a by-product of biology rather than of man-made cultural arrangements; that the attractiveness of material gratifications must, in the end, reassert itself or require an intolerable apparatus of policing), all these and others are the kinds of questions that will inform this book, even if, inevitably, it raises questions more often than it provides answers. Nor can the Chinese experiment be said to answer definitively all the culturally and historically specific, and therefore in many ways quite different, kinds of problems that face us.

I write, however, as no specialist Sinologist, and without being able to speak or write the language, though my specialist colleagues hearten me by their insistence that virtually everything one could wish to read of contemporary published Chinese documentary material is available in English. I intend, too, to stick very close to the facts as I perceived them, and very close, too, to the 'grass-roots'. I saw nothing of administration above the level of the enterprise, such as the hospital, factory or the commune. I do not know the inside story of what happened to Lin Piao; and this must be one of the few recent book-length accounts which does not contain an interview with Chou En-Lai. I wanted, instead, to try to get the feel of life as it is lived by ordinary people. Though my visit was extremely short – three weeks only – I did possess professional experience which allowed me to make a very intensive use of my time, and certain technical advantages, too. Thus I was not part of a group, which necessarily inhibits following up one's personal interests. I was often free to question people for two or more hours after the formal reception and tour around the commune or school. I had the full-time services of a marvellous interpreter, Mr Kou Shu-Pao, whose services were supplemented by those of local interpreters in each place we visited (since differences of dialect are as great as those between Spanish and Swedish). I also had the advantage of a car and chauffeur. Hence I was able to accumulate over two hundred pages of notes and some five hundred photographs. Knowing the kinds of issues I was interested in, from my advance reading, I could concentrate my efforts.

In any case, time is not linear. What one sees, does and thinks are functions of what one has seen, done and thought before. And since my return I have steeped myself in the literature. One reworks experience and, as with seeing a film, continues to wrestle with the significance of what one saw. In a sense, one's whole lifetime is brought to bear on the present. I have not tried to restrict myself, therefore, to direct reportage, but have written into this text the results of a lot of thinking and reading which has at times made me recall vividly the con-nection of the word 'agonizing' with the Greek: of wrestling with one's soul.

To use mixed scientific imagery, the visit which forms the nucleus of this book was therefore a catalyst; it brought about not only a crystallization of past experience and thought, but also a new detonation and distillation of thinking. Part 1 of this book, therefore, is a description: I try to stick closely to what I saw. In Part 2, I endeavour to relate this limited exposure to China to reports of other people's experience of that country, to confront problems it has generated for me against the back-ground of the debates in the literature on China, on socialism and on development generally. Because of these latter concerns, I have prefaced my account of China with vignettes of those parts of capitalist Asia I visited *en route*.

Professionally, because I have always been interested in the Third World and in development, I came to China with a relevant background, even if not that of the specialist on China. I had studied Tanzanian rural development schemes; co-operatives amongst Indians and Metis in northern Saskatchewan in Canada, and had lived for a year among aborigines on a settlement in Northern Australia. More importantly, I had come to this field of study in the first place, not so much because of abstract intellectual professional interest, but because, like millions of other people, I had been swept up by World War II to find myself serving with African troops in East Africa, then in India. After the war, I experienced, as an employee rather than a researcher, what it feels like to be on the receiving end of a development scheme – the débâcle of all 'development' débâcles – the Groundnut Scheme in Tanganyika. My professional formation, then, was an integral part of this life-experience of development, non-development, and change on a world scale. Moreover, my political commitments led me early to involvement in anti-colonial causes and left-wing movements. Hence I was one of a generation reared on Edgar Snow's *Red Star Over China*, published in 1937, and still the best general background book for understanding China. I never doubted thereafter that the Chinese Communists, then confined to Shensi, would sooner or later come to power. Hence I followed events in China closely, reading the early editions of Mao's military and political writings when they were only available in obscure pamphlets issued by left-wing publishing houses. I have tried to keep abreast of what has happened within China since, and to relate Chinese development to development (to be strict, to non-development) in the rest of the Third World.

The opportunity of visiting China had always eluded me, however, and seemed remote. It is not easy even now: access is still difficult, and the expense high. The biggest component in the cost was suddenly and miraculously resolved for me when I found myself invited to act in an academic capacity at the University of Hong Kong. This would enable me also to stop off at other countries briefly, *en route*, but it seemed idiotic to arrive at the front door of China itself and not to knock and ask to be admitted. So I wrote to the Chinese Embassy (then

Legation) in November 1971. Knowing the work-styles of Communist bureaucracies in Eastern Europe, I did not expect any answer, and did not get one – not even an acknowledgement. But I also knew the application would be grinding through the machine somewhere. Five months later, I still had not heard anything, so I wrote saying that if they were unable to allow me to enter, so be it, but that if it were still possible I would soon need to make arrangements. To my astonishment, following five months of silence, I received a telephone call back saying 'Yes'. I had to pay my way, and so I was not able to utilize the full two months period allowed by the visa. This sudden development was probably a very minor consequence of Nixon's visit to Peking, which had occurred only the month before. Possibly, too, the sheer volume of applications for visits had caused the delay (now no doubt intensified, since as many as 500,000 American tourists are said to be clamouring for entry to China after Nixon's visit). It could equally have been that it had taken five months to examine my political credentials. Knowing the primacy given to the political in China, I felt flattered that they could assign to me the status of a 'friend', a wide category, but in this case plainly something different from the 'instrumental' visits by businessmen or the large numbers of overseas Chinese visitors from Hong Kong, Singapore, North America, and elsewhere, or from sponsored 'friendship delegations'. Finally, my university reacted so generously by helping with my expenses that I did not have to bankrupt myself, as I had otherwise prepared to do.

1

1

CAPITALIST ASIA

China has been unknown to us for many reasons, one of them China's own severe control of contacts with other countries. This isolation reached its height at the time of the Cultural Revolution, when such Western correspondents as there were were reduced to trying to make sense of what was happening by asking their Japanese colleagues to translate the 'big character' wall-posters for them. In Peking I delicately suggested to an English friend, long resident there, that our misunderstanding of China had not been helped by the difficulties of access created by the Chinese themselves. 'Hell,' he said, sweeping aside my oblique criticism, 'they closed the country down for two years.' But there has always been a lot more traffic than is normally realized. Business went on with the outside world; parties of visitors still came and went, and anyone who wanted to could find out if he made the effort. There are few guide-books to Europe as detailed and informative, for instance, as the superb Nagel *Encyclopaedia-Guide* of 1,504 pages, published in Switzerland in 1968, even though it is largely devoted to the cultural legacy of the past and does not cover all cities and towns. In the U.S.A., scholarly 'Pekinology' has been as well financed as 'Kremlinology' for a long time now in universities and other less academic institutions; large storehouses of information are available in research institutions in Hong Kong, in particular, that nobody ever suggested to me were anything other than Intelligence outfits.

The drying-up of direct communication was by no means mainly the doing of the Chinese. We are now informed, as if it were a matter of great surprise, that explorations of friendship were made towards the United States, both before the final campaigns which resulted in Liberation, and immediately following the accession to power: Mao even offered to go to Washington. (In the end, as was pointed out to me in China, it was Nixon who was obliged, a generation later, to fly to Peking – 'waving the white flag'.) The Chinese approaches were frustrated by the joint efforts of Chiang Kai-Shek and the American 'China Lobby' of financial and business interests who succeeded in imposing their policies of ostracizing China on the American government of the day, and who stimulated a campaign of persecution of all those whom they conceived of as having been responsible for the policies which had 'lost' China. The majority of experts in Washington were removed, leaving only a handful of people with acceptable right-wing views; nor did the search for scapegoats stop with Government servants. The McCarthyite wrath descended, too, on academics and others outside government: scholars like Owen Lattimore, the great specialist on China's historic relations with the peoples of the Eurasian steppelands, were subjected to the most vicious victimization, and many were hounded out of public and academic life. From thenceforward, policy towards China was shaped by people often ill-equipped to understand China, and determined to ostracize and punish her. Millions of dollars were poured into breeding a new generation of 'safe' China-watchers, who inevitably generated research emphasizing China's undoubted difficulties, internal strains, and, for some, the inevitability of her collapse in the not too distant future. So deep was the persecution and the consequent gulf of mis-understanding created that it was only years later, well after the end of the McCarthy era and the Cold War, that a few courageous souls began to lift their heads. The Committee of Concerned Asian Scholars only came into existence in response to the convulsions that racked American society in the 1960s over the war in Vietnam.

Ignorance of China was in very large measure, then, deliberately created in the U.S.A. The false images subsequently generated inevitably suffused the media in the rest of the capitalist world. In a country with an imperialist tradition as lengthy as that of Britain, generations had grown up filled with ideas about the Yellow Peril, about coolies who could live on a handful of rice or the smell of an oil-rag, about opium dens, Dr Fu Manchu, and other such mental lumber. These images were reinforced by the actual experience of servicemen in two World Wars, who saw the brothels, the poverty, the illiteracy and the starvation East of Suez, and who blamed it on the indolence or incompetence of the Easterners themselves. There were other images, too: of an elegant, exotic and 'inscrutable' world governed by mandarins with long nails: of cultured poets, calligraphers and classical scholars, who led lives of ritualized elegance punctuated with tea, ancestor-worship and resort to concubines. Corrupt to a man, and incredibly vicious beneath this cultured veneer, they cut off men's eyelids or sliced them to death without compunction. The poetic China of the past was acceptable and sufficiently distant for the educated West to enjoy it at a distance. Perhaps symbolically, Arthur Waley, the great scholar who made so many classical Chinese writings available to us in English, never actually visited the country whose literature he spent his life studying. The China of his day was not a very attractive place for a cultured scholar who valued the classical virtues of order, peace and harmony. It was, by then, a rapacious and bloody place, the site of wars, rebellions, and what we would now call counter-insurgency. For ordinary people it was a land of unpredictable mass starvation and misery.

The ancient European myths provided a ready-made explanation of all this: it was the outcome of the character of the Chinese people, or of their institutions, this picture of Chinese society being one from which the decisive, and quite non-Chinese, influence of the last hundred years had been mentally expunged: the gunboats, the expeditionary forces, the opium-traders, the 'concessions' and the consuls. Ancient myths, however, needed updating or supplementing. Given this mythological 'infrastructure', more modern anti-Chinese sentiment was regenerated easily enough during the 1950s, when World War III seemed all too likely to break out, and when, whatever the temptations for individual capitalist countries to act in accordance with an ancient habit of formulating their *own* foreign policies, the U.S.A. soon whipped them into line. Hence, despite Britain's recognition of the People's Republic as the legal government, in 1950, at the same time she abstained from supporting China's right to occupy her place in the United Nations and its Security Council instead of Chiang Kai-Shek's rump-régime on Taiwan. In contacts with the 'peace movements' of Eastern European Communist countries, one has become used to hearing the proposition that formal relations between governments do not necessarily reflect the general attitudes of the peoples of those countries. Feelings of friendship between individual workers in either type of country meeting face-to-face are, however, no guarantee of similar friendly feelings towards abstractions like 'the Russians', or that direct experience of the Soviet State will necessarily be pleasant. Workers saturated with nationalism are anything but 'natural internationalists' (by definition), and the attitude of the people of Britain towards the new Communist China turned out to be anything but friendly. No one of any human sensibility had any time left for Chiang Kai-Shek by 1949; he was a failure, and had made his exit in a flurry of squalid shootings of imprisoned revolutionaries on the streets, and in the back of the neck: the dying excesses of an already excessively brutal régime. The Communists, though largely unknown, had no negative image up to that time. They had fought the Japanese when Chiang had not; they had therefore been on our side in World War II, and effectively so. All reports were of their honesty, efficiency and incorruptibility. Within a few weeks, all that was changed, and the heroic Chinese Red Army suddenly became an enemy: slant-eyed little yellow men – a racist stereotype developed so powerfully during the war against Japan, and easily revived and redirected. In a fit of last-ditch imperialist stupidity, the British government sent a warship, the *Amethyst*, deep into China, up the Yangtse River, just reached by the Communist armies, which were poised to move southwards, to 'protect' British nationals in Peking.

Within hours the Press, and mainly the 'popular' Press, was waving flags. It was not difficult, in a country which was the major ally of the U.S.A. and already deeply involved in a Cold War. Two years later, it had become a hot one. British troops found themselves in action, not just against China's Communist neighbour, North Korea, but against a Chinese army. It was to be two decades and one more horrific war later, on China's southern border this time, before the hostility effectively subsided.

Today, we are able to step back a bit and look more dispassionately at what has been happening inside China since the great rupture. So massive is the transformation that we resort to many different frameworks in our efforts at comprehension, and even then we still feel lost. One framework, in some ways the most apposite, is the one we use least, because we know so little about it: the framework of Chinese culture and history. The Chinese themselves, by contrast, constantly compare their present lives with life before 1949, whether under Chiang or the lives the peasants led during the imperial centuries. We tend, naturally, to measure Chinese development, historically, against the yardstick of our own industrial and agricultural revolutions of the eighteenth and nineteenth centuries. We also make more 'contemporary' comparisons between the lives we lead now and those of the people of China. Secondly, we compare China with other *communist* countries, since we know more about the Soviet Union than we do about China, even though the Soviet mode of life, despite its Marxist line of descent, is so different from that of China that the two countries are more at loggerheads with each other than they are with the capitalist world. A third mode of comparison is with other underdeveloped ex-colonial Asian and 'Third World' countries, mainly non-communist. All these modes of comparison have some utility. In one way or another they reflect different facets of the same central problem: the problem of development. When we make historical comparisons with Britain in the eighteenth century, for example, we are not making comparisons between societies at the same point in *chronological* or *synchronic* time; we are making comparisons in *developmental* or *diachronic* time. Such comparisons are so remote, however, that they are of limited analogical value. Britain's transformation from an agrarian to an industrial society was a capitalist transformation, when capitalism was only just taking its modern form. The Chinese transition has been, by contrast, a communist and revolutionary one, where political revolution was the prior condition of industrial break-through, and was achieved by a party with its mass base amongst the peasants and workers. The Chinese transition, indeed, took place within a quite different *world*: after Western imperialism had brought the world into being, for the first time, as a single social system. The Chinese revolution also represented the beginning of the end of the unquestioned supremacy of world-capitalism, a world-order brought into being by imperialism, and particularly British imperialism. It is a dual opposition: the one of time – at opposite ends of the imperialist epoch; the other of direction – along two divergent social paths. China's revolution, that is, has not been a revolution in the most advanced country on earth, as Britain's industrial 'revolution' was, in the formative period of the emergence of world society. Nor is China simply 'industrializing'; she is developing an entirely different human culture, not only unlike, but opposed to the culture of the capitalist world.

Comparison with Soviet development, also communist and not so distant in time, is more meaningful, for revolutions now take place within the context of world society; they are not to be comprehended simply by studying the history and culture of the particular societies within which they occur. All revolutions stand upon the shoulders of their predecessors, and their predecessors, in this epoch of instant cultural transmission, include predecessors abroad. It will never again be possible for such a traumatic and protracted social upheaval as the Mexican Revolution to take place with virtually no reverberations in even adjoining countries. To the extent that earlier revolutions are the only available models, there is almost a built-in tendency to imitate them. But not inevitably so, for later revolutions face special problems of their own, deriving from a particular historical and cultural experience, and develop new modes of solving their problems. Hence the Chinese Revolution *contains* the Soviet Revolution, and goes beyond it.

Indeed, China was able to observe and avoid the mistakes of predecessors, for people and governments learn from the experience of others, not only positively: by borrowing ideas and experience concerning planning, mobilization, organization, etc., but also negatively: what *not* to do. For the Chinese, the crucial negative lesson of the Russian Revolution, the one which they, of all countries, could least afford to imitate, was the strategy of mounting industrialization out of capital accumulated from the exploitation of the peasantry, a policy which drove the Russian peasants into an opposition so strong that only machine-guns made them toe the Party line.

There is one other final framework we can use in looking at China; in many ways the most illuminating measure of her performance: to compare her with other countries which were in similar political and social circumstances at the time of China's Liberation in 1949. The most appropriate comparison is with India, another huge Asian country which achieved its Independence just after China's Liberation, but remained capitalist. India had been more directly subjected to imperialist domination. China, although dominated economically and effectively controlled from the 'concession' enclaves established by the European Powers and Japan on the coast, was never subject to direct colonial-type government over her whole territory, and successive governments always maintained their claim at least to formal sovereignty, even though, *de facto*, the country was near partition and total occupation at the end of the imperial period and during the inter-World-War warlord era. India, too, has been held up as the major example of Western-style development, political, economic and social, in Asia.

The comparison with India, however, was only an intellectual one at the back of my head when I was actually visiting China. Much more vivid was the recent memory of passing through several smaller Asian countries, formally independent, but part of the capitalist world. What is happening in these countries is, in itself, a transformation so striking and profound that it grips the mind. Compounded with exposure to China, it is a contrast so shattering that it still reverberates, and it is a contrast so necessary to any evaluation of what China's very different development signifies for Asia, the Third World generally, or the world as a whole, that it needs describing.

Modern air-travel makes for sudden culture shock, in any case. I am suddenly plunged into one Asian culture after another only days after taking leave of Europe by sampling some of its most typical products: Copenhagen, with its old city, evoking the culture of the early mercantile and colonial epoch of Danish capitalism; the Tivoli Gardens with their Victorian atmosphere of the well-established order of middle-period capitalist society: the lights, the restaurants, the fireworks, and that communal family atmosphere which the German word *bürgerlich* sums up best: the comfortable sense of pleasures shared with others from the respectable middle layers of this prosperous society. By contrast, the French term *bourgeois* has, to foreigners at least, quite other primary resonances: those of capitalist culture – of class antagonism, domination, and political estrangement, rather than shared identity and membership. But 'late-capitalist' seems to be the best label for contemporary Danish culture, whose ability to compete in capitalist markets is based on high quality of design, whether of furniture or of precision-lathes, together with a maximally-developed consumer culture which supplies all wants for cash, including blue movies and pornography, whether for a night out or for home consumption. The city of the innocent mermaid.

Half a day later, Asia. The winding rivers through the deep green give way, as we begin to descend, to actual fields, then houses, then lotus-plants visible to the naked eye. Out of the plane into the steaming heat of Thailand. The first building that meets the eye is the Royal National Military Bank – an appropriate assemblage of epithets to capture the style of the régime – only 'American' was missing.

Bangkok, the 'Venice of the East', sounds very romantic. The canals that thread through the city are, in fact, not very visible, and when they are, are not at all attractive, mostly dirty stretches of water sandwiched in between buildings and roads filled with noisy traffic. On the outskirts of the main city there are more attractive waterways, threading off the traffic-laden Chao Phraya river, with slim-lined water-taxis and water-buses ripping through the water, their long propeller shafts powered by V8 car engines.

The ancient glories are still there: the lofty gold, saffron, ochre and green temples; the Royal Palace; the royal barges, gilt and red; an omnipresent photograph of the current King, descendant of a monarchy whose antiquity, powerlessness, and modern-style accessibility and middle-class respectability re-mind one of the British Royal Family. Apart from anachron-isms like Morocco, monarchies no longer wield power. One soon found out whose writ ran in Thailand when criminals were apprehended, for the military dealt with them in exemplary military style, on the spot where a murder or serious theft had been committed. A garment with a target on it was put over the offender's head, and he was shot. On the very same street, at dawn, one can see the very antithesis of militarism, as the Buddhist monks (in a country where a high proportion of all boys, particularly in the rural areas, spend a few years leading this devout life) walk from house to house, begging their food from the faithful.

The young soldier at the entrance to the Royal Palace evinces no such gentleness. Conscious of the automatic rifle on his shoulder, he throws his weight about by objecting to the quite demure slacks and shoes the Thai lady I am with is wearing.

Bangkok, like most Third World capital cities, has become a 'primate' city. It vibrates with the energy and noise of three million people, most of them struggling simply to make a basic living, the rich to become even richer. A colleague explains the social composition of the work-force: so many per cent working in government employment; so many in private industry, commerce, business, etc. Then a category that seems unexpectedly large when compared to Britain. 'Entertainment workers,' I ask. 'What occupations does that include?' 'Prostitutes, mainly,' he smiles. One does not need to read the census-volumes to see that this is one of Bangkok's biggest industries. In the centre of the city at night, a sizeable proportion of all the women aged less than thirty-five are working in what the neon signs euphemistically declare to be 'massage parlours'. To satisfy the demand from Australian tourists and Chinese businessmen, recruiters scour the up-country villages looking for poor families with pretty daughters to sell. Chieng Mai, the larger interior city notorious in my professional world for the controversy aroused over C.I.A. activities disguised as anthropological research, is another centre providing these and other kinds of 'rest and recreation' for the American B52 bomber crews, who were not visible in Bangkok itself because they were up-country in the bases from which they were bombing Vietnam, and where their Army counterparts were masterminding 'counter-insurgency' in Cambodia and Laos, as well as against the significant guerilla forces in northern Thailand itself.

From Bangkok to Kuala Lumpur, where I stay in yet another hotel once frequented by Somerset Maugham; but whereas the Oriental in Bangkok is now overshadowed by a massive new tower-block wing dwarfing its parent, this one has hardly been touched since he left. Indeed, the whole dowdy city centre seems to belong to the old colonial era. The new suburb of Petaling Jaya, designed on the American plan, with open-plan lawns, bungalow houses, massive supermarkets, and the modern university for the new élite are different. The less well-heeled are not to be seen, except as servants, but their presence is tangible in the form of the sliding metal grilles across the space where the door might be in a cooler climate, which keep them at bay. The new life-style is only physically American, though, for the new élite's orientation to English culture has changed little from colonial days. Their children go to boarding-schools in the U.K. and take English exams. They follow English pop, English ideas and English football. At moments, I remember the atmosphere of colonial Tanganyika in the 1940s – only to be pulled back into the more affluent seventies by a typical hospitable Indian millionaire who wafts me, together with eighty other guests, on a magic carpet of wealth, to a tropical island, where he hires the ferry, the beach and the whole hotel for our delectation. In getting there, I am passed from hand to hand along a network of kin, from one rich family to another.

En route, we visit rubber estates and tin mines, and find that the British presence is not merely a cultural one, but a continuing stake in the country's economic life, despite political independence. For if Somerset Maugham-like plantation managers are not strikingly visible, the plantations are, though managed now in a style characteristic of the modern multinational corporation. They are still enormously profitable, despite shaky world prices, as are the tin mines which begin immediately outside the city and continue for scores of miles, ripping open a landscape reminiscent of misty Chinese paintings. Not many people can be seen at work, though, for the mines are now capital- rather than labour-intensive, using massive dredgers which need only a few skilled men to work them. I meet one of these skilled workers: he is white.

Further up-country, at the side of the road, are the resettlement villages into which the rural Chinese were herded: the 'sea' in which the guerillas of the 1948–54 'Emergency' (only officially ended in 1960) swam so successfully for a while. There they remain, in neat rows, each with a plot of land attached to them, though now without the security towers and perimeter wire that once enclosed them. When this particular 'sea' was drained and canalized, most of the guerilla fish died or were left stranded. In the deep oceans of the jungle, however, a small force is still at large. A nuisance rather than a menace at present, it is led by Chen Ping, who has never surrendered since the end of the Emergency, though he once engaged in abortive peace talks with the authorities, only to slip back into the jungle he knows so well.

He has been reported as seen in Peking, but the Chinese have very carefully refrained from supporting movements of Overseas Chinese in South-East Asia, whether armed or otherwise, lest their kith and kin be denounced as 'unpatriotic' subversive puppets of 'Mainland China', and thus become isolated from their non-Chinese fellow-nationals, as happened in the Emergency. Hence Chinese policy has been to urge local Chinese to seek their future as nationals of their own country.

The border-road to Thailand is still not a healthy journey, but the guerillas are such a minor force that they might almost be in another country for all the attention even the most left-wing people in Malaysia pay to them. No doubt it was equally hard to believe, in China in 1934, that the 20,000 survivors of the Long March who took refuge in remote Yenan, out of the 250,000 who started, would ever be able to take power from a Chiang Kai-Shek backed by the Western powers.

Whether the guerillas in Malaysia represent a possible 'wave of the future' or not, no one should be too keen to bet that Malaysia can continue to knife-edge its way as it does at present. Class-tensions are severe enough in a classically colonial-extractive economy. But, reinforced as they are by ethnic divisions of labour, inequality and exploitation, an extra, and explosive, dimension is added to class-division.

The foreign corporations make quite spectacular profits even from the smaller estates, and funnel the wealth out of Malaysia into London banks. I visited one small – but immensely profitable – estate.

Inside is a small community of rubber-tappers, locked into the estate by virtue of their lack of any saleable alternative skills. These are neither Malays nor Chinese, but Tamils, descendants of men and women who were brought to Malaya from South India a generation or two back, often from the same villages; on present form, their descendants are likely to be still there in the year 2000, for there is no alternative employment for them. They possess neither financial capital nor 'social' capital, their only equipment being the limited education that a wretched primary school and a Hindu temple can provide. Now the survival rate is going up. Children no longer die as they used to. This obscure closed community is, in this respect, a microcosm of the Third World, for the number of jobs available has not increased as fast as the numbers of people seeking them. The policy is to 'share poverty' by spreading the limited amount of work around more people: by cutting the number of trees each worker has to tap. This is a miserable and precarious substitute for the investment of national capital in developing the country's productive forces, and for mobilizing underdeveloped human energy, creativity and potential.

Not all Tamils are locked into plantations, or all Chinese into poverty-stricken resettlement villages. Many have been successful in business and trade outside. Third in terms of economic success are the Malays, in their own country. But, politically at least, they now run their own country. The British colonial administrators, who always admired the simple 'villager' as against the slick townsman, the untutored and 'unspoilt' folk as against the city slickers, made sure that the powers of the rulers of the Malay sultanates, around whom they built their colonial machinery of administration, were well entrenched before they left Malaya. The scions of these aristocratic houses, anglicized in British public schools and universities – of whom Tengku Abdul Rahman, one-time playboy millionaire and architect of the Malaysian Federation, was the most notable example – made sure that the new state was in safe hands: theirs. After Independence, government service became a magnificent field of opportunity for the Malays, and when Singapore, the centre of Chinese population and business, split off to become an independent city-state, the Chinese political threat was further reduced by adding the backward territories and populations of Borneo (Sabah and Sarawak) to Malaya to form 'Malaysia'. Political life thus runs along ethnic lines, and students I spoke with at the University of Kuala Lumpur were understandably obsessed with race relations as their principal field of interest in sociology. Malay weakness in the economy has given rise to a new determination to use *political* power to protect their future, in the form of a new nationalism at home and pan-Islamic internationalism abroad. Domestic Malay nationalism is represented by the building of another University, in which teaching will be in Malay, cheek by jowl with the existing brand-new University of Kuala Lumpur.

Important changes are taking place in the economy. Rubber's share of total exports fell from 38 per cent in 1966 to 27 per cent in 1972. Agriculture still produces a quarter of the gross domestic product, but manufacturing has gone up from 9 per cent to 15 per cent in a decade. Investment in these new areas of the economy is booming. Hence we find overall growth-rates of 4·7 per cent and 5·7 per cent in 1971 and 1972, while the price of rubber was at its lowest for a quarter of a century. Similar developments have taken place in other parts of eastern Asia: in South Korea and Taiwan, and oil now brings in 60 per cent of Indonesia's overseas earnings, half of it going to Japan.

It is ironic, however, that not only the most massive Communist development but also the most dramatic capitalist development in south-eastern Asia today is Chinese: in the two city-states of Singapore and Hong Kong. Much of Malaysia's wealth that does not end up in London flows to Singapore, that island entrepot which British, American and Japanese capital use as their major base of operations in South-East Asia, even more than Hong Kong, whose stability and future are thought to be more problematic. Most of this wealth flows back to the metropoles of Europe, America and Japan. A minority live luxuriously on the wealth retained locally, as the abundance of apartment blocks and villas indicates. The population is again mixed, but this time the Chinese are decidedly in the majority – 75 per cent. They are descendants of immigrants who quit the poorer parts of Southern China, mainly Fukien and Kwangtung, for Nanyang, the lands of opportunity in the south, or for Hong Kong, Hawaii, Indonesia or California, an emigration comparable in scale to that other huge outflow – from Europe – at about the same period, to the U.S.A., Canada, Australia and South Africa.

The whole region, indeed, bears witness to ancient cultural movements in both directions: the roofs of buildings in the Imperial City of Peking resemble architectural styles to be found here, thousands of miles away, much as Gothic churches are to be found from one end of Europe to the other. This recent exodus, however, was only the latest instance of the radiation of Chinese culture outwards into the South-East Asian perimeter surrounding the Chinese heartland. Nor has the traffic always been one way, the penetration of Buddhism into China being the outstanding case. Though trade and religion made for intercourse over the centuries, China never sought to impose her way of life on foreign peoples, as Western imperialism was later to do. Journeys were made to cultural centres outside China from time to time, to acquire what the outside world had to offer, as when the pilgrims Fa Hsien, Hsüan-Chuang and others journeyed to India, to acquire knowledge of Buddhism between the fourth and seventh centuries A.D. But such expeditions were exceptional, and only once in Chinese history was a sustained policy of overseas adventure mounted, during the Ming period, when, just before Columbus and Vasco da Gama, the eunuch Cheng Ho led a series of expeditions to as far away as Africa. It has even been dubiously claimed that he may have reached Australia, for a Chinese image of the god Shou Lao was found beneath the roots of an ancient banyan tree (not indigenous to Australia) in Darwin in 1879. It was probably conveyed there by Indonesians, who sailed down to the coast of Arnhem Land in their *praus* from the Celebes in search of the sea-slugs (*bêche-de-mer*) which eventually found their way to the market in China, where they are prized still. The reason for going to all this trouble originally was that it was believed to be an aphrodisiac. Since in its raw state it looks like a huge penis, one can see how the belief arose. It had no noticeable effects on the Persian lady I shared some with, nor on me.

The Ming expeditions did not last long. Soon, China ceased exploring the outside world. In the next few centuries, a handful of Jesuits might bring with them European religion and science, but they were cautiously handled, and it was their astronomical knowledge they were valued for. Even Matteo Ricci, the great astronomer, had to live for years on the coast at Canton before being allowed to proceed to Peking for the last few years of his life.

Chinese cultural influence on Asia was by no means as pervasive, therefore, as Hinduism or Buddhism, which spread down into the Indonesian archipelago, leaving populations with different religions, specializing in different types of economic activity. Hence Hinduism and Buddhism extend across and beyond present-day state boundaries. Conversely, there are minority populations within the existing polities which, mixed with other populations, have given rise to multi-ethnic, culturally 'plural', societies in which the different ethnic groupings may or may not be physically separated from each other, but are separated socially by language, religion and endogamy. Where religious, ethnic and class antagonisms all coincide, as they tend to for Tamils, Malays and Chinese in Malaysia, you have a degree of 'overlapping' separation in all areas of life, with no cross-cutting or counter-balancing ties or divisions, so that unity is always problematic and tensions always liable to erupt into riot along ethnic lines when times are bad – as happened in Malaya in 1969. And $7\frac{1}{2}$ per cent of the population is unemployed.

Historically, these different communities only met in the market place to do business: to trade, to buy and sell. Today, modern social mobility and communications systems are breaking down even the rigid Hindu caste-system, especially in the cities.

Cultural segregation, in any case, was not always so absolute. The religious practice of the ordinary man was often a 'syncretic' drawing on several religions. In Buddhist temples in Thailand and Sri Lanka (Ceylon), Hindu fertility-shrines and gods – no part of orthodox Buddhism – can be seen to this day. In pre-revolutionary China, too, scholars have insisted, the 'three religions' of Confucianism, Taoism and Buddhism are not to be thought of as three discrete 'churches' or 'denominations', each with its separate body of believers and local congregations, but as *resources* situationally drawn upon by the peasants according to their need: whether for reassurance about their after-life (when Buddhist cosmology might be invoked), or as guides to practical moral conduct (in which sphere Confucianism was the dominant orthodoxy), or to find solutions to everyday problems of illness, poor crops, and the like, where Taoist magical practices would be resorted to. Ordinary folk *used* these different religions differentially; only the more intellectually-minded religious specialists – monks and priests preoccupied with theological systematization – drew sharp boundaries between one religion and another.

We are inclined, too easily, appalled as we are by the abundant evidence of inter-ethnic and inter-cultural hostility, even butchery, to assume that social differences of this kind are always divisive. But religion and trade can unite and link, as well as divide, communities and countries. Indeed, where national and ideological identity coincide, they generate a singularly powerful double solidarity, as the modern yoking of nationalism and Communism has proved. There is no universal rule, then: common religion can override ethnic divisions; common ethnicity or nationality override religious divisions.

Such older traditional identities are under challenge today; side by side with Westernization *à l'Américain* in Singapore (with a small fossil of the British colonial era around Raffles Square) a vibrant South Chinese culture still flourishes that has now disappeared in China itself. The rats scuttle across the slum side-streets near the waterfront as you make your way to where a spectacular Chinese opera is being performed on a stage built across the street. As soon as that performance closes down, the street is taken over for a performance of a different kind: a possession-séance by a spirit-medium. Only a few blocks away, tourists are eyeing the stunningly beautiful prostitutes, dressed in the ultra-latest Western gear, who parade their wares around the open-air café-bars of Bugis Street. There is nothing unusual about public prostitution in Asia – what is less usual is that these 'girls' are men.

For the many thousands who have no Welfare State safety-net to save them, a living has to be made in such unrespectable ways. Crime is a major industry. My friends who live in a cool, elegant, ex-British Army residence high above the city were burgled five times in their first fortnight; security depends on constant patrols by guards equipped with guard-dogs and walkie-talkies; the obtrusive presence of the poor outside penetrates the sacred enclave of the home. But some of the money channelled through Singapore does filter down to more orthodox workers who inhabit the enormous tower-block housing-estates which dominate the skyline. As a technical achievement in mass rehousing these are impressive; visually, too, they are attractive. The only problem must be living in them, bristling as they do with TV antennae, the air rent by a polyglot cacophony of sound in Tamil, Hindi, Malay, Chinese and English from thousands of television sets and transistor radios.

Singapore society is 75 per cent Chinese. But the housing-units are not allocated according to ethnic considerations: Malays, Indians, Chinese and Eurasians are mixed up. As a result, more than five marriages out of every hundred are now inter-ethnic – an important lesson for countries like the U.S.A. where poor ethnic minorities – Blacks, Puerto Ricans, Mexicans – are segregated in ghettoes. Religion, especially Christianity and Islam, is a more serious and persistent barrier than ethni-city, just as caste remains important in regulating who marries whom in the cities of India, though it no longer determines occupation or place of residence, as it once did. Common ethnic identity as 'Chinese' is inevitably splintered under the kaleidoscopic conditions of city life. For 'Chinese' is a label that covers millionaires and beggars, industrial workers and priests, prostitutes and social workers – and however much people may see themselves as 'Chinese' in some situations (especially vis-à-vis non-Chinese), often the people whom they find themselves up against are not Malays, but fellow-Chinese. The gulf between management and worker is every bit as real as that between Bradford mill-owners and the fellow-Yorkshiremen they employ.

The older Chinese culture, in any case, has now to compete

with powerful new rivals, for the mini-skirt is more characteristic of Singapore Chinese culture today than the tatty temples
and stores of old Chinatown. The new models for behaviour
are acquired from transistors and television sets, from the
thousands of tourists, and from direct visits abroad. So many
strange juxtapositions ensue that they no longer seem
extraordinary. But some contrasts still rouse a response, and
some are even obscene. I travel to Hong Kong in the company
of some of Tokyo's *jeunesse dorée*, 'beautiful people' dressed in
super-Carnaby high fashion. Japan Airlines celebrates its
imitation of American jet-culture by offering free champagne.
Down below is the coast of another country experiencing
another side of American culture, the coast of Vietnam, where
the battle of Quang Tri is at its height. Nobody seems very
interested: the champagne is good. For the businessmen
abroad, no doubt, the war is an opportunity to make a killing
of another kind. Others can even eliminate the war from their
perception of Vietnam. I meet an English girl whose holiday
in Saigon was 'spoiled' by the Tet offensive.

Soon we are skimming the rooftops of Kowloon and
descend to Hong Kong. The natural setting is spectacularly
beautiful – the blue harbour, busy with traffic, framed against
the hills. No bigger than Kent or Long Island, most of Hong
Kong's four million people are packed into the city of Victoria
on Hong Kong Island proper and in the city of Kowloon on
the mainland opposite, at over 200,000 to the square mile.
They are governed by a handful of white officials, for Hong
Kong is that strange anachronism: a real colony. Out of a
population of 99 per cent Chinese, there were only three
Chinese in the top Government posts in 1966, and only two
persons in the top four grades of Administrative Officer (both
in the lowest grade). Attitudes, too, are typically colonial.
While I am there, an unprecedented cloudburst results in a
huge mud-slide, like Aberfan; hundreds of 'squatters' in the
ramshackle shanty-towns are overwhelmed and scores are
carried to their deaths. A large luxury apartment block housing
whites, behind the University of Hong Kong, also collapses.
Local Chinese residents are incensed when, next day, the
newspapers carry big headlines about the European deaths but
give quite subsidiary space to the dead squatters. The tower
blocks lining the harbour and the hills in profusion are
impressive evidence of this massive development, for communist development, as we have seen, is not the only

development in Eastern Asia. Rising production and rising productivity through the introduction of more modern technology
and management in larger industrial units has taken place
to some degree, though most of the rise in living standards
has been earned by sweated labour, and inflation has eaten
up a lot of it. Between 1968 and 1973, money wages for
industrial employees increased by an annual 14 per cent, but
only 7 per cent in real terms. There is, nevertheless, an ever-
growing internal market for consumer goods, and some
evidence of declining family size (as in other urbanized parts of
Eastern Asia) in certain demographically significant groups in
terms of age and their location in the inter-generational cycle
of child-bearing.

As in Singapore, the older Chinese culture still persists,
especially on the outer islands and in the villages of the New
Territories. Western anthropologists go there to study the
dying culture of the rural areas in a society where farmers
constitute less than 4 per cent of the population and where the
young men are away manning the local factories or Chinese
restaurants in Lancashire. The older culture has become almost
a tourist spectacle even for the Chinese themselves, who take
the ferry to watch the 'Bun Festival' on Cheung Chau Island
once a year much as we might go to Blackpool illuminations.
To older people, little girls dressed as the Goddess of Mercy
may still convey religious resonances; the ancient sword
rescued from the sea may symbolize the village's past as a
fishing village, and the antics of the Monkey recall traditional
myth and culture. But the young men dressed as gangsters or
firemen hardly do so. For all that the fantastic eye-rolling
dragons, the ear-splitting symbols, gongs and drums resemble
a religious village fête, the floats are sponsored by different
business and community associations. It is still something
fascinating to see, however, and no longer to be seen in China
itself.

Everyday life is very different. The growth of Hong Kong
historically was a function of conditions on the other side of the
border. From the time of the Taiping Rebellion onwards,
floods of people have crossed over whenever conditions inside
China became intolerable. Tens of thousands fled the Japanese
drive into China in 1941, only to find the Colony itself overrun
a year later. Over 10,000 women were raped and over 10,000
Chinese executed. Of the 1,850,000 inhabitants in 1940, only
500,000–600,000 remained by 1945. Little wonder that the

Japanese occupation is spoken of in China in terms reminiscent of those used of the Nazi occupation of Europe. Though Hong Kong was bedecked with Chinese flags when the Japanese surrendered in 1945, colonial rule was rapidly restored and only five collaborators were arrested, despite the wholesale collaboration of businessmen with the Japanese.

By 1947 the population was back to pre-war levels, and in 1948 and 1949 the push of the Communist armies southwards drove more refugees across the border. (By comparison, the later influx of April/May 1962, when natural disasters in Kwangtung Province in China drove some tens of thousands into Hong Kong, was small.)

The real rise in population, in recent years, has come from natural increase. Half the population is under twenty years of age. The influx that did occur was one not only of poor peasants, but also of Shanghai businessmen and industrialists, who brought their capital and even their machinery, rather than let it fall into Communist hands. The economic boom that followed was extraordinary. Foreign capital poured in in the wake of the refugee capital from Shanghai. Today, American investment occupies first place, Japanese second, and British third. The American presence has been visible in other forms, from the use of Hong Kong as a Rest and Recreation centre for tens of thousands of GIs during the Korean and Vietnam Wars to the warships of the Seventh Fleet riding at anchor in the harbour today. The Japanese presence is less military: the electric signs around the harbour of the big electronic and optics firms: Sanyo, Asahi, Nikon, Saiko. Japanese businessmen are busy ransacking the natural resources of Indonesia, Malaysia and the Philippines; some have even proposed a naval 'presence' in the Straits of Malacca that separates Singapore from Sumatra, to protect trade. With the closing down of the traditional trade with China as a result of American and U.N. embargoes in 1950, during the Korean War, Hong Kong turned outwards. Today, it exports more than India and nearly as much as Norway, mainly to the U.S.A., the U.K. and Western Europe. It is ninth in the world as measured by per capita volume of trade; unemployment runs at only around 3 per cent; real wages in manufacturing went up by about two-thirds over a decade; and over a million people were rehoused in 1958–63 alone. In these terms, Hong Kong's performance outstrips every other Asian country except Japan, Singapore included. So impressive is the growth of manufacturing (employing 40 per cent of the population, including half the women) that it is easy to forget that commerce is still the biggest money-spinner, spawning no less than four Stock Exchanges.

Hong Kong, then, is not some petty unit absent-mindedly left out of the dissolution of the British Empire. Rather, the British economy is perilously dependent on Singapore and Hong Kong assets banked in the U.K. which provide half the backing for the British pound. (If Hong Kong and Kuwait were to go, the sterling area would be doomed.) Hence, Britain's firm hold on this Colony, even during an era where her other Asian possessions have been granted independence, for, as Hong Kong is a colony, the British Government makes her deposit 89 per cent of her assets in London, £900m. worth to date. But Britain cannot adopt the strategy of giving Hong Kong 'independence' whilst retaining economic control, since Hong Kong is due to revert to China in 1997. That Hong Kong is part of China is accepted even by the U.K.

Hong Kong is also important at present to China, though foreign trade is not all that important to China overall. Whereas 20 per cent of Britain's Gross National Product is devoted to foreign trade, for China it is only 4 per cent. But China does need to trade, and gets nearly half of her foreign exchange from using Hong Kong's world-wide banking and related facilities as her base for international trade, and from trade and investments inside the Colony itself. Today, half of the food the Hong Kong workers eat (at less than local farmers' prices), a quarter of Hong Kong's water supply, and half the clothing and a fifth of the textile yarn fabrics and made-up articles which supply Hong Kong's main industry, textiles, come from China.

Hong Kong's prosperity also depends on textile-workers who work the longest working day and the longest working week in South-East Asia, and the looms are in action twenty-four hours a day, 360 days a year. The vast majority of firms, too, are still tiny family or partnership affairs, employing little capital and only simple tools and machines. One in every four workers is an under-age child; there are no legal restrictions on hours of work for men, no minimum wages, and trade unionism is very weak. Even the larger American firms, which practise 'scientific management' at home, seem to forget it in Hong Kong. They are, according to one authority on labour relations, 'authoritarian' and 'production-oriented', and pay their workers flat-rates rather than piece-rates. Establishing branch-plants in Hong Kong pays off: though wages rose by 100 per cent between 1958 and 1968, so did productivity; the share of labour in the proceeds of manufacturing industry therefore *declined* between 1960 and 1967.

The Government spends 1 per cent of its budget on the social welfare of four million people – three times as much is spent on the few thousand students at the two universities. A working party in 1967 described social security provisions as 'conspicuous by their almost total absence', even by Asian standards. Apart from those in Public Service, a local expert remarks, 'it is broadly true to say that workers in Hong Kong had no old age pensions, no medical insurance, little protection against loss of earnings due to sickness, no unemployment benefits, and no guaranteed redundancy payments. Female workers have not been entitled to maternity benefits. As the Financial Secretary [of the Hong Kong Government] said when presenting the 1969 Budget, the Government has been "more concerned with the creation of wealth than with its distribution". Firms expect to get the capital they invest returned in five years, and many in two or three.

The more fortunate are better treated. With profit tax at only 12½ per cent until 1966 (now 15 per cent, but only on unincorporated businesses over 7,000 Hong Kong dollars) and with income tax at 15 per cent (and *declining* for very high incomes), the entrepreneur is certainly encouraged. Some improvements have benefited ordinary people also. As in most countries, modern medical advances have been striking: infant mortality was halved in ten years, and T.B. deaths reduced by nearly two-thirds. But there are still at least 50,000 heroin users (perhaps as many as one in twenty of the population), 12,000–13,000 recorded T.B. cases every year, and the average industrial wage in 1971 was 300 Hong Kong dollars per month – less than £250 a year.

What these figures mean in human terms can be better seen by visiting the squatter shanty-towns and the 'resettlement blocks'. From the late 1940s onwards, homeless people threw up ramshackle encampments of bamboo, canvas, corrugated iron, old packing-cases and whatever they could get their hands on. They were at the mercy of fires, typhoons, disease and gangsters.

Such settlements spread wherever space was available: up hillsides, on vacant lots. They are still there – and the people,

pigs, chickens, dogs, shops and 'cottage industry' workshops
which make up these crazy-quilt communities. The smelly open
drains, full of rubbish, are used as lavatories by those who find
the one tub supplied by Government for every hundred people
inadequate or not attractive enough to use. Water is also carried
in pipes to taps, each one of which supplies five hundred people.
The meandering paths are sometimes cemented over: Government provides the cement, the people the labour. These are
improvements over the early settlements, and the people
themselves, now earning incomes from steady jobs no different
from those of people in permanent housing, have often banded
together to improve their own situation. One settlement I
saw had electricity provided from a generator paid for by
money raised by the residents, organized by the shopkeeper.
Many can undoubtedly afford better housing, and improve
their present homes. But there is not enough better accommodation to move to. So there are still 300,000–400,000
squatters, despite a massive rehousing programme which
began in the early fifties. Between 1962 and 1966 alone, more
than a fifth of the metropolitan population were compulsorily
evicted, but by 1968 there were still more people in squatter
settlements (443,000) than there had been in 1954 (250,000).
(In Kuala Lumpur and Djakarta, one-quarter of the population
lives in such settlements.)

The Government was driven to start rehousing by a series
of fires in squatter settlements in the early 1950s which left
100,000 homeless. Fire-lanes were then driven through the
settlements, like so many afforestation-zones, rendering even
more people homeless. The answer the authorities came up
with was massive multi-storey blocks, not, as in Singapore,
units of several rooms including a kitchen, but soulless
barracks in which people were crammed not even at the legal
minimum space-ration of 35 sq. ft. per person, but at 24 sq. ft.
per person, 'twice the area of a grave' as one authority has
put it. As late as 1968, 350,000 people on these estates had even
less than this. These densities are ten times greater than the
maxima on British housing estates, and eight times greater
than similar estates in Latin America.

In the squatter settlements people are exposed to rain,
typhoons and mosquitoes. But they are also open to the air
and the sunlight, and people generally have more room than
the inhabitants of either the overcrowded private tenements or
the rehoused residents of the public resettlement blocks.

Squatter housing was certainly more tolerable than the appalling tenements from which these people came. Nearly all the older tenements have now come down, but there are still one and a half million people crowded into every nook and cranny of the newer private housing, spilling over onto the roofs, crammed into corridors and verandahs. At night, the noise of thousands of *mah jong* pieces clack-clacking on thousands of boards in the tenements down below can be heard from the geographically and socially higher levels of hilly Hong Kong Island. Hope is poured into gambling as suppressed violence is into the bloodthirsty 'Mandarin' sword-fighting films. The better-off, like their European counterparts, have self-contained flats of several rooms, with their own toilet and kitchen, their television sets, fridges and phones. But one-third of those in private housing have less space than the miserable minima set as long ago as 1935; one-third do not live in rooms, but in cubicles built by dividing up rooms; one-half share toilets, cooking and washing space. 300,000 work in 'domestic' rooms. You can still see women putting together plastic holly for happy Christmases in Britain for fifteen to twenty cents an hour. Fifty hours of this a week will bring in about sixty new pence.

A not untypical cubicle, housing a couple and their children, was seven feet by nine, formed by partitions running off an access corridor, with the use of a tap shared with other cubicle-dwellers and a cooking bench with eleven kerosene stoves on it. For this, they pay 25 Hong Kong dollars per month. Some have not even this: 'cocklofts' are built in the space below the ceiling. Others have only 'bed-spaces' on shared bunks six feet by three feet wide. Their worldly goods are stored beneath the bunks, and covered with wire.

The squatter settlements were first occupied by people fleeing from these private tenements, who were then forcibly rehoused once more. Small as the space-ration was, children were only counted as 'half' persons, and relatives were allowed on top of this. When children married, they brought their spouses to live with them; then babies came along. A dozen people in these ten feet by twelve feet rooms is nothing unusual.

The resettlement estates average 44,000 people, in twenty massive blocks. The sheer noise rising from so many human beings in such a small area is staggering. Half of the housing is still the oldest 'Mark I' type. Mark IV, the 1969 model, is the first to meet W.H.O. minimum standards. A balcony runs round the outside of each of the six or seven floors, giving access to the 120 sq. ft. rooms (often shared by more than one family) which face outwards. They are built of concrete and breeze-blocks, have no water or lavatories inside the rooms, and no electricity fitments are provided. Cooking is done on the narrow balcony, which also serves as a children's playground and as a place where adults try to breathe some cooler air in the steamy heat intensified by the warmth of packed human bodies. Water has to be brought from a central area on each floor, where the lavatories are also to be found – open trenches automatically flushed every quarter of an hour. Human life here is about as close as one can get to the life of a battery hen. To make it minimally tolerable, crazy festoons of wiring run all over the buildings to carry electricity to run rice-cookers and radios, or even televisions, fridges and phones for some. Fans are no luxury in this soaking heat, where vehicles have two or three to keep the air moving. On the roof-tops, gangs of lively kids acquire little more than the three Rs in classes run in shifts by charitable organizations, mainly missions of every denomination under the sun. The spaces between the buildings are not available for the residents' own use but are filled with dozens of hawkers' stalls, selling food and other necessities, their canvas and tin roofs covered with rubbish heaved over the balconies.

Little can be done to improve the old blocks; they can only be pulled down, thus increasing the housing problem. The newer ones are better, and the latest housing for better-paid workers more so. But even this latter only provides 35 sq. ft. for each person, and all reflect a bureaucratic approach that fits people to rooms rather than rooms to families. Even the newest housing provides 'standard' rooms for eight adults, when two thirds of squatter families have less than five persons. In essence, this is *colonial* housing, where people's wants are not considered because people have no voice. 'Hong Kong,' a leading lawyer reminds us, 'is not a democracy. . . . Power, both administrative and executive, is in the hands of civil servants who are in the main primarily responsible, through the Governor, to the United Kingdom. The people of Hong Kong can neither appoint these public servants to office nor remove them. . . .' 'Unofficial' members, appointed, not elected, are only 'consulted'. They include the Managing Directors of the biggest firms – Jardine Matheson (whose prosperity was originally based on the opium trade); Butterfield & Swire; and the Chairman of the Hong Kong and Shanghai Banking Corporation. Less than 1 per cent of the 10 per cent of the population entitled to vote representatives onto the (party-elected) *Urban* Council bother to do so, since it has been described by one of its members as 'an advisory group whose advice nobody takes'.

Cheap labour makes Hong Kong attractive to others than businessmen. For the tourist stopping off on his world tour, it is a magnificent opportunity for a duty-free shopping spree for Japanese cameras and hi-fi. The city, with its tower-blocks spread across the beautiful harbour, looks reassuringly enough like Vancouver, New York, San Francisco or Sydney. Familiar, too, are the pleasure-beaches, the quaint English trams and buses, and the thousands of cars climbing the dizzy hairpin bends of the Island up to the cooler regions where the white and the rich live, amongst their gardens, their schools and their University. Here one can even find specimens of the Guards-and-debs jet-set.

Hong Kong, then, is a marvellous place – if you are rich. Living at the Hilton, at someone else's expense (not my usual wont), I had a wonderful time. If I had stayed in a squatter settlement, and not had at my disposal as much money for my weekly expenditure as most people earned in several months, it would have been different.

Hi-fi sets and cameras are not the only kinds of consumer goods as readily and cheaply available. There are special attractions not so available at home, like the army of 22,000 call-girls, hostesses, bar-girls and just straight prostitutes stocking the brothels and bars, the latest in a succession of generations who have ministered to the wants of British, Japanese and American servicemen, where every taste, including copulation by (and with) children can be catered for. The tourist is not likely to run across the less attractive inhabitants of Suzy Wong's world: the gangsters who, I was told, stop you, knife in hand, demanding to 'see red'. Red is the colour of the Hong Kong 100-dollar bill. If you do not produce it, your assailant will satisfy his need to see red another way – with the sight of your blood. If you only have, say, fifty dollars, the (perhaps apocryphal) story goes, you are asked which arm you would like it in. (One speculates about the in-between amounts.)

Criminality in other forms flourishes amongst those professionally employed to stop crime. While the going is good,

the police – as recent scandals involving British senior officers
have indicated – line their pockets at every level of the service,
with bribes from gangsters, businessmen and anyone who
wants anything at all done, in a spirit of *après nous le déluge*. It
is not that these men are corrupt: it is that Hong Kong society
is corrupt as a whole.

Poverty, luxury and vice are common enough elsewhere.
Here they have an extra exotic flavour. The floating restaurants
of Aberdeen, and the 'flower girls' in their lantern-bedecked
floating brothels, are only a small part of the community of
thousands who live, die and give birth on sampans. To the
visitor, the beach where the Japanese received the British
surrender is simply a pleasure beach (like Changi, the notorious
prison-camp at Singapore).

Local people are aware that Hong Kong could be taken
easily by People's China, and that the police and military are
only there to keep internal order, not to defend the colony.
No one expects any such invasion, though, for China intends
to get Hong Kong back as she will get Taiwan back – by
negotiation. Hence the major sign of China's presence in
Hong Kong is the huge Bank of China (its Chinese lion
matched by the British lion a few yards further down the road,
outside the Hong Kong and Shanghai Bank). One of over a
dozen banks controlled by China, hard by the Hilton, the
Bank of China towers over the greensward where British
expatriates play cricket.

In 1966, the atmosphere was not so sporting. There were
riots over increased ferry prices, and, in the next year, the
Cultural Revolution inside China spilled over into Hong Kong
in the shape of much more political riots. These were firmly
repressed, and did not seem to evoke unambiguous backing
from Peking. In nearby Macao, Portugal's oldest colony and
contemporary centre of gold-trading and gambling, the outcome was different. Portugal, incapable of holding down her
African colonies, could not even keep her grip on Macao.
The Portuguese Governor was brought to his knees and
signed an agreement which left the local millionaires who
represent People's China effectively in control of what is still
constitutionally part of Portugal.

The people who fled to Singapore or Canada when the 1967
riots broke out were soon back, though some of their capital
stayed in Singapore, which has become the dollar financial
capital for Southern Asia. People go on living, some struggling

to survive; others captured by consumerism, without much thought of a morrow which will inevitably mean reintegration with China. Only a handful, like the left-wing students, ask what the future will hold for them and for others when that day comes, for their skills and experience will scarcely equip them for life in People's China. In general, the problem of adaptation will be less of a problem for younger people: the diminishing but still powerful anti-Communist population, from Kuomintang supporters of Chiang Kai-Shek to their business partners, and some of the more recent escapees who swim across from the mainland, will no doubt move on once more.

The majority of their fellows pursue the unquestioned Western style of life which television holds up for their admiration. Pop music, cars, girls, and their future business careers preoccupy them more than China. The posters of the Christian societies in a University full of *Chinese* students seem to symbolize this cultural marginality.

There is no doubt that revolutionary China will absorb Hong Kong as efficiently as she did when she took over similar cities like Shanghai and Canton. Back in 1949, it was necessary, I read at the time, to train the People's Liberation Army soldiers, overwhelmingly peasants who had never lived in the city, how to use the things of the city, such as tramcars, by building bamboo 'mock-ups'. Since then, a generation has emerged which has built a whole urban-industrial sector.

A few of the students I met had been across the border to visit relatives in their home-villages in Kwangtung Province. I found their descriptions more credible than the accounts given to me by the 'China-watchers', that mixed, strange population of academics, spies, journalists, and intelligence personnel, who monitor life inside China and produce masses of material ranging from propaganda to useful records of Chinese provincial radio stations.

Almost imperceptibly, the time has come to leave this Oriental offshoot of the West, where I am able to watch Newcastle United play Santos. As on other days, I take the regular commuter train from Kowloon Station to the New Territories. We pass through Lion Rock Tunnel into the ever more thinly-populated rural areas.

But today I do not get off at the station for the Chinese University. I am going further. At station after station people get out; the carriage is nearly empty. Suddenly, we are there, at

Lo Wu, the border station. With about as much fuss as arriving at a country station, I go through the British passport control and am crossing the famous bridge. I look back and see the monitoring radar station high on the hill beamed into China. I look ahead, and see the Red Flag, a few People's Liberation Army men in olive green, and hear the strains of the *Internationale* issuing from the loudspeakers. In that couple of hundred yards, one crosses much more than a river.

2

ACROSS THE BRIDGE

The strains of the *Internationale* and the presence of P.L.A. (People's Liberation Army) soldiers remind you that you are entering a country where political power was won by the Communist Party in armed revolutionary struggle. In Europe, Communism has also come to symbolize bureaucracy and rigid control. I therefore expected to be subjected to punctilious and suspicious inspection at the Chinese customs. The inspector said something I didn't catch, so I prepared to open my cases, anticipating total disarrangement. I asked him to repeat his remark: 'The Customs inspection is over,' he said. But I did have to register my camera and watch, plus imported film, and had to change my money into Chinese *Renminbi* (People's Currency, the basic unit of which is the *yuan* – 'dollar' – which exchanges at just under six *yuan* to the pound sterling, and is divided into 100 *fen* – 'cents'). The Chinese dollar was thus equivalent to 17p, but I was to discover that it would buy very much more than 17p would in Britain.

Each visitor or party then proceeds to an airy and comfortable room where he and his interpreter work out an itinerary. The interpreter assigned to me, Kou Shu-Pao, who was to stay with me throughout my visit, was pleasant, efficient, and had excellent English which he had learned from Chinese teachers at Nanking University. I had been given no clear notion of costs at all by the Chinese Embassy in London, a disturbing uncertainty since I never knew what I would have to pay until, late in my tour, a bill was presented for a ludicrously small amount.

I had expected to see people in great masses, working away in a state of high mobilization, urged on by bugles and loud-speakers: the kind of scene that I had seen in a film in the fifties showing *millions* of people working on the Huai River Dam. Such scenes can indeed be seen today, but only on massive construction sites, such as the project not far from Peking, where thousands of city folk, including civil servants, go out on their weekends off to help with the work.

What I did see when I looked out from the vine-covered balcony of the modern white reception building was the exact opposite: a quiet rural scene, with a few red flags here and there against the green mountainous background, some Hong Kong Chinese from the train walking over to the bus station with their bundles, *en route* to their natal villages elsewhere in Kwangtung. Then came a crocodile of children, on their way home from school, a red flag at their head, some with Red Guard armbands, and singing, not too vigorously, at the end of a day's school, under a broiling sun. It was a scene of deep peace. I have not the slightest doubt that had I been there during the Cultural Revolution, peace would hardly have been my dominant impression, but this sense of calm was to remain with me throughout the stay. One has the sense that the Chinese feel that they have *arrived*, and that their revolution has been consolidated. Not that their revolution is over, or that the 'heroic' period has given way to staid routine, for the achievements of the original revolution – the Liberation of 1949 – have been constantly extended, expanded, and eventually – in 1966–7 – gave rise to what was virtually a second revolution, the 'Great Proletarian Cultural Revolution'. The convulsions of that latest revolution have now subsided but the consolidation has been no conservative 'settling-down'.

In fact, there has never been a period of comfortable coasting along, ever since 1949. In less than a quarter of a century, China has gone through a series of changes, each one of which would have been major happenings in most other countries.

For several years after 1949, China tackled the formidable task of dismantling and replacing the former political and administrative apparatus, and the neutralization of opposition; the process of rebuilding 'civil society': of establishing an elementary infrastructure of food-supply; of reconstructing a road and railway system devastated over decades by war and the corrupt inefficiency of the warlords and Chiang Kai-Shek; the beginnings of a school-system and a health service; the revival of agriculture and industry. This period of economic reconstruction and the establishment of an effective political organization lasted until about 1953.

Then the Chinese took stock, and were able to think not just about survival and revival, but about creating socialism. Revolution is not just a matter of seizing power – itself a complex enough operation: this is merely the first step. Nor is it a matter of transforming some abstraction called 'society'; it involves changing *people*, or, more accurately, people changing themselves, and society, in the process. A revolution is, indeed, a series of emergences, not an event, and in China, a process without end, because China has not experienced the fate of most post-revolutionary societies: that it is not the State which 'withers away', as Marx had it, but the revolution.

The Chinese leadership never allowed the loss of revolutionary *élan* to occur. As early as 1950, when military operations were still going on in some parts of the mainland and on Hainan Island, new laws on marriage reform, agrarian reform and on trade unions were put into operation. Nor did the enemies of the Revolution allow China any respite. In 1950, the Korean War began; within a short time, American armies had reached the border of Manchuria, and General MacArthur was talking of dropping atomic bombs on China's main industrial bases.

Only five years later, in 1958, the 'Great Leap Forward' was launched. In the West, only the excesses and the failures (abundant enough) were reported. Few noticed or, if they did notice, understood, the import of the beginning of a new mode of life: the establishment of the People's Communes in the countryside, where most of China's population lives.

Hard on the heels of this upheaval, and threatening the all too delicate balance of the new social order, came three quite disastrous years from 1959 to 1961, when natural calamities, both floods and drought, brought the countryside to the edge of disaster. Before 1949, millions would have starved. Now, nobody did. A quite different disaster, right in the middle of this, was man-made rather than natural: the withdrawal of Soviet assistance. Overnight, Soviet technicians and advisers left the country, taking with them the blueprints of the 300 industrial plants they had agreed to provide between 1953 and 1967, half of which remained uncompleted or uncommenced.

The major outcomes were the emergence of a new military threat on the northern borders, the political rejection of the Soviet model which was to mature in the form of the Cultural Revolution, and the development of a policy of self-reliance. The Russian withdrawal, the Chinese now say, was the best thing that ever happened to us. We had to do it ourselves. But it was an anxious period, especially since, all this time, the Vietnam War was becoming more vicious and threatening on China's southern borders.

Neither the Chinese leadership, nor the outside world, then, has ever allowed the Chinese Revolution a breathing space of more than a few years at a time. And yet the atmosphere, today, is one of confidence and calm. People work hard, sometimes, by Western standards, appallingly hard. I saw a pedicab driver load up at the station with a monstrous pile of bags and cases, then with three passengers. But it is not Stakhanovite overtime, or Western speed-up. They work hard, but it is a solid eight-hour day, six days a week, fifty-two weeks a year (with public holidays). They are still poor, but they know that the only way they will get out of their poverty is by hard work.

*

Having arranged an itinerary, every item of which was later fulfilled, we move onto the first major city, Canton, a few hours inland by rail. The carriages and engine are Chinese-made, huge and solid, and the service runs to the dot. Crossing a big bridge over a tributary of the Pearl River, windows are pulled down, and I am asked not to take pictures: the only time, apart from at airports, that I received such a request. Otherwise, I took anything, anywhere, as long as people did not mind being photographed.

Kwangtung is tropical: sugar-cane, lychee trees, bamboo, tapioca, banana trees, pawpaws, all flourish along the margins of the irrigated rice-fields. It is green, beautiful and rich country. The hilly outcrops stand out dry and infertile, but many of them are covered with young trees, mainly eucalypts and pines, which a Canadian doctor I travel with remembers first seeing as young shoots in the great afforestation campaign of the 1960s when $2\frac{1}{2}$ million trees were planted. The village forts stand out like the towers of English churches, reminders of an era which only ended twenty-five years ago, when defence of the village against one despoiler after another was a basic consideration.

We arrive at Canton. Like Shanghai, it is a monument to Western imperialism, from the days when it began to grow as a result of the opium-trade forced on China. The Chinese Emperors, for centuries, had channelled most external sea-trade through this and other ports, well away from the capital. The barbarian traders were confined to a ghetto in Canton, and allowed there for part of the year only. The stage was soon reached, however, when the trade had become so enormous (£11m worth at Canton by 1828) that the profits on opium exported to that city from India, the heart of the British Empire, covered not only the cost of the tea purchased from China (over £8m worth in the same year), but also the cost of the cotton goods imported into India from Lancashire (Britain having destroyed India's indigenous textile-industry). From the point of view of governments, this was an equally satisfactory commerce, for the revenue from the opium trade covered a considerable part of the costs of administering India, whilst at home the duty paid on tea imported into Britain contributed as much as 10 per cent of all government revenue.

The barbarians were not going to let trade of that importance slip from their grasp, no matter how many edicts banning the importing of opium the Chinese Emperors might promulgate (the first in 1729, then again in 1796 and 1800). By mid-century, the trade had created at least ten million addicts in China.

The last major effort to stop it led to the first major Western intrusion into China. On 10 March 1839, the famous 'patriotic Commissioner', Lin Tse-Hsu, arrived in Canton charged with suppressing the opium trade. He wasted no time, and is duly celebrated in China today for his courage in burning the chests of opium and confining the traders to the comfort of their own quarters. The result was inevitable: the First Opium War: 10,000 troops arrived from India to blockade Canton. Today, the ancient guns that were used in vain to fire on the invaders have been re-installed along the Pearl River waterfront of Shamian Island, as a monument to men like Lin, who first resisted Western imperialism. Hundreds of people now stroll under the trees in the 'concession' formerly reserved for foreigners, and read the inscriptions on the guns, while their children clamber over these great mementoes.

Driving through the streets, I am reminded strongly of a more recent colonial era I knew myself. The open-fronted shops look like India or Malaya. The topees worn here (as in Vietnam) are colonial hangovers. The avenues of trees look French. My camera broke down the minute I arrived, so I was taken to a shop which seemed devoid of anything to sell. The principal business was obviously taking portraits and developing customers' reels. It reminded me of Indian shops in Nairobi in World War II. People flocked around to see this curiosity, a visitor from Europe with some expensive gadget that didn't work. I have to record that my Russian camera broke down four times, with different illnesses each time (though I am assured they are normally excellent machines). Not once did anyone take the opportunity to make the slightest anti-Russian remark, except, I am ashamed to say, myself, in a moment of extreme frustration (it broke down as I entered the 'Forbidden City').

Most of the shops looked bare and ill-maintained, as compared, say, to Chinese stores in small towns in Malaysia. There were comparatively few large buildings (unlike Shanghai, later), and, apart from the tall towers of the complex where the famous Trade Fairs take place every year and the splendid new bridge across the Pearl River, little sign of major modern building. The apartment blocks, too, looked run-down, and much of the housing looked like candidates for demolition (which will probably be their fate). Little transport was to be seen other than the olive-green trucks, the buses, and thousands of bicycles. At night, the streets are illuminated by weak lamps, well-spaced. The effect is eerie, with ghostly cyclists, many without lights, silently gliding through the shadows.

I was not very impressed. The people were adequately, but plainly, dressed in shirt and trousers, men and women not very dissimilarly, with few varieties of shades of grey, light blue and dark blue. They all looked healthy enough and as attractive as healthy people anywhere. But the contrast to the dollies of Hong Kong, who make even the dedicated followers of Carnaby Street fashion look positively dowdy, was staggering. The only concession to 'fashion' one can speak of is a minor variation between one pigtail or two, slight differences in length, or the replacement of a rubber band by a piece of coloured thread. Older women tended to wear their hair bobbed.

We arrive at a large hotel built in Stalinesque baroque style, not my favourite architecture. Its interior fittings are equally solid, and, to British eyes, poor in design and aesthetic appeal. The epithets in my notebooks are jaundiced: 'execrable design', 'tasteless', 'bilious', 'style twenty years out of date', 'poor quality'; fittings were broken and cracked, cementing 'poor', furniture 'very heavy'. Just as I kept underestimating the ages of people in China, especially older women, who are remarkably well-preserved as compared with their Western sisters, I kept overestimating the age of buildings and furnishings by as much as two decades. The Russian stylistic influence – itself strongly Victorian or 1930s 'Art Deco' at best – has been laid on top of the predominantly colonial legacy of the 1930s and 1940s.

We immediately go to the famous 'Five-storey Pagoda', dating from 1380 and rebuilt in 1686, in a leafy park overlooking the city. My guidebook details the wonderful things I will see among the historical exhibits on display here, for it is now a museum.

Some good things there are, plus a few appalling pieces of 'socialist realism' depicting revolutionary incidents. But the displays listed in the guidebook have been completely changed. Many of the famous items have been transferred to Peking's national museum, I am told. I am to discover that since the Cultural Revolution many museums are closed completely; the displays are being reorganized so as to present a sharper political line.

Since our guide, a sweet girl, is less knowledgeable about Chinese history than I am, and appears simply to have learned her lines by rote (heavily larded with political comments), I feel irritated at having to sit through it all. We look down into the courtyard where the Krupp guns remind us of the imperialist era, across the beautiful park, past the Sun Yat-Sen Monument and the fine sports stadium to the city. I cannot help observing 'So you have a pollution problem, too!', a remark which elicits the (correct) observation that (a) it is nothing like as bad as in the West, (b) they are working hard to eliminate it. Later, I read that no less than 100 industrial establishments in Peking alone had installed pollution-control devices in the last six months, including the printing-house of the main newspaper, the *People's Daily*, which has converted a storeroom into a smoke-control facility.

There is little of historical interest in such colonial cities, except from the colonial period itself (notably in the building where Mao gave his famous lectures at the Peasant Movement Institute). So I determine to make up that deficiency by maximizing my exploration of the present. We go to the Cultural Park I'd glimpsed from the car. Mr Kou insists on escorting me, together with the local interpreter who is provided everywhere we go (partly owing to dialect differences, and partly because of his local contacts and knowledge). I am reluctant to bother them in the evenings, and think of going on my own, but there is very little one can do without the language (I could only read two characters: those for 'men's lavatory'). Far from being impeded by an interpreter, the visitor gains immensely by being able to converse (indirectly) and have things read for him.

We go by car. Gates are specially flung open, and I have the unpleasant feeling of being a privileged tourist come to observe the workers on their evening out. That is exactly what they are doing, thousands of them amongst the trees and the lights. The first thing we see is a stage performance of excerpts from revolutionary operas such as *The Red Lantern* (set in the time of the anti-Japanese struggle), and dances of the minority peoples (Mongolian and other 'peoples of the grasslands', the Korean minority, and Tibetans are among those very commonly represented), and other dances, all with a strong political content, very colourful, well-executed and enthusiastically received by the crowd of over 2,000. The performers are local worker-amateurs. In two large halls, basketball and (of course) table-tennis contests are taking place. We sit, embarrassingly, on what would be the 'trainer's bench' in English football, and are clapped in and out. The sense of being a conducted voyeur begins to be dissolved by the enthusiasm of the welcome.

There are soft drinks and ice-cream (served by women wearing masks over their mouths), and a sweet stall, but all very simple and doing little business. There were no expensive restaurants, as in the Tivoli Gardens. By European standards, there isn't really much to do. There was a 'Big Wheel', a television screen and a theatre, none in operation. Two main attractions would be quite absent at home. The first is an art exhibition, nearly all by ordinary workers. Contemporary Chinese art displays a most curious association of different kinds of medium with different kinds of subject-matter. Painters are still producing the most magnificent water-colours of Nature, with misty mountains, swirling rivers, trees and bamboos in the style we think of as quintessentially Chinese. Huge reproductions in this style adorn hotel lobbies. There is a difference, however: beneath the great mountain, crossing the river at the foot of the painting, is a tiny detachment of soldiers and a small patch of red flag. Oil-painting is a European medium, and largely acquired from the U.S.S.R.: hence the typical oil (like the sculpture) is banal, didactic, naturalistic 'socialist realism', representing heroic workers or soldiers. These are said to be very popular. Finally, there is a whole range of techniques, including paper-cuts, wood-cuts and other popular styles, which derive neither from the 'high art' styles of China's past nor from Europe. By far the most exciting, vigorous and most varied in style are the paintings by peasants and workers which reminded me of Douanier Rousseau or Grandma Moses and other 'primitives'. The themes are equally political: scenes of production mainly, but they were exciting, full of the vigour of rural life, sharply felt and realized. Unfortunately, it is usually the more 'professional' and rhetorical art that gets seen abroad.

We are taken to the most crowded hall in the Park: an exhibition of products of Chinese industry. Mao Tse-Tung's emphasis on military power and political mobilization is well-enough known: everyone is familiar with the aphorism 'Power grows out of the barrel of a gun'. They are also aware of the strong Chinese emphasis on 'moral' incentives, and on ideological conviction as major sources of revolutionary energy. But they are less aware that Mao, being a Marxist, has always paid the closest attention to economic factors, and has insisted that, to maintain the confidence of the masses, they must experience socialism as something which materially improves their lives. Maoism is thus no simple *Realpolitik*, no idealistic voluntarism, no mere economistic 'materialism', either. It is a synthesis of all three – the three modes of motivation, interestingly enough – 'moral', 'coercive' and 'remunerative' – that the sociologist Etzioni uses as the basis of his typology of kinds of authority-system.

The hall, and its counterparts in other cities, contains the latest goods, mainly consumer goods: shoes, kitchen equipment, clothing, musical instruments, canned foods, medicines, furniture; as well as more specialized things: jade-carvings and other works of art, embroidery, etc. One interesting speciality is 'props' for performances of revolutionary opera, costumes, etc., which are sold on a mass basis because, as we will see, the dances and operas are highly standardized, and certain of them performed again and again, at every level of social life, by performers of many kinds, mainly worker and peasant amateurs.

If anyone thinks the Chinese rely only on 'moral' incentives, he is being misled by an uncritical acceptance of a Chinese rhetoric which, since the Cultural Revolution, has been fiercely directed against 'material incentives'. Indeed, it is because people's material wants are so strong – and because China is still poor – that the campaign against 'material incentives' has to be so fierce, and these wants have to be met if there is not to be gross dissatisfaction. No amount of ideology will substitute: force (basically rationing) is even less satisfactory and counter-productive as a way of controlling demand.

The importance of Mao's injunction that the people must experience real and steady improvement in their living standards – that socialism must 'pay off' – could be seen in the eyes of the people, old and young, grandmothers and kids, as they gaze at these goods. This is perhaps a combination of Western window-shopping and Western advertising, to some extent, but it is devoid of any function as a generator of profits from 'planned obsolescence' or phoney changes of fashion. Such exhibitions in China are a response to, rather than an encouragement of, consumer wants. The political message, moreover, is not that these things are there for individual consumption, but that they are available now to the working masses collectively, who – as collective consumer – are reaping the reward of their own labours as collective producer of these goods. These improvements, too, are common improvements, everyday commodities for all, not just luxuries reserved for a rich minority. And they are only made possible as the product of collective organization, under Communist leadership.

Training Teachers

Next day, we visit Kwangtung Teachers' Training Institute, formerly the South China Training College, the biggest in the South. It is a massive building with three wings, set in a park, and established in 1951. But only 1,000 students were in residence, since the first year's intake after the Cultural

Revolution was just reaching the end of their first academic year.

We have this explained by the reception committee, four of them administrators, four academics, and three student representatives. Amongst the teachers was a Professor of Sociology who had been at Harvard with Kluckhohn; a Professor of Biology, a Physical Eudcation Professor, and a lecturer in Politics.

The Institute is run by a 'Revolutionary Committee', with a chairman who is a P.L.A. officer and makes the customary 'presentation'. It is a change from the usual assemblage of big business representatives, civic worthies, and party hacks, who constitute the 'lay' element in British higher educational institutions. The Cultural Revolution only seriously reached the Institute as late as 1969. The result was a massive exodus of teachers and students to the factories and the countryside, to renew their contact with the people. Then things started up again: an experimental class was tried out, at introductory level, finally a full new intake of 1,000 from the middle schools. Evidently, the former student population was being largely replaced. The new intake were workers, peasants and P.L.A. men, chosen by their fellows in communes, factories and Army units. The impact of the Cultural Revolution was visible also in the Departmental structure. Five of the seven Departments were familiar enough: Politics, Foreign Languages, Maths, Chinese Literature, and Physical Education. But 'Basic Knowledge of Agriculture' and 'Basic Knowledge of Industry' are the rubrics under which Chemistry, Physics, Biology, etc., are now to be located.

Recruitment thus aims at selecting 'ordinary' people, i.e., drawn from the masses. Everywhere one goes, the formula is used *'The poor peasants and the lower middle peasants'*. These are the sections of the masses whose interests are being promoted with special attention.

The Cultural Revolution changed radically not just the pattern of recruitment, but the character of education itself. Traditional classwork is, of course, fundamental still, but there is a new emphasis on production, on the 'unity of theory and practice', and on the breaking-down of the walls separating the student from the world outside. Students had been, they said, 'three-door students'. They had come from privileged backgrounds – sons and daughters of 'cadres' – Party and Government officials, professionals, managers, etc. – very much on the

Soviet pattern. The first 'door' led from home to school, usually a good school; the second, from school to University; and the third, from higher education to a privileged job as an official, professional or manager: a beautiful, cyclical and self-reproducing class-system. They were determined to break the cycle, which, under the appearance of meritocratic open competition, in fact meant the emergence and consolidation of a new kind of technocratic and hereditary élite.

Three methods had been adopted to 'open the doors' of the Institute: getting involved in the work of factories and communes outside; setting up workshops and farms inside the Institute itself; and linking theory and practice by combining scientific research with production and educational training and with active teaching in schools. They were 'walking on two legs': one 'leg' was the new style of work inside the Institute; the other, their new external involvements. Mobile teams had been sent to coach middle (secondary) school teachers in their schools, including remote mountain areas, and 13,000 teachers had attended classes held for three or four months at different points in the countryside. They had also helped the teachers in the counties to organize their own mobile teams. This was their 'output' contribution, a professional one. The 'income' was a political one: the re-education in social values they received from working with peasants, workers and the Army. Had not Chairman Mao declared that the major problem of education was the problem of educating *teachers*? Many of the new teachers had, like students, been recruited, therefore, from the ranks of peasants, technicians in the factories, and school-teachers. The existing staff, the 'intellectuals', had been 'remoulded'. Many had then returned, others were teaching outside.

They were keen to show me the evidence of the new 'unity of theory and practice'. We visit the radio-workshop, the 'practical' manifestation of the Physics Department. Now we have 'practical' work, too. But this is not a 'lab', where experiments are carried out: it is a *production-unit, a factory*, in which teachers, students and workers (usually technicians or skilled workers brought in from outside factories) are manu-facturing oscilloscopes, transistors, frequency-correctors, tape-recorders, amplifiers, etc.

This production policy had begun as early as the Great Leap Forward of 1958, but, they said, had wound down during the period of Liu Shao-Ch'i's revisionism. I ask the students, mostly sixteen or seventeen, what they had been doing before they came here. The first girl had been a farm-worker; another an electro-plater in a factory; the next, a girl, a mail-clerk in an office; another girl had just graduated from senior middle school, so had another man. The next girl had been in charge of assembling amplifiers in a factory; the next, a peasant. Evidently, these were not 'three-door' students.

There are two Chemistry workshops: for Inorganic and Organic respectively. It is a Chinese plant: instead of glass-ware, ceramic jars. The main product is a chemical whose name means nothing to me. But I do understand the Institute's farm, which has both irrigation crops and rainfall plots on the vegetable side, and fish-ponds, chicken-hatcheries, piggeries and hen-runs on the animal side. I cannot elicit clearly how much time is devoted to theory, and how much to practice, but I find that 'Basic Knowledge of Agriculture' includes Botany, Zoology, Biology, Microbiology, Chemistry, Genetics and Physiology. They refer, too, to a half day per week devoted to 'experimental' work and a half day every fortnight to 'physical labour'. The verbal emphasis on productive labour, then, seems exaggerated, and the courses are much more orthodox, at least in terms of the amounts of time devoted to 'theoretical' as against 'applied' work, than they are said to be.

The emphasis on self-reliance is clear. They seem to know nothing of the 'Green Revolution' when I ask. Most of their seeds come from Research Institutes, especially the local one. Foreign seeds are said to have high yields, but to ripen slowly under local conditions, and they are experimenting with improving these strains by treating them electrically. The Danish and English pigs in the spotless piggery (where I mistake the straw-hatted Professor for a swineherd) are used for cross-breeding.

These pigs from Yorkshire or Zealand must realize they are now in China, because my first encounter with acupuncture is to see the needles being stuck, not into humans, but pigs. The surprise is further compounded, for the 'traditional' needles are carrying a quite un-traditional electric charge from a transistorized stimulator. The needle, moreover, is, in this case, a hollow one, through which a piece of surgical suture is inserted beneath the skin, and left. I cannot elicit a clear rationale for this experiment, but it is quite clear that it *is* an experiment to them. Since acupuncture still lacks a general theoretical explanatory framework, despite its pragmatic success, experiments such as these must have a largely 'suck it and see' rationale (like so much practical science). Many people argue that acupuncture only works because the Chinese are receptive to persuasion if the persuasion is backed by authority, Confucian or 'Maoist'. (There are also more explicitly racist versions which suggest that it couldn't work on critical Englishmen.) But would they, I wondered, argue that Chinese pigs, too, are fatalistic and deferential?

Now a class where I can understand the subject-matter – English. The teacher is a former teacher of Russian, who taught himself English in eighteen months by self-study; his English is excellent. He can only be a few steps ahead of the students, who have been studying it for nine months. The text they are using concerns Comrade Chau Yu-lu, Party Secretary in Lanchau county. Now this interested me very much because I had been listening to the Cantonese language-lessons given on Hong Kong radio. Sitting in the Hilton Hotel in Hong Kong, I had learned such phrases as 'This nightclub is very noisy; couldn't we go somewhere quieter?' or, 'I rang the theatre six times for tickets today, but had no luck' – the kinds of phrases vital to the everyday life of the white élite in Hong Kong. Here the subject-matter of everyday life was somewhat different.

'What was the situation like in 1962 in that countryside?' he asks. He selects someone to reply (who uses his own para-phrases of the words in the text): 'Lanchau had suffered from serious natural disasters.' 'What was the life of the peasants like?' 'Many poor peasants were in want of food and clothing.' 'Did everything go well in 1963?' 'No, they were hit again by natural disasters.' 'What happened to the crops?' 'Two-thirds were washed away by serious floods.'

'So,' resumes the teacher, 'for two years running there were serious natural disasters.' 'What about the situation in 1964?' 'The situation in 1964 was getting better.' 'How was the life of the peasants?' 'The life of the peasants was getting better.' 'Yes,' he says, 'the county was now able to support itself. How was this possible in so short a time?' 'It was possible because the poor peasants and lower middle peasants followed the line of the Party and the Thought of Chairman Mao.'

Here was language linked to life – and political life – with a vengeance. The Party Secretary in the text exemplifies the virtues of 'serving the people'. He gives the lead, the example, he works on the land himself, he encourages others to co-operate in building socialism higher, faster, further, and economically and in a self-reliant way. He also used his theoretical equipment to do research in order to evaluate the situation and 'seize the principal contradiction': he carried out studies in the homes of poor and lower-middle peasants, went to the fields, observed the crops and the animals. This is what, in China, they mean by having a 'high level of political consciousness', a phrase which we take to mean blind obedience to the Party line and parrot-like repetition of the Little Red Book. A better equivalent, in our un-political culture, would be '*social* consciousness'.

I asked for a copy of this textbook, which was only roneoed. They were apologetic. It was only provisional, they said, a text they had produced since the Cultural Revolution, so it would undoubtedly be modified, and they were not really proud of it. All that was true enough, I thought, but they were also probably not empowered to give such materials to foreigners, and that they did not say.

'Had I any criticisms of the English class?' I had to say I was amazed at the teacher's command of the language, and that the students' fluency, too, considering they had had less than a year and that none of them had had access to a native English-speaker, was remarkable. (So I tape-recorded a few pages from a book on the history of the revolutionary struggle in Shensi in the 1930s.)

But I did have a non-linguistic question. Why were there constant references to 'poor' and 'lower middle' peasants when these, in Marxist terms, were categories which related to ownership of the means of production, and the land had been collectively owned since 1958? The teacher began a quite competent answer, but was soon politely interrupted by a student who said: 'Would you mind if I tried to give an answer to that question?' I was bowled over at this initiative, and at the idiomatic English he employed. He then discoursed on how the elimination of private *ownership* did not necessarily mean that capitalist *attitudes* had disappeared: exactly the Marxist answer, in terms of 'base' and 'superstructure', that I had expected. But the confident competent use of language was the striking thing, together with his self-assured, though quite un-arrogant intervention.

We went back for a general discussion. We discussed the 'three-in-one' structure of the Revolutionary Committee, the body that runs the place. They try to build in a spread of ages amongst its members: older, middle-aged, and young. The 'three', however, are not age-grades, but representatives of the Army, cadres and masses. The 'Army' element, in fact, seems almost invisible. What it means is the presence of a *political* person in the key seat(s), in this case the Chairman of the Revolutionary Committee. There were only two students on the Revolutionary Committee. What did they think of our radical students' demand for '50–50' representation or 'one man, one vote'? Smiles. 'Numbers are not the important factor,' the answer came, 'but which class they represent and the lines they advocate. The key thing is to ensure that the class interests of the masses are given priority and that the political power of the Party is there to ensure that these interests are met.' Following up my presentation of the student-radical line, I asked them why the two student members present were serving the tea. A cheeky question got a perky answer. 'Well,' the chairman laughed, 'it wouldn't do for you, as a guest, to have to do it, would it? And I, as chairman, have been busy explaining, so someone else does that job. We adopt a division of labour.'

They are certainly no mandarins in terms of income. The average staff salary was 80 *yuan* a month. They started at 61·5 *yuan* (a wage an industrial worker would be earning after nearly ten years' service), and could reach a maximum of 320 *yuan* (over two and a half times the highest normal wage for an industrial worker). But few were at this top end of the scale. The financing of the College, both capital and recurrent expenditure, is provided for out of national funds, the State Budget, and based largely on student numbers. The Budget Finance Section of the Institute draws up a provisional Plan, which the Revolutionary Committee and the Party Committee then discuss and send up, with any changes, to the Provincial Planning Commission and the Provincial Bureau of Finance. A great deal of written and verbal exchange then goes on within and between these bodies.

They work very hard by our standards: forty-eight periods a week, thirty-eight of them 'vocational', seven on political and current affairs. They are up at 5.40 (I think of my colleagues and students – and myself – 'struggling in' for 9.30 lectures). Classes begin at 7.40. There are four periods up to 11.30. From then to 2.45 is set aside for private study. Classes begin again at 2.45, until 5.20. The evening between 7.30 and 9.30 is again for private study. So classes amount to six hours and twenty-five minutes a day; private study to five hours and fifteen minutes – comparable with the hours worked by science students in Britain, in terms of formal classes, but much heavier than a non-scientist's day, and only a small minority of either ever put in so much additional private study.

They also work a six-day week. They get Sundays off, plus public holidays, and the summer vacation lasts four weeks, mainly devoted to revision, rest, visits, preparing for next year, and some practical work. Only 10 per cent of the students are from the city of Canton; over 80 per cent from the rural areas.

I turn to my own field. In the social sciences they study Politics, History, and Marxism-Leninism. The political texts they use are Lenin *On Dialectics, Empirio-Criticism* and *Imperialism*; Engels' *Ludwig Feuerbach, Socialism, Utopian and Scientific*, and *Anti-Duhring*; Marx, *The Gotha Programme, Wage-Labour and Capital*, and selections from *Capital*; Stalin, *Economic Problems of Socialism*; and, of course, the works of Mao Tse-Tung.

Chinese and foreign classics are studied, though 'critically'; Western books where they are 'useful', avoiding mechanical 'imitation'. History, naturally, focuses on China and South-East Asia, with special seminars and 'reports' on the Soviet Union, the Third World, and the capitalist countries. They refuse to suggest which countries are ripe for revolution: Marxism, they say, is not crystal-ball gazing, and each country has different historical circumstances. The path of revolution will be different in different countries. It was one of *urban* revolution in Tsarist Russia, but there is no developed proletariat in underdeveloped countries. What will happen is the outcome of an interplay between a 'universal law' of social development, and the 'concrete practice' in each country. The emphasis is not so much on 'circumstances' producing a revolutionary situation, but on *men* producing revolution, on practice: power, in the final analysis, has to be *seized*; it does not fall into one's lap when times become ripe. Indeed, times will never *become* ripe; they have to be made so.

As a small *quid pro quo*, I offer to try to answer questions on Britain. It is the three senior men who consult to produce the questions. 'What jobs do your students go into?' and, 'What happens to those who fail?' We discuss this, exchange compliments, and part.

*

Next day we quit academia for industry and agriculture. On leaving the hotel, I pass the 'Lost and Found' glass-fronted cabinet (such as I later see on the streets), containing one nail file, three combs, two pairs of spectacles, a lighter, four watch-straps, a receipt for a 'small container made of copper' (sic) – all the minutiae of socialist honesty which is so astoundingly normal in China that – as nowhere else in the world – I leave my passport, cheques and banknotes in a drawer with the door of the room unlocked. They are perfectly safe.

Of course, foreigners may be specially treated, and there are places where thousands of bicycles are 'parked' and locked up. How far this is a matter of sheer organizational control or of fear of theft one cannot judge, but obviously the Chinese are not all saints. Nevertheless, there was absolutely no need for the peasants to pick up the packet of Gauloises the Swedish girl I met had thrown through the train window! Two days later, they were returned to her in Shanghai. And she had wanted to 'kick the habit'. So the apocryphal stories are true.

Sha Chao Commune

Heading through the suburbs of the city, we can see that farming is practised well within the city limits, wherever land is available. Soon we cross the 'off limits' sign for foreigners – (in English and Russian), and are in the country proper. In order to strengthen ties between town and countryside, how-ever, no less than twelve of the communes surrounding the city are under the administration of Greater Canton, as is the ceramic-producing district of Foshan, a town of 230,000, where numerous new chemical and other factories can be seen. When the Japanese left, only 90,000 of the original 300,000 in-habitants remained. Traffic is heavy: bicycles with massive loads and passengers into the bargain crowd the 10-metre tarmacadam centre of the tree-lined road, so that we drive almost continuously on the horn.

The commune is a good way inland. Eventually we turn onto a gravelled side road and arrive at Water Pond Pro-duction Brigade People's Hall, where the reception com-mittee is waiting. They are typical of the men at the grass-roots, the cadres who have organized the building of the new China. Now they are aged between thirty-five and forty-five; at the time of the Liberation they were teenagers.

Guo-Pau, full-time cadre, member of the Revolutionary Committee, reminded us that this area of Shunte county had been occupied by the Japanese, who had burned most of the houses and killed over 200 people. Some of the villagers had fallen victims to Chiang Kai-Shek, too; others had fought in the underground militia or went North to join the Red Armies.

There were today, we learnt from Guo-Pau, 66,000 people in Sha Chao Commune. It was a big one, and densely-populated with 15,200 households cultivating over 68,000 *mou* (over 11,000 acres, with about 1½ families per acre). The commune divided into twenty-two Production Brigades, and these subdivided into 296 Production Teams. The size of the commune was the first striking feature. In this region of myriad waterways, half the productive activity of the commune was devoted to fish-farming in ponds (hence the Brigade's name), and most of the transport was by sampan (the Japanese too, had come mainly by water, not by road). Nowadays, they had gone over to building small ferry-boats of up to 130 h.p., too. At Liberation the only other industry had been a silk factory employing about 100 women. Today, it had 900 workers, 800 of them women, but there were also 57 other mini-factories of all shapes and sizes, some run by the commune, others by its constituent Brigades. They were obviously very proud of this industrial progress: a chemical factory made medicines, including vitamin extract, out of silk-worm dung which, before 1949, used to be thrown into the fish-ponds. Now it brought them in 13,000 *yuan* a ton. Bamboo, wooden and iron utensils were turned out on lathes in one workshop; electronic components in another; and they processed food, too. Since the pumps and motors used in agriculture were made on their own lathes, and they repaired their own agricultural machinery, they were remarkably independent of the outside world for many key items and services.

This was no purely rural village, then. No less than 9,000 of the 33,000 people in the labour-force were working in industry, but industry closely tied in with agriculture. For them, water-control had been the great initial problem. The biggest job had been building a 34 km. dyke between the two rivers on either side of the commune's land-area, and levelling no less than 65 per cent of the total area of farmland. Beginning with the Great Leap Forward in 1958, they had built a network of 195 km. of HT and LT electricity supply, 2,000 kilowatt capacity in all, which had not only brought power to the houses but had enabled them to construct eight major irrigation and drainage stations (plus 539 small reservoirs).

The resulting improvements in production were proclaimed

on the walls of the Hall. Taking 1961, the base year, as 100, rice-production had doubled (208); pig-production, 635; sugar, 132; fish, 177; and the production of silk-cocoons was up by a third. But these are averages: there were large differences between the yields of the more advanced units and those less so. Some Production Brigades could get over 10,000 kilos of sugar per *mou*, others only 7,000, in part because of variations in soil fertility, but also because there was still an inadequate supply of machinery.

We go to have a look at the production side: to the mulberry-fringed fish-pond first, where we watch men up to their necks in water closing the net on the cornered fish, which leaped and splashed; an operation performed every fifty or sixty days, yielding over 750 kilos a time. I have my photograph taken lifting a shoulder-pole with two wooden buckets full of fish on each end. I am mightily relieved to be able to drop it smartly after four seconds of supreme effort to keep it in the air. Not only is it heavy, but I am already soaked through with walking even a few yards in this hot, damp atmosphere. Then, industry: the silk-factory, with its racks of cocoons and worms in various stages of growth, and, finally, the looms where the (to me) quite invisible thread is spun onto reels.

The machinery is Chinese-made (in Kwangtung), and new. The fans stirring the air were not too effective, but over each girl's head was an air-duct leading off a plywood main supply running the length of the shed. It was needed in this heat. I noticed it looked brand-new, and was told that these had been installed, at the workers' demand, after the Cultural Revolution. (Behind the girls were photos of their predecessors: emaciated-looking women workers of pre-Liberation days.) So not only the Liberation, but also the Cultural Revolution had directly paid off! The women wore plastic aprons; older women sat, and their machines ran at a slower pace.

It was an eight-hour day – no overtime. Wages averaged 45 *yuan* a month, ranging from 30 *yuan* to 50 *yuan*. One girl told me, with a rather shamefaced laugh, that in the days of Liu Shao-Ch'i's revisionist line they used to be paid overtime and other bonuses not only in cash, but even in kind – pencils, enamel cups, and pork. 'Such a reliance on material incentives,' she remarked, 'was truly disgusting'.

A shift that had finished its day's work was sitting, doing their one hour's political study, laughing from time to time and not working particularly hard at it, it seemed. Then we saw the end-product: two-kilogram reels of 'Blossoms' White Steam Filature silk, labelled in English, being tested for thickness and tension on a simple modern machine with a graph-cylinder recorder, and then baled. Defective skeins were being teased out to make padding for quilts and pillows by women wearing face-masks.

Sha Chao was no ordinary commune, then. In the best Brigades, annual incomes in agriculture ranged between 220 *yuan* and 550 *yuan*; in industry, from 150 *yuan* (children and unskilled farm-workers) up to as much as 700 *yuan*. People also raised pigs privately which brought in 60 *yuan* a time (selling two or three a year was common).

We went to see what they spent this income on. Some half of it they received not in the form of cash, but in rice, sugar-cane and fish. The biggest luxury 'consumer durable' was the bicycle, costing 120 *yuan*, say, three to six months' income. But 5,000 bicycles had been purchased: one to every three households. The village shops, too, were full of smaller everyday household and agricultural necessities, of decent quality: plastic cups, cotton shirts, straw hats, hoes, sandals, dacron materials, buckets, pharmaceuticals, and so on. It was a pretty large village, containing no less than 15,000 people in 2,000 households. They were grouped into three different Brigades, two on one bank of the river running through the village, one on the other bank. This was much larger than the normal village, which usually contains either one or two Brigades, and those much smaller, too. I found myself corrected, in speaking of 'the village': it was either this 'Production Brigade' or that. The traditional self-enclosedness of the village is thus being broken down, in two ways: firstly, because the village is only part of a much wider entity, the commune, and, secondly, because it may be internally divided into more than one Brigade. The people of this village were plainly mixing widely with people from other villages as a result: at film-shows and basketball competitions as well as in their production and political meetings. It was tantalizing to speculate upon what had happened to the traditional lineage-solidarity, under the influence of these wider ranges of contact, intellectual horizons, and foci of new solidarities. Certainly, my English reverence for the past was rudely treated. I admired the old tiled roof on the former clan-temple across the river, but lamented its state of disrepair. 'What use is it?' the Chairman replied. 'We only use the central room now as a primary school.' It is muddy underfoot in tropical Kwangtung, so the village paths are paved with huge stone slabs. One, however, bore characters upon it. 'What's that?' I asked. 'Oh, you know, the scholars in feudal times used to put up steles (stone monuments) to themselves when they passed the State examinations – they thought they were really superior beings. What use are they now – except as paving-stones?' Finally, the village-fort had its embrasures bricked up. 'Couldn't you use it for something?' I asked. 'For what?' came the answer once more.

With these utilitarian, irreverent attitudes to the culture of the past ringing in my ears, we went to see the culture of the present and future. In the factory kindergarten, for children from two and a half to seven years (they had a nursery, too, for infants, who could be accepted fifty-six days after birth), beautifully-rouged and lipsticked little tots were waiting to welcome their 'uncle' raucously and perform songs from revolutionary operas. One sweet little thing sang a delightful melody. 'What is it?' I asked, 'it's very pretty.' 'Yes, it is a nice song,' said Shu-Pao, 'it's about the notorious scab, hidden traitor and revisionist, Liu Shao-Ch'i.' I was shocked, even annoyed, at this indecent haste to politicize the young, and brooded for a while, until I thought back to my daughter in Canadian kindergarten saluting the flag and singing 'O Canada', and to the Salvation Army Brownie troop she had belonged to, later, in Yorkshire. Was it a case of 'You are political; we are patriotic; they are chauvinist pigs'?

Evidently, the commune had had its share of 'excesses' during the Cultural Revolution. They had tried going over to communal feeding in canteens, but these had been abandoned as – standard Chinese euphemism – 'inconvenient'. Now they ate at home, like the family of ten I visited. The husband, a peasant and nearly sixty, earned 360 *yuan* a year (the *maximum*, you will recall, for staff at the Teachers' Training Institute per *month*). His wife, aged fifty-one, had worked in the silk-factory, and had retired on the advice of the commune, but now used her 'retirement' to work for socialist construction in the factory nursery we had seen. The Brigade's midwife had been kept busy by this family: four of the children were now at work; the youngest, a boy of thirteen, was still at school. Three daughters were married and had left home. The three youngest girls (sixteen, seventeen and nineteen, all peasants), earned about 30 *yuan* each a month; the twenty-five-year-old son, in the shipyard, over 59 *yuan*. Between them, then, they brought in 260 *yuan* a month (leaving aside income from the sale of six pigs, and other subsidiary occupations) – about £5 a head.

It was a pleasant house, cool, clean, privately-owned, and built, free of charge, in 1968, by the members of the Brigade, which also helped with providing the materials and gave the land for nothing. An outhouse had been added in 1970. Neighbours build each other's houses by this mutual aid. Families which have savings in the bank may use them to improve their housing, though they are encouraged to save by getting interest of 18 cents per 100 *yuan* on current accounts, and 27 cents on fixed accounts. Those who need to borrow can do so from the Production Team Credit Department, for the higher, but equally modest, rate of interest of 36 cents for every 100 *yuan* they borrow.

The floor of the house was tiled; they had their own well; the children wore coloured patterned shirts. There was electric light (five 25-watt bulbs), as in 95 per cent of the Commune's houses, which cost them only 60 cents a month (about 12p). The cooking was done on a four-hole stove fuelled by home-made coal-dust briquettes. For the future, they hoped to add further rooms once the children had left home. The younger boy would soon be going to middle school. Previously, children from this commune had to travel by bus or board at the county town if they went on to senior middle school. Now the commune had its own, and every Brigade had a junior middle school. Over 4,500 children were in middle school, compared to only 300 before the Cultural Revolution.

A Factory

It had been impressive, and people looked happy and prosperous. For me, it had been pleasant to be away from the city. But now we were going further inland, to the medium-sized county town of Kiang Men. We pass a hillside covered with graves in poor state of attention. 'The people don't bother much!' (Shades of Confucius!) The hills themselves were in better condition, with reafforestation much in evidence and much needed. We cross a couple of tributaries of the Pearl River by ferry, each a very large river in my vocabulary, and slide through the bright green fields smelling of the chemical spray the peasants are using on the rice.

In the evening, an entertainment by a Mao Tse-Tung Thought Propaganda Team of artists and local performers. I find myself a guest of honour, together with the leading cadres of the factory and town Revolutionary Committees. (They are well-read in the Marxist classics: Engels' *Socialism, Utopian and Scientific*; Lenin's *Imperialism*, Marx's *Civil War in France*, etc., etc., but all of them, too, to my delight, had read the classical novels, *The Dream of the Red Chamber* and *The Romance of the Three Kingdoms*.)

The performance opens with incidents from the life of Chairman Mao; a Mongolian dance ('Searching for the Lost Sheep'); children of about seven do a skipping dance next about the Thought of Chairman Mao. Then 'Half of a Basket of Peanuts' – a very commonly-staged sketch about how an ideologically-advanced mother tests the political conscious-ness of her children by exposing them to the temptations of stealing a few peanuts from a bowl she is giving to the com-mune: a Garden of Eden situation which seems to me very naive, but which arouses gales of appreciative laughter. Whatever the content, one cannot but admire the vivid colour, especially the red flags, which contrast with the dimly-lit streets outside.

Then an equally common Vietnam sketch. Three guerillas (a shoeshine boy, a waiter and a girl paper-seller) lure a G.I., who has a ridiculous long, sharp nose and carries a flask of whisky as well as his pistol, on his hip, into getting drunk, and then rob him of his weapons. In the background are signs reading 'Beautiful' to represent the brothels of Saigon, and the G.I. is lured by girlie magazines as well as by drink. 'Vietnam Will Win' is blazoned across the stage, in Chinese and English, at the end. A final cimbalom solo version of a song from *The Red Lantern* ends an immensely popular evening.

Next day, to business. Kiang Men was a small town in 1949 – only 30,000 people. Now it has 130,000. Then it was a con-sumer town; now it has over 110 factories. The plant we are to see is the Kiang Men Sugar-Cane Chemical Plant. The Chairman of the Revolutionary Committee is Li Yung-Shen, a man of forty-two, who was assigned by the Party to the plant after the Cultural Revolution. Previously, he had done propaganda work in the Army and then in the Propaganda Department of Kwangtung Province. The former Chairman, whom he dis-placed, was 'criticized' for his shortcomings and mistakes, but had been helped to put them right, and was a leading cadre once more (the former Director of Sha Chao commune silk factory had also been 'criticized' but subsequently reinstated as one of the four Deputy Chairmen of the new Revolutionary Committee).

The plant is a post-Liberation development. Construction began in 1957 and was completed in 1959, but in the middle of the construction work, Chou En-Lai visited the site and suggested that they might 'leap forward' ('following Chairman Mao's teaching') by combining sugar-cane processing with paper-production, using the *bagasse*, the fibrous residue left after crushing the juice from the cane. In addition, the waste liquids and other residues could be turned to agricultural use. This strategy of 'multi-purpose utilization' meant that five different kinds of products, not just sugar, started being produced in 1959; over 3,600 tons of sugar a day; 120 tons of paper-pulp; six tons of yeast, from which twenty-four tons of alcohol was produced daily; and ten tons of solid carbon dioxide a day. By the time of the Cultural Revolution, ten different products were being turned out.

But the Cultural Revolution was the watershed. (I was now getting used to thinking of 'before' and 'after' the Cultural Revolution – not 1949 – as equivalent to B.C. and A.D.) Thirty different kinds of products were now produced, including cement made from filtered sludge; No. 702 insecticide and other chemicals; adhesives and fertilizers from waste liquid; bricks from the ashes, and steel from the coke-ovens fired by pyrites cinders. Sugar, which had once constituted 80 per cent of the value of the output, was now only 64 per cent, and the total value of production was three times the 1958 level.

This was the first way they had developed 'multi-purpose utilization' – by using formerly waste raw materials to produce new products. Secondly, they had made 'multi-purpose' use of their machines, for purposes other than those they were designed for; thirdly, they had trained workers in new skills: what had only been a metal instrument repair-shop now also produced electronic silicon controls for rectifiers. Former sugar-cane processing-workers were now producing calcium carbonate and lime, or working in the repair-shops. The new diversification also reduced seasonal fluctuations in the demand for labour. Previously, a third of the work-force was only needed during the peak 'golden period' from November to March, when the cane was ripe for cutting; now the demand for such temporary labour was only for 300 workers out of a total labour-force of 3,500 (one and a half times the number employed when they started in 1959).

It is a big plant now, spread over 63,000 square metres, with twelve large workshops, sited on a river where cargo vessels are loaded by electric cranes, and take the products down-river to Canton. Sugar production still has pride of place, though, and had risen from 30,000 tons in 1959 to 40,000 in 1972. Diversification also means diversification of control; two Ministries, Foodstuffs and Light Industries, are now involved.

To enter the works, we leave the workers' settlement area where I have been staying, pass the young sentry at the works entrance with rifle and bayonet (which he cheerfully lets me examine), and walk up the tree-lined avenue. Small diesel engines are pulling trucks loaded automatically with the cane-stalks. The workers wear masks. A large blackboard carries chalked records of production-performance by each team, and of electricity consumption. There are three shifts, changed weekly, those on night-shift getting an allowance for the cost of their evening meal.

This electrical machinery was all designed and manu-factured on the spot. Mechanization is on quite a high level, and there are safety devices on all moving parts. Only two workers man the huge purification plant, and one controls the next stage of filtration. Massive vats hold the liquid which ends up as sugar. The next workshop turns the *bagasse* stringy residue into paper-pulp sheets and into paper of varying qualities, from packing-paper to high-quality duplicating and air-mail paper. Sheets rejected by quality control are re-processed. This machinery is from Shanghai; the driers and rollers carry the date '1956'. 'Some of this machinery is quite old', they comment as I record the date. After visual inspection by a woman sitting under the moving sheets, who marks every impurity with chalk, and a second inspection, small trolleys on rails take the sheets to the loading-bays, where, instead of hand-packing as in the past, there are two men on an hydraulic press who bale the sheets into 100-kilogram bales.

Some of the machinery in the repair-shop is quite sophis-ticated, with an electric crane running on an overhead track, and the workshop is cool and airy. The machinery is partly Chinese, made in Canton, and partly Dutch. Here they now manufacture liners for the crushing machines, where once they could only re-bore them. The gear-cutting machinery has an accuracy of ·003 mm.; the lathes, from Dalien in Manchuria, tolerances of one in 10,000 mm., and they can now even make their own here.

But the power supply comes from three Czech generators producing 17,000 kilowatts per hour, made in 1957, and the control-system is Polish (1958). They go out of their way to point out, however, that the turbines have been improved here, stepping up output by 20 per cent. The boilers supplying the steam for the electric generators, too, are Polish (Poznan, 1957), and one has been adapted, experimentally, to take a proportion of coal cinders which have already been used once. The yeast plant, again, has Polish and East German fermentation, separation, purification, and drying equipment, for turning out tablets and sheets. In the Metal Instrument Workshop, the machinery is mainly Chinese, the oscilloscopes from Kwangsu, the province where Shanghai is located, and the electric vacuum machines made here in the plant – all highly automated, with only four workers attending the machines. On the whole, the strong impression is that for all the emphasis on self-reliance the bulk of the key machinery is East European in origin.

I see one quite remarkable machine that is purely local. A strange-looking truck in one workshop prompts me to ask: 'Is that a relic of the Japanese invasion?' Shocked silence, then the reply: 'No, it is a truck the workers made themselves in their spare time from scrap.' The body-panels were full of welding: obviously bits of sheeting fitted together like a big jigsaw puzzle. The prop shaft, gear-lever, and other timers looked like old bits and pieces 'cannibalized', modified, converted from their original uses. It looked Heath Robinson-like. But *it worked*, and the winch on the back was useful for pulling and lifting things around the plant. I asked myself: 'What for?' Obviously it was useful to have an extra piece of machinery, but this was something else. It was certainly not a prototype – they were not going to produce trucks. It was, no doubt, primarily a one-off exercise in do-it-yourself economizing. But it was also a profound expression of self-development as well as self-reliance. They were not just doing it, but developing the confidence to dare to do it in the first place. And if ever the need came to produce their own vehicles, by hand if necessary, they could do; if ever the request came to supply relevantly-skilled labour for new automobile plants, they could supply that, too.

On the way out we watched not only hundreds of workers,

but also their wives and children (who don't get school-meals
at primary school) having their midday meal in the canteen.
It is a utilitarian building, with a tiled floor and cooled by a
huge fan. They were eating from metal plates off wooden
tables. The girls doing the cooking were wearing face-masks.
A large bowl of rice cost 4·5 cents (just over 1p); a similar
bowl of meat 10 cents (2½p); and vegetables were 2 cents.
Top-priced dishes are only 11 or 12 *fen* – say 3p; the menu is
changed daily. A good meal for less than a shilling, in old-
style British currency. The atmosphere is very 'family', and,
with the workers' housing cheek-by-jowl, a degree of inter-
connection between home, work-place, school and community is possible which cannot be achieved in the large city,
or even in the commune, where the family household is still
very much the key domestic unit. It was something like the
kind of industrial village the Rowntrees or Cadburys had
wanted, probably *too* communitarian for the average middle-
class Westerner, though less so for working-class people used
to the more communal estates and 'traditional' slums. The
workers' settlement is a series of four-storey blocks of apartments, with trees shading the paths, chickens running around,
and the ends of each open space between the buildings leading
off into the surrounding rice-fields. There are heaps of coal-
dust at the end of each space, deposited for the free use of each
family to make their own briquettes in moulds provided. An
hour or two's work makes a month's supply.

Family life for Ho Derh Chau had not always been like this.
He was fifty-one, his wife fifty. To my surprise, after twenty-
five years of marriage, they had only one daughter of eighteen
living with them. Little wonder, for they had lost three
children of starvation before Liberation (which they didn't tell
me until I probed). He was a store-keeper, fourteen years in the
factory, having previously worked in a paper mill in Canton.
Though he had been assigned here, he was not a Party member,
and held no office. He was earning 78 *yuan* a month, a decent
enough wage; his wife worked in the general office for 46 *yuan*
a month; and the daughter was an apprentice pastry-cook in
the canteen, on only 15 *yuan*. Unlike the peasants, these people
had no ancillary source of income.

But the home looked like a home. They had a transistor
radio (cost 40·96 *yuan*, about a third of their monthly collective income), another radio, a *pipa* (a lute-like Chinese
musical instrument), an alarm clock, a sewing-machine (cost

140 *yuan*), and a bicycle (a 'Flying Pigeon', cost 159 *yuan*, which they all used to go into the town centre, since this estate was on the outskirts). There was a calendar on the wall, a framed portrait of Chairman Mao, and four of his pamphlets. The walls were papered, the windows glazed, plenty of flowered cloth in evidence, the food-cupboard fly-screened and the high double bed had its mosquito net. Washing hung from the window, catching the breeze from the fields. The chairs and other furniture were plain, wooden and bamboo, no frills.

The rent of these middle-storey apartments was dearer than the floors above and below, because ground-level is more humid, and top level hotter. They paid 10 *yuan* a month, one-fourteenth of their joint income, plus 2·60 *yuan* for piped water and electricity. The indoor lavatory was flushed by a hose attached to a tap; the bath was a metal one which also had to be filled by hand. For this rent, they had the use of a living-room measuring 9 feet by 12 (12 sq. m.), a bedroom 9 feet by 9 (9 sq. m.), together with a lavatory and kitchen, 28 sq. m. in all – about the same size as the accommodation in Hong Kong resettlement blocks, but, there, there would have been half a dozen or more people extra, and this was infinitely more pleasant, with proper 'mod. cons.'.

The industrial worker buys his food out of his wages just as in England. As in England, his wife cooks it. Mr Ho's wife was cooking something special for him, because he had a bad stomach condition, an appetizing enough meal of meat and vegetables, over the concrete 'stove' (she also had two portable rice-cookers). They reckoned themselves to be a medium-income family: bigger families had more living-space, *pro rata*. Their rice-ration, of 31 *catties* (about 15 kilos, or 40 lb.) for a man, and 30 for a woman, was plenty and cost them about 4 *yuan* each a month, to which has to be added the cost of meat, another 17 or 18 *yuan*. With a joint income of 139 *yuan* a month, food is obviously their biggest single expense, about a third of their income.

*

On the way back, I count the traffic: in sixty kilometres before we pass Foshan and get into continuous traffic, there are twelve tractors – six with trailers – eleven buses and twenty-two trucks, mainly five- and three-tonners – not exactly the paucity of mechanized transport I'd read about in Hong Kong.

3

STABILITY
AND
REVOLT

The older cities still take the breath away: Nanking's lakes with the five islets representing the five continents (the Imperial archives were housed on 'Australia'); the ferry chugging across on a still morning; the city wall where the Taiping rebels made their last-ditch stand in 1864; the spectacular Sun Yat-Sen Mausoleum on the slopes of the Purple Mountains.

Chinese culture had existed in recognizably continuous form for over two and a half thousand years before the Communists came to power. A centralized state had first come into being two centuries before Christ, when the prince of Ch'in – Ch'in Shih Huang Ti – succeeded in defeating his enemies in less than a decade, and uniting an area stretching from near modern Tientsin to as far south as Indochina, and westwards to the lands of the Hun. In the next ten years he laid the foundations of the Empire (and gave us the name 'China'): he standardized weights and measures, the coinage and the script, and linked up existing fortifications to form the Great Wall to shut out the Huns, the Wall of which it is said that a million men died in building it and every stone cost a human life. The feudal nobility experienced his ruthlessness as well as the ordinary people, for he broke their power by dispossessing them of their estates, and made them reside at the capital. It was the officials manning the new system of centralized administration who now wielded decisive power. The Emperor's hostility to feudal culture was so thoroughgoing that all books except the archives and works of medicine, divination and agriculture were destroyed. Even when those who had suffered under him seized power after his death, the attractions of wielding power over a now unified society, and quarrels between contenders for that power, led those who finally established the succeeding dynasty, the Han, to consolidate rather than dismantle the system he had built.

Throughout the oscillations between disunity and unification in subsequent centuries, the institutions created under the Ch'in were to persist, if only sometimes as ideals, and the direction development took was one of increasing centralization.

The legacy of a culture of such antiquity, a culture as complex, extensive and impressive as the entirety of Western Christian culture, still impinges everywhere. Visiting the Great Wall with hundreds of Peking residents at the weekend, one looks out towards the steppelands from whence the nomad horsemen periodically erupted to attack China. The cameltrains on the roads are a reminder of just how near those lands are. One school of thought attributes the early centralization of China to the necessity for the agricultural Chinese to develop and maintain permanent defences against the nomads.

Another school of thought emphasizes the need for control of water – irrigation works, dams, canals, dykes – as the centralizing factors. Certainly state works made possible extensive and intensive improvements in agriculture, and improved communications by water made possible the expansion of trade and a more effective administration and taxation system. The great break-through was the linking of the Yangtse region with the North by the construction of the Grand Canal.

The broad contrast between the irrigated rice-lands of South China and the rainfall agriculture of North China, where wheat, millet and *kaoliang* are the staples, is the main obvious division, though geographers distinguish as many as nineteen natural regions across the whole of the vast territory of China.

But four 'key economic areas' have been the decisive ones in
the country's history: the North China loess plain, the Valley
of the Yangtse, the 'Red Basin' of Szechwan in the mountainous South-West, and South China. When, periodically, central
government weakened, China fell apart along the lines of
these geo-economic zones. The title of the fourteenth-century
classical novel, *The Romance of the Three Kingdoms*, thus refers to
the kingdoms of Wei, Shu and Wu, during one of these periods
of disunity in the third century A.D., corresponding roughly
to North China, with the Yellow River as its core, Szechwan,
and the Yangtse Valley.

Over the centuries, the population increased massively,
from sixty millions in 1290 to 179 millions by 1750, largely
owing to improved varieties of rice and the introduction of
new crops. The Han – the people we call 'Chinese' – had been
expanding southwards and westwards for centuries, conquer-
ing and absorbing many other peoples. Those longest under
Han control and influence were absorbed – 'sinicized'. But in
the far west and in the ethnic 'shatter-zone' of the south-
western marches of Yunnan, the penetration has been too
recent for complete assimilation to have been completed.
Hence these regions were racked by the periodic revolts of
what are now called the 'national minorities' – who occupy
two-thirds of the land area of China (though with only 6 per
cent of the population) – right into the twentieth century.

Continuity of political institutions and political culture did
not mean continuity of a single polity. China was overrun
many times by nomads. The earlier conquerors usually carved
out smaller states, but in later centuries, as with the Mongols in
the thirteenth century and the Manchus in the seventeenth,
they took over what was an increasingly integrated society *in
toto*. In the end, Chinese culture took *them* over, or reasserted
itself, as when the Mongols were driven back beyond the Wall
in a revolt led by a peasant.

Peasant discontent could equally be directed against indigenous dynasties and often expressed itself via the more
heretical Buddhist or Taoist sects. But the rebels themselves,
once established in power, followed the classical principles of
State organization. For the principles themselves were not seen
as wrong, even by rebels: the Emperor had been surrounded
by evil advisers, or had himself forfeited the 'mandate of
heaven', and, even where the Empire split into smaller states,
they were organized along similar lines.

The crucial principles were hierarchy and obedience; they governed all relations from those between father and son to those between Emperor and subject. Indeed, the hierarchy of the Empire was represented as a cosmic, not just a human order. The Emperor, as the apex of earthly society, mediated between man and the heavens. At the Temple of Heaven in Peking, in grounds taboo to his subjects until after the establishment of the Republic in 1911, he went, at the winter solstice and in the first month, to 'speak with the heavens' about the events of the past year, and to perform the harvest and other rituals vital to the health of the whole society. The Imperial ('Forbidden') City is elevated above the rest of Peking, where lesser mortals dwelt, for symbols of superiority were matters of great significance. The very alignment of the buildings follows the axes of the Universe: North, South, West, East. The steps of the terrace of the Three Great Halls are in sets of nine, the largest number, hence an apt symbol of imperial majesty. The colours, too, have symbolic significance, and the magnificent bronze incense-burners, shaped like cranes and tortoises, are also symbolic of immortality. The influence of the heavens on the fortunes of men underlie, too, the pride of place among the branches of knowledge given to astronomy. For centuries, the only Europeans tolerated in the capital were the Jesuits manning the Observatory.

Earthly society – according to the dominant Confucian ideology – was part of a divine, eternal order. Though other societies and cultures existed outside her borders, China was the centre of the world, the 'Middle Kingdom'. It *was* civilization; the rest merely 'barbarism'. When Emperor Ch'ien Lung accorded Lord Macartney an audience in 1793, the British envoy was treated as a respectful inferior bringing tribute; the Emperor naturally understood that European countries needed Chinese products: silk, tea and porcelain; but the Chinese themselves had no need of barbarian manufactures. However, in magnanimity, a few Europeans would be allowed to live in a trading ghetto at Canton. The suggestion that they might reside in Peking, and, if need be, adopt Chinese dress and customs, was dismissed, since 'the distinction between Chinese and barbarians is most strict'. George III was enjoined to 'display even more energetic loyalty in future', so that he might 'deserve for ever Our gracious affection'.

Though there had been periods in which foreign contact flourished, only during one extraordinary period, during the reign of the third Ming Emperor, Yung Lo (1403–24), did China ever herself turn to engage directly with the world outside her borders. Yung Lo's energy was first evident in his seizure of the throne, then in his rebuilding of Peking, and in the commissioning of the *Yung Lo Ta Tien*, a virtual compilation of existing knowledge in 11,095 volumes, completed by over two thousand scholars in only four years.

Five weeks after his accession, he began dispatching missions abroad: to Korea, Tibet, Mongolia, Annam, Java, Japan, South India, the Ryukyus, and to Champa and Samudra in contemporary Malaysia and Indochina respectively. He moved the capital to Peking to counter Mongol power, and under the eunuch, Cheng Ho, sent no less than six expeditions in enormous vessels, specially built, to the Indan Ocean and beyond. The early voyages were more clearly straightforward shows of Chinese military and political strength, designed to establish or re-establish Chinese suzerainty. Later he was more content to maintain his moral power. Though the spread of ties of this kind assisted the security of trade, too, the expeditions themselves involved more giving than receiving, as demonstrations of Chinese superiority and benevolence. The exotic products of many lands flowed back to Peking as amusements and as evidence of the range of China's influence. One voyage even reached Africa, and brought back ostriches, giraffes and zebras to delight the court: the 'auspicious' or 'tribute' giraffe, in particular, was recorded in a delightful painting.

But the expeditions began and ended with Yung Lo; they exhibit a desire for direct relationships with the outside world which was never repeated, and reflect in part, perhaps, the insecurity of a usurper, or, more fundamentally, the insecurity of an indigenous dynasty which was only re-establishing itself after a century of Mongol rule.

More secure rulers had no such uncertainties. For them, the classical principles upon which the empire rested were unquestioned. It was taken for granted that China was the centre of the civilized world: no expeditions were needed to reaffirm this. China, then, never saw herself as part of an international system of states until forced to in the nineteenth century, when she was shocked to discover that her status in the new world system was a low, semi-colonial one.

The internal principles of ordered social life were unquestioned, too. In such a system, even rebels thought within this framework. Hence, though there could be rebellion and revolt – even *legitimate* rebellion against a dynasty that had lost the 'mandate of Heaven' – a revolution transforming the economic and status orders and the political institutions of society was unthinkable. In the *Romance of the Three Kingdoms* the heroes swear, in the famous Peach Garden oath, to 'serve the state and save the people'; their first contribution is to help suppress the 'Yellow Turban' rebellion which the incompetent government generals could not contain, and even the rebels of the classical novel, *Heroes of the Marshes* (also called *Water Margin* or *All Men are Brothers*) are men unjustly outlawed, like Robin Hood, not revolutionaries. (Hence there is great public controversy in China today about the correct political evaluation of these novels.)

In the closed world of Confucian orthodoxy, however, these romances, written in the vulgar literary form of the novel, often by men who had failed in their careers as officials, were enormously popular. The illiterate masses would be more likely to hear them from storytellers or watch them as colourful operas than to read them. Young peasants like Chu Teh or Mao Tse-Tung enjoyed the stories of rebellions most. So did Mao's school-fellows and the old men of the village alike, but since the schoolmaster hated these 'wicked' books, the boys had to hide them behind copies of the Classics.

The orthodox culture the schoolmasters inculcated was rooted in a stable system of social relations in the countryside – and China was one huge countryside. Yet it was a social order in which even the land-owning gentry were socially inferior to the officials who manned the machinery of the State, unless, like most of the officials, they had passed their examinations. The contemporary revolt against the superiority of mental over manual labour has to be set against this traditional pre-eminence of the *literati* who ruled China for centuries. In the traditional status hierarchy, scholars (including officials and teachers) came before farmers, then artisans, then merchants; below these the military, and, of course, the mass of the people.

Non-Marxist scholars reject the label 'feudal' as a description of this system, since they conceive of feudalism as a *political* system of loyalty and dependence, based on the holding of land granted by a superior and involving the lord in duties of protecting his vassals. At the top of the hierarchy of vassalage and fealty were the great landowners, who were also the great political magnates. Such a system did once exist in China but only briefly, during the Ch'in dynasty. It was replaced by a system which persisted for over two thousand years, up to the establishment of the Republic. Non-Marxist scholars refuse to call this system 'feudal' because those who exercised decisive political power were the men who controlled the State, not the landowners. The wealth pumped out of the peasantry, too, took the form of taxation paid to the State, not rent paid to the landlord. Hence, in China, the State was strong; in medieval Europe, the king was always hard-pressed for sources of finance.

But the differences were not all that fundamental: in China, much of the State's revenue found its way back, albeit by different routes, to the land-owning gentry, who were well-paid for their local services to the State. Moreover, Marxists continue to consider the use of the term 'feudal' as quite justified, since, for them, the essence of feudalism is that it is a *mode of production*, not just a political system. Hence they argue that the extraction of a surplus from the peasants who worked the land, by the use or threat of extra-economic sanctions (political power), is the characteristic form of exploitation under feudalism. Under capitalism, the form exploitation takes is quite different: the extraction of surplus value from the labour of free men working for wages. Under feudalism, the surplus extracted from the peasant is 'rent', according to Marxists, whether it is handed over to the State or paid to the landlord.

The State also, as we shall see, drew its officials mainly from the ranks of the landowners, great and small, and kept the merchants, the owners of workshops, and the towns generally, firmly under control: manufacturing was small-scale, capital-scarce and labour-intensive and the right to engage in it was monopolized by the State, which might own workshops itself or license others to do so. Though the relationships between the landowners and the State differed from that of European feudalism, it was an agrarian social order in which, sym-biotically, the State's revenues depended on the health of agriculture, as did those of the landowners, and in which the gentry's capacity to enjoy its wealth was ensured by the State, even if they did not, as a class, run the State directly or even develop any significant organized political power. (Even the great princely houses, if they fell from imperial favour, could decline, a situation the great novel, *The Dream of the Red Chamber*, movingly shows.) An industrial or commercial bourgeoisie would have threatened both the gentry and the officials; it was not allowed to develop at all. And the system of inheritance, which divided the land between the sons, contributed to the decline over time of even the great land-owning families.

The way to make a fortune in imperial China was to become an official. Hence the land, though a valuable source of rents, was not the main source of income even for the minor local gentry, whose income from the State in return for such services as arbitrating in local disputes, raising and command-ing bodies of militia, maintaining public works, performing rituals, etc., brought them at least as much as did the rents they extracted from their tenants. The higher up you were in the State machinery, the greater the opportunity to become wealthy, not so much from your official salary and other rewards, which were small, but from the 'extra-legal' extortions which made up 90 per cent of an official's income. In one extreme case, under the Ch'ing (Manchus), an official with an estimated salary of 180 *taels* a year acquired 180 *million* in moveable property alone! In some periods, only about half the taxes collected reached the Imperial treasury.

To become an official one had to pass the examinations: the status of degree-holder could not be passed on to one's descendants. Hence each generation had to renew its access to the source of wealth, the State, by putting its sons in for the examinations. Some historians, indeed, regard the cessation of the Imperial examinations in 1905 as the beginning of the end for the Imperial system, for it cut the crucial bond between the landed gentry and the State. It closed off the major avenue of social mobility for the ambitious sons of the landed gentry – and even many of humbler stock – who gathered in Peking from all corners of the Empire every three years in the third lunar month, to retire into special cells for three days and two nights with their examination papers. (They were required to wear special clothes so that notes could not be smuggled in.) Those who had taken their lower degrees at provincial or prefecture level were now aiming at the highest degree of all. Like nineteenth-century British Civil Service examinations, it was a meritocratic system. But the Civil Service was not just a career for younger sons excluded from inheritance of the family wealth, as in Britain – like the Church or the Army, a lesser, though respectable, alternative to landowning. In China it was *the* highroad to wealth. As in Britain, there were other ways to high office, but this was the principal route, even for noble families, for the chances of their children being successful were high.

In similar fashion, the British upper class sent their children through Oxford and Cambridge. As with the nineteenth-century British examinations, the content of their education generated a 'gentlemanly' style of life. It put a premium on ability, but ability of a particular kind: that of regurgitating the classics, in the Chinese case, within the rigid framework of the 'eight-legged essay' style.

The rich families were aristocratically remote from the world of work. Pao Yu, the hero of *The Dream*, on his way to a funeral, enters a farm:

> He had never seen the various farming implements before. He did not even know their names, and had to ask the servants . . . to explain their use and purpose. When told, he could not get over his astonishment . . . He came to a room in which he saw . . . a strange implement, which seemed to him even more curious than the others. That, he was told, was a spinning wheel with which was made the yarn that was later woven into cloth.

Even the waiting maids brought up in this hermetic world of luxury cannot recognize a pawn ticket when they see one: 'Oh goodness!', Black Jade and Little Cloud giggle, 'what funny ideas people come on in order to make money!' Their ignorance is praised as 'innocence' of this 'wicked world'.

The unworldly culture of the great houses had its counterpart in the unworldly leisure-time pursuits of those most worldly of men, the mandarin officials. Imbued as they were with the Confucian ideology of loyalty, and indebted to the State for their position in the world, their rapacity in office was combined with a professed gentlemanly disdain for the materialistic and practical. They saw themselves as men of culture, set apart from the rest of society not just by special legal privileges, but by their cultural values.

The duty of subject was to obey, and to leave the affairs of State to the officials. But even for the officials the highest ideals, their duties done, were those of quietistic self-cultivation, and the pursuit of the spiritual and the ideal, rather than activistic involvement in the world. Once his duties were fully removed, on retirement, he could pursue higher things more single-mindedly. He could concentrate on perfecting his skill

at writing poetry in classical styles, at calligraphy, painting and
writing, and on deepening his knowledge of the Classics, concentrating on the ultimate in exclusiveness – on cultivating
himself and his cultivated friends. The detached and ultimately aristocratic mood is beautifully captured in Shih
Nai-An's ironic introduction to his great classic novel of the
fourteenth century, *Heroes of the Marshes*:

A man should not marry after thirty years of age; should not enter
the government service after the age of forty; should not have any
more children after the age of fifty; and should not travel after the
age of sixty. This is because the proper time for these things has
passed . . .

What excites pleasure in me is the meeting and conversing with
old friends . . . When they come they drink and chat, just as they
please, but our pleasure is in the conversation and not in the liquor.
We do not discuss politics because we are so isolated here that our
news is simply composed of rumours, and it would be only a waste
of time to talk with untrustworthy information. We also never talk
about other people's faults, because in this world nobody is wrong,
and we should beware of backbiting. We do not wish to injure
anyone, and therefore our conversation is of no consequence to
anyone. We discuss human nature about which people know so little
because they are too busy to study it.

My friends are all broad-minded, and well educated, but we do not
keep a record of our conversations. The reason for this is (1) we are
too lazy, and do not aspire to fame; (2) to talk gives us pleasure, but
to write would give trouble; (3) none of us would be able to read it
again after our deaths, so why worry; (4) if we wrote something this
year we should probably find it all wrong next year . . .

But someone may ask: 'As you did not write down your friends'
conversations why have you written this book?' To which I reply
(1) because it is just a hotchpotch, and cannot make me famous or
even discredit me; (2) I have only done this to fill up my spare time,
and give pleasure to myself; (3) I have written it so that the unedu-
cated can read it as well as the educated; (4) I have used this style of
composition because it is such a trifle.

Alas; Life is so short that I shall not even know what the reader
thinks about it . . . So why think anything further about it?

Some retired to the country; others, literally, cultivated their
garden in some lotus-land like Soochow. The gardens are still
there, with names like 'The Garden of the Forest of Lions' or
'The Garden of the Plain Man's Politics' (named in this Confucian spirit by a former censor, because cultivating one's
garden to meet one's daily needs was a plain man's politics),

'The Garden of the Master of the Nets', 'The Garden of the Pavilion of the Waves', 'Precious Belt Bridge', the 'Tomb of the Good Wife', the 'Temple of Mystery'. The names evoke the lives of those leisured scholars who shared the pleasures of wine and poetry, and projected their philosophical concepts onto Nature in their arrangement of water, hillocks, buildings and vegetables. Lord Macartney's retinue, in 1793, were impressed not only by the gardens, but also by the silk industry and by the scholars, the artists, the acrobats, the delicate women, the gondolas on the canals. 'In heaven there is paradise,' it was said, 'on earth Soochow and Hangchow.'

Such were the exquisite rewards for a lifetime of rapacity, in which the only constraints were those set by what the traffic would bear: the point at which the peasantry would revolt. If they did, they risked death in equally exquisite torture. But periodically there were revolts, and dynasties were even overthrown when peasants withdrew their loyalty on a large enough scale.

Continuity of political institutions and ideology was the counterpart of stable social relations in the countryside. But the degree to which they were stable fluctuated considerably over the centuries, and the fragility of the social order was such that, at times, as R. H. Tawney said of twentieth-century China, 'the rural population was in the position of a man permanently up to the neck in water, so that even a ripple is sufficient to drown him.' Conversely, long periods of prosperity also occurred. The crucial variable was the efficiency of those who controlled the State; there could be no prosperity when the water-works were not maintained in good order, when marketing was unsafe or unprofitable, or when central authority was so weak that local officials could, with impunity, bleed the peasants white with taxation.

The continuity and stability of Chinese society has also been greatly exaggerated by the Confucian ideologists who were its main recorders. For it is also a history of remarkably persistent peasant protest, erupting at times into revolt.

The form that it took most typically was that of the secret society. These societies were usually primarily religious associations, often subscribing to heterodox Buddhist or Taoist beliefs, such as the millenarian belief in the return of Amida Buddha and the belief in the 'Western Paradise', rather than any Confucian orthodoxy. They also subscribed to utopian social ideals: dreams of the 'Great Peace', of universal abundance, and a primitive egalitarian belief in taking from the rich to give to the poor. At times of disorder and distress, their numbers would be swollen not only by starving peasants, but by unemployed craftsmen, boatmen, pedlars, and labourers, and by unorthodox Taoist and Buddhist monks – the equivalent of our Lollard 'hedge-priests' – who provided the intellectual leadership.

In many ways, the secret societies resembled Western masonic lodges, with their elaborate initiation-rites, ordeals, tests and trials. In normal times, some societies might be not only passive, but even quite conservative: though there were secret societies of the poorer peasants, there were also those which were concerned to protect men of property from those who lacked it. But most societies were *trans-class* in their composition; they recruited people from the local community, irrespective of their standing, in a way that de-emphasized their class status and stressed, instead, their identity as 'brothers'. Hence they were often little more than mutual-benefit or 'friendly' associations, or, at times, 'communities of the afflicted', to use the term Victor Turner has employed to describe similar African societies: places where those who had lost their family, their kin, or their lineage status, could find a substitute identity and brotherhood.

Much of the time, they would be principally preoccupied with their elaborate cult-practices. But in times of disorder, they became ready-made vehicles of protest. They were remarkably continuous over the ages, and references can be found to a society, or to its successor, in the same part of China, over centuries. In times of rapid change and dis-location, or of the degeneration of dynasties, they often became very violent. Sometimes peasants would simply take to the hills in order to live by banditry. But the scale of protest could turn into virtual peasant war. At this point, the State would be obliged to step in, not always successfully, for the fall of the Ch'in, Han, T'ang, and Sung dynasties was in each case accompanied by massive peasant uprisings.

By the turn of the nineteenth century, the population had grown enormously: from 82m. in 1751 to 432m. by 1851. Yet the areas of arable land only increased by 8·5 per cent. The arrival of the Western Powers was thus only a final but crucially disturbing force on top of major changes already going on inside China.

After the establishment of the Republic in 1911, landlord

and official, together with the militia and local Kuomintang party leaders, constituted a 'grain-controlling minority'. But the peasants often discriminated between these separate elements within the ruling class. Thus, much peasant protest was directed against the State rather than the landlord, as in that other autocratic and archaic régime, Tsarist Russia, where, as Shanin has shown, though there were many uprisings, they were primarily directed against representatives or actions of the State (rather than 'class-war'). Chinese peasants, too, resisted increased taxes, recruitment for the Army, the requisition of labour, and so forth, often entirely as a local resistance simply aiming to protect their village. If they could persuade the officials to move on to do their dirty work in the next village, so much the better. There were also 'horizontal' conflicts, as Lucien Bianco has termed them, with other villages and districts. Peasants tended to defend what few rights they had got and what little property they possessed, and to react against changes which threatened to make their situation even more precarious. The task of changing the whole social order was something quite beyond their vision, except as a dream, and, indeed, frightened them normally. They also tended to feel bound by ties of kinship, custom, and dependence even to those who exploited them. They might feel gratitude and loyalty – a double 'indebtedness' – to those who had lent them money or rented them land or farming equipment, even at high rates of interest, and a sense of identity with those richer than themselves who were nevertheless fellow-villagers.

Many people are inclined these days to think of peasants as 'natural' revolutionaries. The only trouble with this theory is that it runs counter to the experience of most of recorded human history. For it is very difficult indeed to get anyone, peasants included, to risk their lives when faced with total repression and with no idea of where they are going. They are often more interested in surviving than rebelling: in this century, Chinese peasants often deliberately got themselves sent to gaol for short stretches – for at least they would be fed in gaol. Hence the Communists were later to find them unresponsive to appeals to 'stand up', and sometimes made the fatal mistake of trying to force them to do what the Communists wanted: the so-called sin of 'commandism'. At other times, since peasants were not forthcoming, the Communists made do by filling their armies with desperate and disorderly people who had lost everything and would try anything, even

Communism – the people Mao later termed 'declassed elements'.

Peasants themselves usually only rose when they were very desperate indeed, when organization and leadership presented itself, often from outside or from 'marginal' elements in society, and when they felt that others across the land were moving too. Otherwise, even their violent protest remained limited to *'risings'*, desperate local *jacqueries* in which they savagely attacked local wielders and symbols of power, whether landlords or officials.

Just how serious peasant revolt could be became evident when a new factor of instability was added – the arrival of capitalist imperialism. By the middle of the nineteenth century, the internal decay of the Manchu dynasty and the growing intrusion of the Western Powers had given rise to a series of rebellions, each of enormous scale, the largest of which, the Taiping Rebellion, established a régime based on a new kind of ideology and novel principles of social organization (together with some quite traditional elements); it succeeded in maintaining itself over very large areas of China for nearly a decade and a half, despite losses numbered not in millions of lives, but in tens of millions. It was at once the greatest war of the nineteenth century (far dwarfing the American Civil War), the greatest rebellion in Chinese history, and a war and revolution of a magnitude that has scarcely been matched in world history. Yet it is virtually unknown in the West. Since it also profoundly foreshadowed much that occurred in the later Communist revolution, it repays study.

The Rebellion was a portent of the approaching end of not only the imperial régime, but also the social order sustaining it. Previous rebellions had taken 'Overthrow the Ch'ing [Manchus] and Restore the Ming' (the last indigenous Chinese dynasty) as their slogan. The Taipings had quite different goals and ideals. Though they were nationalistic in that they were anti-Manchu, and their followers cut off the pig-tails the Manchus forced on the Chinese as a badge of inferiority, initially they were not anti-Western at all. Indeed, they borrowed Western religious ideas as the foundation of their new ideology. Their leader, Hung Hsiu-Chüan, who had been instructed by Protestant missionaries in Canton, claimed to have received his authority through dreams and visions which told him to spread the new doctrine. It included belief in God, the Ten Commandments, baptism, and many other Christian elements (as perceived through Chinese eyes). He was also very open to Western social ideals. The Taipings abolished slavery and prostitution, forbade gambling and opium-smoking, and gave women a new and higher status than they had ever possessed. They proclaimed universal love and brotherhood as their ideal in regulating both internal and external relations. But they soon found that acceptance of Christian beliefs was no assurance of the friendship of the Western Powers, who were more interested in profit than piety, and who proceeded to help the Manchus – whom they now easily dominated – to suppress this dangerous threat to established trade and to social order.

From their beginnings in South China, in the mountains of the south-west and Kwangsi, the Taipings marched north through central China and the Yangtse valley. In 1853, they proclaimed the establishment of the 'Heavenly Kingdom of Great Peace' (from which their name is derived – 'T'ai P'ing': Great Peace), with its capital at Nanking. (They never succeeded in taking Peking, the imperial capital.) Archaic elements and modern ideas jostled each other in the ideology and practice of the new State. The main leaders were designated *wang*, an ancient term for 'king', and bitter struggles were later to break out between them. The peasants who flocked to join them also stamped their mark on the movement. Wealthy landlords and corrupt officials were put to death, their property distributed to the poor, and tax-records, land-registers and records of debt were destroyed. In these areas where the rebels succeeded in securely establishing their authority, over more than a decade, trade flourished. But, as time wore on, Taiping leadership became a ruling class itself, forgetting its principles and increasingly squeezing the peasantry. The latter began to withdraw their support, and this made it easier for a handful of 'modernizers' in the Imperial court, such as the mandarin Tseng Kuo-fan, with the crucial support of Western imperialism (notably the forces commanded by Gordon, and the denial of Shanghai to the rebels), to pull the imperial armies together and develop a counter-offensive which ended with the capture of the rebel capital, Nanking, in 1864, when Gordon's engineers blew breaches in the walls. The real slaughter began after the surrender of the rebels. When Lord Elgin visited the city shortly afterwards, he found five hundred people in a city where there had been five hundred thousand. Between twenty and thirty million people at least had perished altogether in what had been perhaps the most destructive war in history.

Their victory allowed the Manchus to deal with the other major rebellions: that of the Nien amongst the peasants of North China (1853–68), and the 'ethnic' rebellions of the Muslims in Yunnan (1853–73) and in the north-west (1863–73), and of the Miao minority in the south-west. Accounts of the Nien, a much more decentralized movement than the Taiping, show that guerilla warfare in China is something much older than communism:

> ... [they] were entirely devoid of firearms, which made it difficult if not impossible for them to capture walled cities where any resistance was offered. They carried no tents, and had no permanent encampments, but if night overtook them they scattered to the near-by villages ... They were able to move with incredible swiftness ... Whenever their enemies came too close for comfort, they managed to wear them out by marching in circles ... As a rule they avoided battle with troops sent against them, certainly never attacking first. (W. J. Hail, *Tseng Kuo-fan and the Taiping Rebellion.*)

The collapse of these massive revolts gave the Empire a breathing-space. It was wasted. Reforms were proposed by the modernizers at court, who wanted to introduce Western technology and to modernize the army, and some of whom even contemplated social reforms (though without encroaching on imperial authority or changing the basic political order). This was enough to alarm the reactionary Empress Dowager, Tz'u Hsi, who counter-attacked, smashed the reformers and imprisoned the boy-Emperor, Pu Yi (who later became the puppet 'Emperor of Manchukuo' – Manchuria – under the Japanese, survived a war crimes trial, and ended up as a gardener in Peking, where he wrote a fascinating autobiography subtitled 'from Emperor to Citizen').

Peasant revolt and modernizing reformers might have been suppressed but new threats were emerging in the cities. In any case, the forward policies of the imperialist Powers at home and abroad meant that the end of the Empire was imminent. China's traditional suzerainty over Annam in Indo-China was threatened by the French, that over Korea by the Japanese, who were soon to annex that country. In 1894, Japan attacked North China: Formosa (Taiwan) and parts of the North China mainland itself were ceded. But the foreigners were also 'within the gates': they controlled the customs, the railways, and the great rivers, and their banks and armies in the 'concession areas' were the real government of China. Russians, Germans, British and French were rapidly parcelling China into 'spheres of influence'.

Tz'u Hsi fiddled in truly Neronic manner. She had the tastes, but not the political ability, of Catherine the Great. While the Empire crumbled, she occupied herself with lovers imported into the Palace in covered sedan-chairs on what was often their last journey. She picked at sumptuous meals with dozens of courses, and slashed the eunuch attendants who offended her with two special clawshaped thimbles made of gold. The ultimate memorial to imperial decadence stands in the lake at the Summer Palace today (the Palace burned by invading Western troops in 1860): the beautiful Marble Boat built with funds earmarked for the modernization of the navy. Meanwhile, an international military guard (British, American, Japanese, Russian, German, French, Austro-Hungarian and Italian) was stationed in the Legation Quarter of Peking adjoining her palace. From the high walls, the troops could easily rake the city with fire. No Chinese had the right to live in this quarter; Chinese troops and Peking police were forbidden entry.

In 1900, popular hatred exploded in the anti-foreigner 'Boxer Rebellion'. Frustrated by the indignities heaped upon China by the Powers and anxious to court some easy popularity, a commodity in very short supply by then, Tz'u Hsi at first covertly supported the rebels. Later, bowing to foreign pressures and scared of the forces she had helped unleash, she turned and slaughtered them.

After the suppression of the Boxers, it was clear that it was necessary now, not to reform the Empire, but to abolish it. The time for protest, revolt or rebellion, or for a purely *political* change, had passed. The time had come for *social* revolution. A young doctor, known to us as Sun Yat-Sen and to the Chinese as Zhongshan, now began a brilliant campaign of recruiting young students, not peasants, into a revolutionary society, the 'Dare-to-dies', collecting money from Chinese overseas to finance the revolution. The political chaos following Tz'u Hsi's death in 1908 gave him his chance. He had to operate principally from abroad, and travelled between Hawaii, Japan, the U.S.A. and Europe organizing the revolution. Once he was 'shanghaied' and dragged into the Chinese Legation in London, from whence he said he would have been smuggled back to China and had his ankles crushed and broken by hammers, his eyelids cut off, and his flesh sliced into slivers. (He was rescued due to the efforts of his former teacher, Dr James Cantlie, who raised the case in the courts and with the Foreign Office.)

Back in China, the different elements among the ruling classes were at each other's throats. Government proposals to nationalize the railways brought the indigenous capitalists to the edge of revolt. In this climate, Sun's movement flourished; the ability of the government to crush one revolt after another was not enough to deter the revolutionaries. After no less than ten unsuccessful attempts to launch risings in the South, mostly across the Indo-China border, a successful rising began on the Double Tenth (10 October 1911) at Wuch'ang. This time, Sun's limited forces were joined by whole armies under defecting generals. The Chinese Republic was born.

*

Young men growing up at this time were living in a world where Confucian order was just a memory. The problem was what to put in its place. The village in which Mao Tse-Tung was born, Shaosan, was affected by the same upheavals that racked countless other villages across the length and breadth of China as the Empire gave way to the Republic.

Mao, the son of a middle peasant who had become rich, was not born an instant revolutionary. Like others of his generation, he had gone through a period of enthusiasm for the mandarin reformers in Peking who had tried, unsuccessfully, to modernize the Empire. Disillusioned by that failure, Mao and his school-fellows cut off their pigtails in symbolic rejection of Manchu rule. It was now necessary, it seemed clear, not to reform the Empire, but to overthrow it. When the uprising began at Wuch'ang, Mao joined the rebel army in Hunan.

He was ready enough to act, but he and young revolutionaries like him needed an intellectual system which would not only help them to make sense of all this turmoil, but also show them what they needed to do to put China on its feet as a modern and just society. They ransacked the whole range of literature flooding in from Europe and Japan. At this stage, Mao later remarked, his mind was still 'a curious mixture of ideas of liberalism, democratic reformism, and utopian socialism'. He had 'somewhat vague passions about "nineteenth century democracy", utopianism and old-fashioned liberalism' and was 'definitely anti-militarist and anti-imperialist'. But these doctrines did not provide what he was looking for, and he needed access to newer ideas and the opportunity, too, to work with people of like mind willing to translate these ideas into action. The search led him, firstly, to high school at the provincial capital, Changsha, and finally, in 1918, to Peking. Other young men, like Chou En-Lai or Chu Teh, the future Commander-in-Chief of the Red Armies, had gone off to Europe and Japan. Mao felt the need to deepen his knowledge of China. In the North, he visited the historic places of Chinese culture, climbed T'ai Shan, the sacred mountain of Shantung, visited Confucius' grave, and walked on the ice in the Gulf of Pei Hai. He also saw the walls of Nanking where the great Taiping Rebellion had been drowned in blood half a century before. And rebellious peasants were still being slaughtered: Mao himself had seen the corpses of their leaders lying in the streets of Changsha.

In Peking, he quickly found what he was looking for. He got a job as assistant to Li Ta-Chao, the Librarian of Peking National University. Li also happened to be the founder of Chinese Marxism. The influence Li had on him is said to have been the source of the 'populist' elements in Mao's thinking, for Li was well acquainted with the writings of the Russian Narodniks. One small direct echo of Li can be detected in Mao's writing: here is Mao making fun of those peasants who rely on the gods to protect them:

One who believes in the Eight Characters hopes for good luck; one who believes in geomancy hopes for the beneficial influence of the burial ground. This year the local bullies, bad gentry and corrupt officials all collapsed within a few months. Is it possible that till a few months ago they were all in good luck, and all under the beneficial influence of the burial grounds, while in the last few months they have all of a sudden been in bad luck and their burial grounds all ceased to exert any beneficial influence on them? . . .

The gods? They may quite deserve our worship. But if we had no peasant association but only the Emperor Kuan [the god of loyalty and war] and the Goddess of Mercy, could we have knocked down the local bullies and bad gentry? The gods and goddesses are indeed pitiful; worshipped for hundreds of years, they have not knocked down for you a single local bully or a single one of the bad gentry!

Now, you want to have your rent reduced. I would like to ask: How will you go about it? Believe in the gods, or believe in the peasant associations?

'These words of mine', Mao says, 'made the peasants roar with laughter.'

And here is Li, writing at almost the same time about the Red Spears secret society, whose peasant members, though militant enough, only had knives, shovels and forks to fight with, and traditional boxing and breathing techniques as their military training. They supplemented these, Li says, by appealing to traditional extra-human assistance – the gods, the characters of the popular romances like Chu Ba-jie, the wondrously strong pig or Sun Wu-kong, the clever Monkey, or by using talismans, divination by sand, '*yin* and *yang* jargon', and the like. 'With talismans on one side and machine-guns and rifles on the other, it was bound to be an unequal battle,' he remarks. 'Once the peasants have modern weapons in their possession their belief in the five elements and the eight diagrams progressively loses its force.'

The thought of Mao Tse-Tung, at this stage as afterwards, was very much part of the furious new thinking going on all around him.

Through the study-circles Li organized, Mao was brought into contact with similar tiny groups in the other major cities. Later, he was able to visit the largest of these, Shanghai, at once the centre of imperialist power and of new movements among the working class which imperialism had brought into being. Mao was back in Changsha as a teacher when the patriotic May 4th Movement, protesting against a further instalment of the Japanese dismemberment of China, broke out in 1918. It gave him his first major opportunity to try his hand at mass organization. By this time, however, his thinking had gone beyond nationalism, to Marxism.

The *Communist Manifesto* had only been translated into Chinese in 1920, and when the scattered Marxist study-circles were linked together to form the Chinese Communist Party in 1921, there were only twelve delegates representing fifty-seven permanent members of the circles. Yet such was the forced-draught temperature of the political climate that within six years of this microscopic beginning, the Communist Party had become firmly established among the workers of the cities and was attracting many of the most able young radicals to its ranks.

Yet the major party, best placed to harness most of this revolutionary energy, was not the Communist Party, but the Kuomintang, the party of the founder of the Republic, Sun

Yat-Sen, now headed by Chiang Kai-Shek. Sun had been unable to maintain himself in power as President, since he had no
military force to match that of Yuan Shih-K'ai, the general
who displaced him for a while and set himself up as dictator
(and would-be Emperor). Nor could Sun defeat the armies of
the warlords who competed for control after Yüan's death in
1915. He needed a modern Army, and an efficient Party
machine to imbue civilians and soldiers alike with revolutionary determination and coordinate their actions. He turned for
help to the leaders of another new revolutionary country,
Soviet Russia, whose revolution was very different from Sun's
– which was based on the 'Three Principles' of Nationalism,
Socialism and Democracy – but who nevertheless sent him
advisers to reorganize the Party and Army. The alliance with
the Bolsheviks abroad was paralleled by an alliance with the
Communists at home, for the two parties united to prevent
the country's dissolution at the hands of reactionary warlords
who had seized large regions of China as their private empires.
Sun died in 1925. His successor, Chiang, was a military man
who had trained the new officer corps in his military school at
Whampoa near Canton. By 1927, Chiang was ready to strike
out on his Northern Expedition to bring all of China under his
control. By March the following year he was in Shanghai, and
the whole of China south of the Yangtse was in his hands.

Now he no longer needed Communist support. Even before
the Northern Expedition, the growing power of the workers'
organizations in cities like Canton had frightened the urban
capitalists in his party, and driven Chiang to repressive action,
sometimes by passing laws discriminating against the Communists and the trade unions, sometimes by shooting and
imprisoning their leaders. When Chou En-Lai organized a
strike of 600,000 Shanghai workers in 1927, and then an
armed insurrection which drove out the local warlord and
made the entry of Chiang's army into the city bloodless, he
rewarded their action by wholesale massacre. Mao's mentor,
Li Ta-Chao, was strangled; the Soviet advisers were sent back
to Russia. The left-wing of the Kuomintang ineffectually pro-
tested, but Chiang held the guns, and the right-wing of the
Party – the wealthy businessmen and landlords – was firmly
behind him.

The landlords had equal reason to be scared of the Communist alliance, because in the countryside, too, during the
drive North, Communists like Mao had encouraged the

peasantry to rise in revolt, not just against the warlords, but against the landlords themselves.

In 1927, Mao Tse-Tung submitted a report on his activities among the peasants of Hunan to the Central Committee of the Chinese Communist Party. (He also held office in the Kuomintang (Nationalist) Party of Chiang Kai-Shek at that time, since the two parties were in alliance.)

Revolutionaries expect to be sent into situations which are not only dangerous, but also totally unfamiliar. With Mao this was not the case, for Hunan was his home province. The explosion of class-war in the countryside, however, was by no means something a handful of revolutionary organizers could claim credit for. When Mao got back to Hunan he found that the peasants had already organized themselves into peasant associations which had grown from three or four hundred thousand to two million strong in less than a year and embraced half the total peasantry, and in many counties virtually the entire population. They had also armed themselves with spears – 100,000 in one county alone, enough to counter the rifles of the landlords, whose armed forces were defecting, anyway. A force of twenty *million* peasants armed with spears should be organized quickly, Mao urged.

Instead, some of the revolutionaries arriving in Hunan thought that the peasants were 'going too far' and committing 'excesses', and allowing themselves to be diverted into bizarre and marginal activities. Even Mao himself, intimately familiar with the peasants of Hunan as he was, wrote of 'many strange things' that were going on, 'that I had never seen or heard before'. So he set out to try and analyse the situation in the countryside.

He started by an *Analysis of the various classes of the Chinese peasantry, and their attitude towards revolution* (1926), following the classic model provided by Lenin in his analysis of *The Development of Capitalism in Russia* and other writings. This careful analysis was to lay the basis not only for his subsequent turn to the countryside as the locus of the revolution, but also for land reform in the liberated Soviet areas and ultimately in post-Liberation China as a whole. It therefore repays attention.

To analyse the balance of class-forces in the countryside might not seem anything other than the most obvious of starting-points for those setting about to change the whole pattern of rural society, but even today, in a country like Tanzania, the Ujamaa programme of rural development along socialist lines has been launched without any prior analysis of social differentiation in the countryside, largely because it has been assumed, *a priori*, that classes do not exist there or do not matter if they do, and that assertion to the contrary is a Marxist delusion.

Mao distinguished no less than eight separate classes in the countryside, and several groups within each of these. First came the *big landlords*, some the descendants of officials and nobles, others urban merchants who had bought land, and yet others who had 'raised' themselves by expanding the scale of their farming operations. They were the 'deadly enemies of the Chinese peasantry'. The *small landlords* were mostly hard-working peasant proprietors who had similarly raised themselves, others among them, once more, urban merchants and descendants of officials. Some of these could be influenced in a left-wing direction at times when peasant militancy was high, but normally they followed the lead of the right-wing majority among the small landlords – and *they* followed the big land-lords.

Then came the *peasant landholders*, about 10 per cent of whom were able to accumulate a little surplus money and food over and above their daily needs, but about half of them, even with very hard work, found survival precarious, constantly threatened as they were by rapacious landlords, militarists and by foreign imperialists. They were therefore not unsympathetic to the revolution, but would not stick their necks out. The third group among the peasant landholders, about 40 per cent of them, did not even make ends meet. Many had known better days. They were therefore quite amenable to revolutionary appeals.

Below them came the *semi-landholders*, who had some land but not enough for their needs and hence had to rent extra land. To pay the rent, they had to borrow from money-lenders at exorbitant rates; to repay their loans and to tide them over between harvests, they had to go out to work seasonally or supplement their income from petty trade. The *sharecroppers* were even worse off, because they had no land of their own and had to rent it all, but only received half of the crops they grew, as did the semi-landholders from the land they rented. Even if they owned no land, the sharecroppers did at least have a little working capital and some farm-implements, and could supplement their income by growing side-crops, raising chickens and pigs, and fishing. But the lot of the *poor peasants*, who had neither land nor implements, was one of permanent indebtedness, periodic resort to begging, and endemic hunger, at times famine. The landless *farm labourers*, who lived by working for others, were even more uncertain of regular employment (though the rural craftsmen, however insecure, did own their tools and had more specialized skills to sell). At the bottom of the heap were what Mao called the *éléments déclassés*, the vast 'underclass' – all twenty million of them – who had lost all place in normal society: beggars, prostitutes, thieves, bandits, and (not much different) soldiers. 'But', said Mao, 'they are all human beings.' They were also brave people. They tried to protect themselves and to survive by joining secret societies which sometimes resembled mutual aid societies and sometimes criminal gangs. If properly led, these people could even become a revolutionary force, Mao concluded. (They were indeed recruited into the early Red Armies, but given a thorough political indoctrination.)

So far, Mao followed Lenin's mode of analysis. But in a *Report of an Investigation into the Peasant Movement in Hunan*, written shortly afterwards, he went further and deeper into peasant society than Lenin, an urban intellectual dependent on official statistics, was able to do. Mao still concentrated on the mode of production as the key to the understanding of social relations in the villages as well as of class relations at societal level. But the system of exploitation could not be adequately described by looking at work and ownership alone. Each class had its own characteristic way of life, and the dominant class attempted to impose its customs on the peasants they exploited, representing its culture as superior. The rebellious peasants resented and attacked the whole style of life of the landlords, including the symbols of their dominance. Here we can see that Mao's conception of revolution as a process of totally remaking society and man, replacing the culture of capitalism by the culture of socialism rather than changing only economic or political arrangements, was not just drawn from the Marxist classics but grew out of his experience of revolution by peasants in rural China.

The peasants, Mao reported, had had their revenge on the landlords: they had punished them for their misuse of public funds and for their private exploitation by fining them, banishing, imprisoning, and even executing the most 'evil' and 'lawless' amongst the 'bad gentry', the corrupt officials, and their strong-arm squads, as well as the bandits and vagabonds, and the people who hung about the temples and bullied the citizenry. They had also called a halt to extremes of exploitation (though they had not seized the land, or even set up co-operatives): rents, leases, interest rates and grain movements were all brought under control. But they had also destroyed the *moral* supremacy of the landlords, their legitimacy, the respect they had been accorded for centuries, by exposing them to public shame and ridicule: for instance, they had made them wear paper hats. And they had attacked a whole range of 'patriarchal ideologies' and 'evil customs'. There were four kinds of authority to be demolished – not just *political* authority but also *clan* and *theocratic* authority, and the authority of the *husband*. They burned the idols in the clan-temples, and outlawed opium-smoking and gambling (*mah jong* sets were burned by the basketful). Sedan-chairs, too, were smashed (until this hurt the carriers; then carrying-rates were raised instead). Then wine-making and sugar-refining, the keeping of pigs, chickens and ducks, and sumptuous feasts were all banned. Conversely, the slaughter of cattle was prohibited, because of their value as draught-animals (which the poor often had to sell). The 'flower drum' entertainment was denounced by the puritan peasantry, together with other forms of conspicuous consumption, frivolous display, waste and idle behaviour, Mao reported: chanting New Year greetings to the accompaniment of castanets, praising the local deities and singing lotus rhymes, paying New Year calls (a 'foolish custom'), festival processions in honour of the god of pestilence, the purchase of pastry and fruit for ritual presents, the burning of paper clothing during the Festival of the Spirits, the pasting-up of posters for good luck in the New Year, the smoking of water-pipes, and the letting-off of fire-crackers and firing of shotguns, Taoist and Buddhist services for the dead, gifts of money at funerals, and other prohibitions 'too many to enumerate'.

Mao concluded that these prohibitions represented a revolt against 'bad social customs' associated with the landlord class. They were also a form of peasants' self-protection against exploitation by the city merchants in the face of which the peasants had to cultivate 'frugality'. The peasants were exhibiting their rejection of existing cultural forms in other respects, too. Thus they had established their own schools, with curricula related to their needs, in contradistinction to the education they received both in the old-style Chinese schools and the foreign schools that used text books designed for the city-dweller. The peasants' ideas of their own educational needs were sounder, too, he said, than those of the 'so-called educators for popular education, which for all their hullabaloo has remained an ideal phrase' (for 'educators for popular education', today, read 'community development workers').

Mao did give due recognition to the strategic location of the industrial proletariat, concentrated as the latter were in the cities. But he pointed out that there were only two million of them, as against 320 million peasants. The Chinese Communists have, to this day, continued to insist on the 'major' or 'leading' role of the proletariat and 'their' ideology, Marxism, but the massacre of 1927 had revealed that power could be concentrated in the cities not just by the workers, but also by their enemies – the armies and police forces of Chiang and the foreign powers. Increasingly, after 1927, a rural-based strategy became the only viable one. Yet the whole conception was so unorthodox to Marxist eyes that the policy was strongly resisted, and Mao's report was not published.

Mao's admiration of the peasants' militancy did not blind him to their limitations. They might fight bravely, but they lacked both theory and organization. And for revolt and rebellion to be transformed into revolution, direction and continuity were required. What was needed, then, was an agency that would provide these things: the Party. A modern revolutionary party of the kind that developed in those years is a singularly potent organizational device. It brought together several overlapping elements, each of which would have been powerful enough, taken separately, but when taken together, constituted an irrepressible combination. Firstly, it provided an intellectual map of the world. It identified the social system the people were living under: capitalism. It also located that system within history: it was capitalism in its late, dying phase: imperialism. It then identified the component elements of that system: the rival capitalisms and the antagonistic classes within each. It also provided a new kind of social identity: the individual was no longer just a member of this or that particularistic local unit: his clan or village. He was a peasant or a worker, an identity he shared with millions, even with people in other countries. This structural identity also had ethical dimensions: he was an *exploited* peasant or a *downtrodden* worker. Next, the Party identified for him his friends and his enemies: the 'middle peasantry' and the 'Soviet people', or the 'rich peasants' and the 'foreign imperialists', respectively. The revolutionary ideology did not stop short simply at an analysis of the present; it also provided him with a set of goals for the future and a promised solution, with a model of the alternative society towards which he should aim, a programme of action to be followed in order to reach it, and with the actual agency which would communicate these ideas and co-ordinate action.

Given this crucial agency, the Party, an enormous liberation of human energy could occur, and the very personality of the individual could be transformed. For revolution, indeed, nothing less was required than the ultimate commitment: preparedness to die.

But to 'stand up', even short of offering one's life, required great courage; and to develop the courage to challenge the landlords' power, to confiscate their land and challenge their moral domination, and to generate the confidence and the skills needed to set up new alternative institutions, more than socialist vision and education were needed.

Though radical romantics do not always realize it, poverty is not necessarily a stimulus to militancy. It can also induce fatalism, resignation, passivity, hopelessness, compromise, and avoidance. Peasants, classically, have endured poverty and oppression for centuries. Watching starving Chinese peasants in the north-west in 1929, even Edgar Snow was puzzled by their passivity. 'For a while,' he remarks, 'I thought nothing would make a Chinese peasant fight.' It was not that they never dared to revolt; the history of peasant rebellion disproves that. Rather, they would never dare to do these things as long as the landlords could always call up superior force to put them down. Hence more was needed even than a Party: no less than an Army in an area entirely under Communist military and political control, a secure 'Red base' where the peasantry could be protected from landlord thugs and counter-insurgency forces, where continuity in the work of political education, land redistribution and social reform, in the proper training of the Army and improving agricultural production, could be ensured.

Contemporary fascination with the romantic figure of Che Guevara and the theorizing of Régis Debray (theories he later renounced) has encouraged a whole generation in the West to think of all armed revolutionary struggle as guerilla struggle, the guerillas being conceived of as tiny bands of 'hunted men', living '24 hours out of 24 neither in the day nor the night but in the half-light of the enervating, humid, protecting forest'.

Debray argues that during the first phase of guerilla operations, the guerillas experience a period of 'absolute nomadism', in which they are independent of the civilian population and avoid going to the villages. 'Constant vigilance, constant mistrust, constant mobility' are the three 'golden rules': a group of armed propagandists should abandon all hope of remaining unnoticed, 'like fish in water'. The last phrase is significant, for here Debray is quoting Mao's classic injunction that the guerillas must learn to swim in the peasant sea. Thus he quotes Mao only to reject him. Debray's conception of guerilla warfare, fundamentally different from that of Mao, was at the root of the Bolivian débâcle. Its crucial error was the notion of a guerilla movement without a popular base.

The Chinese certainly practised guerilla warfare on a massive scale in the regions occupied by the Japanese or controlled by Chiang. But they were directed from a secure base, and within that base the Red Army survived, not by constantly keeping on the move, but by becoming, in Mao's classic phrase, 'fish' who flourished in the medium that supported them, the 'sea' of peasants. The Party, unlike other parties, had no constitutional or traditional authority; no access to private wealth which could be used to buy support. They could only survive by virtue of the support, shelter, transportation, information, guides, food and protection afforded them by the people. To win over the peasants they had to become rooted amongst them. They also had to bring improvement to their lives. They could not win support; they had to earn it. Power might grow from the barrel of a gun – and the Red base would not last five minutes without guns – but guns could not win men's minds. They could not afford to *make* the peasants do what they wanted by pointing guns at them; their survival depended on trust, not force. Force was something used by and against the enemy.

The Red Army had to become part and parcel of village life, not a foreign military force living in their midst like some foreign army of occupation. They had to identify completely with the lives of the peasants: to work in the fields with them, indeed to *become* peasants themselves, for the Army in China *to this day* grows its own food and helps the communes grow theirs. 'We must', Mao said, 'go to the masses':

... arouse them to activity; concern ourselves with their weal and woe; ... work earnestly and sincerely in their interests and solve their problems of salt, rice, shelter, clothing and childbirth ... The women want to learn ploughing and hoeing ... The children want to go to school ... The wooden bridge over there is too narrow ... All such problems concerning the living standards of the masses should be placed on the agenda ... We should make the broad masses realize that we represent their interests, that their lives and ours are intimately interwoven.

Perhaps the most graphic illustration of this close rapport, however, comes from another country which learned from the Chinese example, Vietnam:

To get a footing amongst our national minorities our political workers have not simply learned their language, but have pierced their ears when the minority pierces its ears, filed their teeth when the minority files theirs ... Without patience, you cannot make a revolution ...

In principle, the revolutionary political workers scarcely ever leave the villages. They know the terrain, the people, their own families. We have political workers who have lived for years like this, hidden underground by day and coming out only at night. Some of them have become blind through never seeing the light. (Nguyen Van Tien, quoted in Basil Davidson's *The Liberation of Guiné*.)

From their earliest days, then, the Communists operated as part of the fabric of everyday life in the villages. But they did not leave it unchanged, or simply become absorbed. They were an activating and mobilizing force which linked together all social activities and related them to the overall policies of the Party. They showed people where to go and what to do, however, not simply by preaching at them or propagandizing them, but by involving them in struggle, drawing out lessons from what had happened, and by involving them, too, in new, socialist ways of living, rather than treating socialism as something that would be put into operation *after* the elimination of capitalism. New ways of living of this kind, and new ways of waging people's war, could not easily be extracted ready-made from classical Marxist writings and handed down by some Party élite. They had to be worked out in dialogue with the peasants themselves, and entailed the closest possible involvement in peasant life.

But, for effective policies to emerge, Marxist theory had to become part and parcel of everybody's thinking, and for this to happen efficient organization was a *sine qua non*. Within the organizations created, too, everyday relations had to be based on socialist premises. Hence relations between officers and men in the Army, between cadres and peasantry, between Government and Army, differed fundamentally from those typical of capitalist armies, governments and officials. Differences of status as between officers and men were therefore reduced to the minimum. In battle, decisive authority had to be exercised, but this did not necessitate an officer caste, rather the opposite. 'The Eighth Route Army', Israel Epstein reported in 1937,

from Company upwards, has elected economic committees which supervise rations, the proper expenditure of men's money and so forth. Officers and men sit on these committees in equal terms, and the committees, which must produce their accounts on the demand of any soldier, see that everyone shares equally.

There were those, as ever in radical movements, who took these principles to extremes, demanding that everyone, irrespective of age, physical condition or the nature of his responsibilities, carry the same loads, and who criticized the allocation of larger rooms to staff for their use as headquarters. Such tendencies towards ultra-democracy or 'absolute egalitarianism' were denounced as 'petty bourgeois individualism'. Organization and discipline were regarded as vital, as was obedience to orders, although there was to be maximum involvement in formulating policy whenever circumstances allowed. Petty criticism, ignoring the central issues and concentrating on minor faults, was regarded as equally destructive.

In the marginal areas, far from the reach of the authorities in either of the adjoining provinces, the harassed Reds could find some security, as their rebel predecessors had done. And like their predecessors, local units, in their isolation, would sometimes lose sight of the overall struggle and become preoccupied with local hostilities – the deviation condemned by the Party as 'mountain-topism'. By the spring of 1928 they had grown to 100,000. The logic of warfare was then driving them towards extended peasant-based guerilla warfare directed from base areas; it converged with the 'social' logic of revolutionary land-redistribution which could only be defended by armed forces. But Mao's strategy only represented a minority view at this time. In the end, he, Chu Teh, and others were forced to commit the ultimate Communist sin: to defy the decisions of the Party leadership.

But the Right of the Party, the proponents of a more cautious city-based strategy, recoiled from militancy for a time after the defeats. Since they included the Party's Secretary, Ch'en Tu-Hsiu, Mao's role in the launching of the Autumn Harvest Uprising lost him his position in the Politbureau. Ch'en's successors, however, under Comintern influence, then swung to the other, Left, pole – with militant action everywhere in the hope of reviving a faltering revolution; risings in the big cities; the concentration of the rural armies to capture provincial towns, and terror in the villages directed against the landlords. The results were even more disastrous: though the workers rose in Canton, their 'Commune' was drowned in blood; at Changsha, the rural armies were smashed. Mao's wife and sister were amongst those taken and executed.

It might seem that there was now little alternative to the strategy of protracted warfare in the scattered areas where the Reds had either a 'Soviet' or networks of guerillas in areas under the formal control of Chiang, and replacing positional warfare and large-scale head-on clashes with superior enemy forces by short, sharp attacks where local superiority could ensure success. But the Left militants did not give in easily, and even staged an unsuccessful armed revolt within the Kiangsi Soviet zone.

Some Marxists use the notion of Marxism as a 'guide to action' in a purely logical, though quite un*socio*logical fashion, as if 'correct' policies can be unambiguously derived from first principles in a way that will command the natural assent of all right-thinking men. The actual history of Communism, as of all political life, shows that mutually incompatible derivations can be made from the same basic principles and that these rival policies give rise to 'factions' whose contention can be quite as fierce as any between Marxists and their enemies. They then use a version of what they conceive of as 'the test of praxis' as an explanation of why one or other of these rival 'lines' of policy wins out over the others. By this, they often mean nothing more than that the best policy is that which works, a notion that reduces Marxism as theory, to vulgar pragmatism, and, as practice, to cynical *Realpolitik*, a divorce of ends from means that can justify the use of any means – brute force, material inducements, deceit – that promises to pay off.

It is obviously not the case that only 'correct' theories are equipped to survive, as if, in some Darwinian sense, they were the 'fittest'. Very bad theories survive, indeed flourish, because if one has enough power, they can be *made* to work. To use terms like 'bad', 'correct', or 'success', in this way, of course, implies some relationship between them, which is a long way from either pragmatism or *Realpolitik*. It implies that policies do not just 'work' in themselves, but that they 'work' in ways that realize different kinds of *values* for different kinds of people. Conservative politics consist in manipulating political institutions so as to channel the goods of society, material and immaterial, into the hands of the dominant social class, usually by a combination of pragmatism – staying in power by using whatever policy works (and to hell with theory) – and *Realpolitik*: using whatever *means* pays off (and to hell with ideals). Though as contemptuous of 'pure' theory as it is of 'pure' ideals, it implies a very definite set of social values: the maintenance of an order of things in which the few benefit from the labour of the many.

Socialist politics is based upon a quite different set of values, and hence uses different yardsticks to measure success: not the successful preservation of the existing system of production and appropriation of wealth; not even the reallocation of that wealth between social classes. Reallocation is only a step towards breaking the power of the dominant class and abolishing class society altogether, and replacing the existing value-system by one based on co-operative rather than exploitative relations between men: in short, the measure of 'success' of policy is the extent to which it has helped to move the society towards socialism.

Socialism, then, implies a relating of means to ends. It is not something that begins after the seizure of power: if it is not practised along the way, it will never develop at all. Negatively, to use means which contradict socialist values, such as inhuman brutality or diffuse terror, may frighten enemies; it also frightens potential friends. A more humane order of society cannot be achieved by inhumanity. But if socialist values preclude some kinds of actions, they indicate others. Egalitarian relations should obtain between socialists, and between revolutionaries and the people they work amongst. Socialism, too, has to be *better* than what exists: people's lives should be improved: by giving them protection against those who exploit and terrify them, and by positive instalments of new

modes of socialist organization: by giving them land or
establishing co-ops.

'Praxis', then, is the *collective* accomplishment of actions to
realize such goals, by groups of men, such as classes and
parties. It is not to be thought of in terms of the individualistic,
essentially *bourgeois*, image of that kind of 'testing' of theory
practised by the scientist with a test-tube in his laboratory (a
quite inadequate model, actually, of modern science, which
involves the interaction, direct and indirect, even international,
of thousands of people in large institutions; it is a poor model,
in any case, even for older science).

Policies aiming at transforming whole societies are far more
complex and difficult to evaluate than the outcome of controlled experiments in laboratories. It is difficult to know
definitely who is right and who is wrong for quite long periods.
At the time of the 'Left' and 'Right' deviations, as the Chinese
call them, in the 1920s, the chances of *any* revolutionary
strategy achieving success against the infinitely superior forces
of Chiang Kai-Shek looked slim in the extreme. Chiang had
extended his control over most of China. He had entered
Peking in 1928, and had then defeated the 'Christian General',
the warlord whose armies retreated before Chiang into the
north-west. The last major remaining warlord, the 'Young
Marshal', in Manchuria, now declared his loyalty to the
nationalist régime, which established its capital at Nanking.

The time had come to deal with the Communists definitively.
They proved more difficult. Chiang, between 1930 and 1934,
launched no less than five major campaigns against the Red
areas. Hundreds of thousands of Kuomintang troops were
launched against the tiny Communist bases. They were all
successfully defeated; equipment fell into Red hands on a large
scale, and large numbers of troops defected to them.

Chiang's German advisers attributed these failures to the
strategy of thrusting troops forward into the Red zones.
Instead, they counselled encirclement and starvation. The fifth
campaign against the three main Soviet areas involved no less
than a million men. It was the Red armies, rather, that now
allowed themselves to be drawn into premature positional
warfare, and suffered severely in so doing. By 1934, retreat to
a more secure base had become imperative. The remote
province of Shensi, in the north-west, where a Red base
already existed, was selected as the goal. To reach it, they had
to undertake one of the greatest epic journeys in history: the

Long March through the south-west of China, through the mountains which rise towards Tibet and Sinkiang, for six thousand miles across some of the wildest country in the world. For 5,000 of these miles they marched nearly twenty-four miles a day, but they had to do more than march; they were continuously attacked by Kuomintang armies and had to fight an average of almost one skirmish a day. Fifteen days were spent in pitched battles.

Half the main body of troops were lost in breaking through the successive lines blockading their entry into the south-west. Many thousands died from disease and from wounds or were captured and executed by Kuomintang troops. Much of their equipment and their transport, which included industrial *matériel*, had to be abandoned. But they fought their way through into Kweichow Province, the column sometimes stretching fifty miles across the countryside, then turned into Yunnan, the province adjoining the Burmese and Indo-China borders. Crossing the Yangtse into Szechwan, and then storming the famous bridge of iron chains across the Tatu River, were both perilous moments when they were not far from total disaster.

They supported themselves by confiscating supplies from the rich. The surplus they distributed to the peasants, and they gave them land, too. Pockets of fighters were left along the route to delay and harass the pursuing enemy; many of them were to carry on guerilla warfare for many years. Millions were thus exposed to the revolutionary message of the Red troops and to their policy of taking from the few to give to the many.

In Szechwan came the greatest disaster, one from within their ranks rather than from outside: the decision of Chang Kuo-t'ao, commander of the largest Red force, not to march north with Mao to Shensi, but to stay south of the Yangtse. Though Mao had been invested with the leadership of the Party shortly after the March had begun, he was unable to control Chang. Mao, P'eng Teh-huai, Chou En-lai, and Lin Piao continued northwards with their troops, crossing eighteen mountain ranges, twenty-four rivers and twelve provinces. During the March, the Reds captured sixty-two towns and cities and fought off the armies of ten warlords, in addition to the greatly more numerous and better-equipped armies of Chiang. They went through areas where the inhabitants were ready to kill any Chinese, Red or White; then into the Grasslands, where men sank into swamps and where for ten whole days no human beings were seen at all. Fewer than 20,000 survived to reach Yenan. At their height the Red armies had numbered nearly a quarter of a million. 180,000 of them had been lost. The men who survived were extremely experienced, extremely efficient, dedicated and tough. They were unyielding on Communist principle, but had learned tactical flexibility the hard way. They were the men who were to beat Chiang and build People's China. By 1960, of the 800 who had survived the whole period between 1927 and 1960, a quarter were members or 'alternate' members of the Central Committee.

Remnants of the other armies straggled in to take refuge in the loess caves, including the battered survivors of what had once been Chang Kuo-t'ao's army of 100,000 men. But from these inauspicious beginnings, Shensi, part of the Yellow River 'cradle' of Chinese civilization, was to become the base where the policies painfully developed in the south came to fruition, and the base from which the rest of China was to be liberated and a new, Communist civilization brought into being. The key to their success was a land policy which won over the mass of the poorer peasantry without alienating the rich peasants or even the majority of the landlords. They had learned to avoid dogmatic wholesale nationalization or collectivization. To keep as wide a basis of mass support, consistent with ultimate principle, they refrained from advocating or practising taking the land off even the rich peasants during the national struggle against Japanese imperialism, the key political issue, for if they had done, they would have provoked resistance and internal division, and might have caused lowered production. If they turned the highly influential rich peasants against them, these would tell the others, less rich, that their turn would come next. Hence everything had to be done to establish confidence and to raise living-standards. The only categories who were expropriated were gross exploiters and those who collaborated with the Japanese.

American scholars, notably Chalmers Johnson, have argued that this change of policy was not only an abandonment of unpopular communist policy of class-struggle, but the substitution of a more successful nationalist appeal in its place. This is not so, for the position of the peasantry was greatly improved during this period, despite the switch away from direct expropriation. Taxation was sweepingly reduced, and was progressive: the richer you were, the steeper your taxes (in contrast to the former exemption of the wealthy from the payment of tax). Where land was in short supply, it was certainly taken from the landlords and rich peasants, but they were left with as much as they could actually cultivate themselves. Where land was plentiful, no confiscation took place; elsewhere, new land was brought under cultivation, so confiscation was unnecessary. Cheap loans were made available; consumer, production and credit co-ops established, and such petty private industrial enterprises as there were outside agriculture were allowed to continue, though new State and co-operative enterprises were established to produce basic commodities such as salt, cotton and paper in primitive workshops. It was a 'mixed' economy, not a socialist one. There was even trade with White areas.

Political power, too, was still decisively based on the poorer peasants, who were given greater representation in the Soviets, but every effort was now made to win over those 'enlightened gentry' who were prepared to struggle against the Japanese. But though even the landlords were not to be expropriated outright, and were allowed land as individuals, their power had been broken as a class.

In a province where recent famine on a massive scale had brought about a concentration of land in the hands of those able to buy it cheaply off their starving neighbours, and where taxation, especially to support the repressive militia, had been inordinate, the stabilization of the economy, the fixing of reasonable rents, the lightening of tax burdens, the distribution of land, and improvements in agricultural practice initiated by the Communists quickly brought about a tangible improvement in the lives of the peasantry. So secure did the régime become, that the Army could be overwhelmingly concentrated at the front, the peasant organizations taking care of civil administration.

Here, then, were the rudiments of the policies of self-reliance and of the scrupulous utilization of all assets, including 'waste', that were to be repeated, on a China-wide scale, after Liberation, when the whole country was thrown back on its internal resources as a result of capitalist blockade and Russian withdrawal. Here, too, evolved the practice and philosophy of equality in shared poverty, a philosophy which might be a Marxist ideal, but was also now a political necessity. Mao himself only earned 7 *yuan* a month – less than he had received as a young soldier in 1911.

Only a year after arriving in Yenan, the Communists launched a major offensive against the Japanese. Their land policy and social reforms won them support even in areas not under their control. But they now also emerged as the only force seriously resisting the Japanese and protecting the people against them. These combined policies won them the moral leadership of the nation. In contrast, Chiang refused even to co-operate with the Communists until his capture at Sian by the 'Young Marshal', the warlord whom he had appointed to wipe out the Communists, but whose experience of the Japanese in Manchuria had converted him into an advocate of national unity to defeat them. Chiang was now obliged to enter an alliance with the Communists, but his resistance to the Japanese remained passive in comparison to the Communist armies. He was waiting for his allies to win the war for him, and then to equip him to destroy the Reds.

After the collapse of Japan, Chiang moved his armies into position, all four million of them, including thirty-nine divisions trained by the Americans, and with considerable air power. Confident, he overstretched himself, attacking towards Shantung, Manchuria and Yenan simultaneously. The Communists, classically, decided to retreat and abandon their capital, Yenan, in face of overwhelming enemy superiority, under the dialectical slogan 'To keep Yenan is to lose Yenan; to lose Yenan is to keep Yenan'. By now, they were so strongly established over vast liberated areas of northern China that Yenan was less important.

Within a year of the outbreak of hostilities, Lin Piao had captured thirty-six Kuomintang generals in Manchuria alone. By January 1949, the whole of China north of the Yangtse was in Communist hands. Peking fell without a battle. In the South, the Kuomintang armies disintegrated.

Such rapid victory posed enormous organizational problems. It meant taking over thousands of villages with no experience of Communist government. In these villages people feared a 'change of sky' which would bring back Chiang, or the Americans. They were still fearful of the landlords. To get them to 'stand up' was a very different proposition from doing it in the long-established Red areas. *Fanshen*, William Hinton's classic account of the course of Liberation in one village, Long Bow in Shansi, shows just how difficult it was. A few brave souls finally dared to lead the attack on an authority which had lasted for centuries, and when they began to examine the landlords' exactions and extortions in public session of the whole village, the flood-gates were opened. Recounting how they had been starved, cheated, beaten, tortured, imprisoned, drafted into the army, the peasants 'spoke bitterness' right in the face of the men who had done these things to them. And they worked out to the last *yuan* just how much rent had been extracted from them, the value of the implements they had been cheated out of, and proceeded to get it back, by seizing moveable property, digging up hoards of valuables, and by taking the land itself. But nothing could compensate for the political crimes of collaboration with the Japanese, or for a lifetime of unremitting misery. So bitter were the memories revived that the peasants' fury could not be contained. In this village of one thousand souls, no less than twelve men were beaten to death – 'excesses' repeated in countless other villages.

This cathartic outpouring of revenge and hate broke the fear of the landlord for ever. They had 'turned over' themselves; it had not been something done *to* or *for* them.

The positive phase of land-reform could now begin. And the most powerful weapon of the Red armies was the Draft Agrarian Law of 1947, which abolished the rights of all landlords, and of the ancestral shrines, temples, monasteries, schools and other land-owning institutions. Twenty billion dollars worth of land was distributed to those in need by the peasant associations. All rural debts were cancelled.

But the Communists had not fought for a quarter of a century to bring into being a system of microscopic private plots. They wanted to *socialize* agriculture.

2

4

THE HEART
OF THE MATTER:
THE COMMUNES

We are all familiar with the effects of technological inventions upon our lives, from steam-irons to nuclear weapons. We are less often aware that our lives have been fundamentally transformed, too, by social inventions: by trade unions, co-operatives, department stores, parliaments, school systems, and revolutionary parties. And we forget, too, how rare the more major social inventions are.

One such invention is the Chinese commune. It is likely to transform the face of the social landscape, in this century and the next, quite as much as the trade union or the co-operative has done in the last century and in this. For, with all due allowance for local variation and circumstance, it is likely to become an institution so relevant for the strategy of making the change from a backward agrarian and capitalist society to a modernized agricultural-cum-industrial life that other countries are bound to use it as a model.

Indeed, one can foresee within the near future the emergence of advocates of the transplanting of this or that aspect of Chinese-type commune organization to underdeveloped capitalist countries as new, technocratic 'social engineering' techniques. The only trouble is that the prerequisites for success are mass revolution, the abolition of private property in land, and the 'communization' of capital and work.

In the West we have only the dimmest idea of what a commune looks like, partly owing to its novelty, which makes it hard to grasp, partly owing to the propaganda which until recently has shrouded China in a mist of obscurity, half-truths and lies.

China is studied by three sets of specialists: sinologists, mainly interested in imperial China; 'China-watchers', mainly interested in communism from a hostile point of view; and people on the Left, sympathetic to China and to socialism. The first two categories converge ideologically: their usual message is that contemporary China has not really changed all that much; that however revolutionary and modern Chinese communist practice might seem, it is really *Chinese*, and even the Party, Marxism-Leninism and Mao Tse-Tung Thought have their analogues in classical Chinese culture.

This is at once true and untrue, though more untrue than true. The opposite view is emphasized by those who stress the importance of Marxism as a revolutionary *rupture* with Chinese tradition and as an independent source of values and policies. They de-emphasize continuities in Chinese history and culture (which they generally don't know much about anyhow). Yet the present is profoundly shaped by what has gone before. Even when the new is brought into being so as to be quite different from the past – opposed to all that is traditional – that, *ipso facto*, is a response, albeit a negative one, to the past.

The commune is a typical locus for this kind of talking-past-each-other debate. On the one hand, the commune undoubtedly corresponds to 'natural' (i.e., man-made and long-standing) marketing zones which link together the innumerable villages of China. People who have lived in villages in this country know this well enough, for they, too, have journeyed to the county market-town, on 'high days and holidays', to buy household necessities and luxury goods, and to sell farm produce. Analysts like Eric Wolf, for central America, and G. W. Skinner, for China, have turned this everyday experience into theoretical terms, showing how Mexican or Chinese villages are linked together via marketing centres which act as points of economic exchange for the specialized products of the different villages as well as for town-made goods. They

also bring the villagers into social contact and intercon-
nection over and above the requirements of trade. In England,
the farmers meet in the pub after the sale; in Latin America,
personal, political and religious ties are woven: marriages,
pilgrimages, festivals, county fairs, link villages into *socio-
economic* zones. The village, therefore, is by no means the
isolated entity the 'townie' thinks it is.

For China, Skinner has distinguished three ranges of market-
areas within which the village is involved, each one shaped over
long periods of time, each one successively wider and including
several of the lower-level areas. The first is the 'standard' area,
served by a market-town which most villagers can reach by
walking only four or five kilometres. The next largest is the
'intermediate' area, which links together several 'standard'
market zones, just as the 'central' places, at the highest level,
link each of these intermediate market-areas together by
providing wholesale supplies and specialized services not
available in the smaller towns. The central towns also link the
larger market-areas up with the provincial and national
economies.

Skinner, and later Shillinglaw, traced the swings and turns
of Communist policy, which sought to break down the traditional isolation and parochialism of the village, but ran into
trouble when they set up communes 'which bore no relation to
any possible trading system at whatever level'. In the end, the
boundaries of the 78,000 communes finally established coin-
cided remarkably closely with those of Skinner's 80,000
marketing communities, and, more roughly, with the older
administrative unit of the *hsiang* (sub-district).

But there the continuities cease. For never in Chinese
history was the *hsiang* a collective unit of production and of
legal ownership of land and other economic assets. And never
before, in this or any other culture, was an economic organization of this size, simultaneously, the unit of local government
responsible for education, security (the equivalent of both
police and 'Home Guard': in China, the militia), the administration of justice, finance, housing, marketing, communications,
banking, and the like.

The very name 'commune' gives us an important clue, for no
such name existed in the Chinese past. The term comes, of
course, from the Paris Commune of 1871, via the writings of
Marx and Engels. Few commentators seem to have noticed
how important the Paris Commune is in the thinking of Mao

Tse-Tung. He took literally Engels' famous remark, in the latter's introduction to *The Civil War in France*, when Engels told the bourgeoisie that if they wanted to know what the dictatorship of the proletariat looked like, they should look at the Paris Commune.

There is a special practical reason why the Commune became so significant to the Chinese Communists: because it was not just a utopia, an abstract ideal, a dream, or a theoretical construct, not even a blue-print or an experiment, whether artificial or pilot. It was an actual or 'natural' experiment, albeit very short-lived, in socialist mass participatory democracy. The only other practical example available, when the Chinese Communists came to power, was the macrosocietal experience of Russia after the 1917 Revolution.

Hence these two historical precursors have always been studied as models, for Marx himself left few explicit or practical guide-lines about what to do once you had seized power, or on how to turn socialist principles into institutional reality. He snorted, typically, that he would have nothing to do with 'writing recipes for the cookshops of the future' as to what a socialist society should look like.

But he did say that there would be a transition period before communism proper could be realized, if only because the full flowering of communism required a massive development of productive forces. Without this, the socialist principle of 'to each according to his needs' could not be put into effect. The needed expansion of production would come about through the liberation of human energies repressed and unfulfilled under capitalism, and via rational and collective self-management in which human and social need would be the key consideration. In the meantime, there would remain shortages, and work would remain a more constraining necessity than under socialism proper, or, as we generally term it nowadays, communism. No 'communist' society today considers itself to have reached this second stage, but to be in the transitional – but 'non-antagonistic' – stage of 'socialism' (though Mr Krushchev, shortly before his fall, did claim that the U.S.S.R. had actually arrived at communism).

Marx foreshadowed this much, but he did not envisage as clearly as subsequent events have demonstrated the extent to which the victory of the proletariat in the class struggle was not the end of that struggle; that even when private property had been brought into social ownership, there were problems of creating forms of organization which would truly involve people in the running of their own lives; that the culture of capitalism: the values and attitudes of individualism, competitiveness, acquisitiveness, of inequality, deference, authority: would not die away overnight. Nor would its myths: myths of illusion and mystification, of attributing what happens in life to non-human entities – to gods, 'market forces', or Fate – instead of identifying the actions of real and powerful men as responsible for what happens: all that is summed up under the rubric 'alienation'. These notions could not be dissolved or switched off simply by passing laws or setting up institutions, because they were lodged in men's minds. It has become abundantly clear since Marx's day that nationalizing industry or proclaiming the equality of women does not necessarily make much tangible difference to the miner at the coal-face or the wife in the kitchen. The human psyche has to be transformed through the re-socialization of people in new, positive, humanistic socialist values so that they will not behave capitalistically, thinking only of themselves or their families, but instead of the contributions they can make to others: as producers, to the general stock of material goods, but, more widely, as whole persons, through willingly helping, not just some abstract 'Society', but their concrete fellow-men in their everyday activities. Socialism, that is, is not just about forms of ownership: it is about participation, democracy and altruism: a human texture of life.

Such sentiments are likely to produce hoots of laughter from those long accustomed to capitalist society. Like drug addicts, they have picked up the habits of capitalism. They have also become quite cynical about socialism after the Soviet experience. Sentiments of this kind applied to China would have seemed even more ludicrous to those who knew the old China: the China of the supremely individualistic and familistic Chinese peasantry, of grasping, ruthless landlords, or exquisitely competitive shopkeepers, micro-traders and merchants. Less promising human material for the construction of socialism could scarcely be imagined. And the 'old China hand' would have been right, for the structures which produced these deformations of personality and character had to be changed before their potential humanity could be unlocked.

This could not happen simply via some revivalist change of heart, some equivalent of the dreamy idealism preached by the

latest *guru* imported into California. It has to be brought about
by organization. In the commune today, the Party is still,
unambiguously, the decisive force. But it is a Party leadership
which has undergone a big change.

After the Cultural Revolution, thousands of P.L.A. cadres
were sent to the communes (and to factories, schools, universities, etc.) to stiffen the political leadership along Maoist
lines, to undo the policies of Liu Shao Ch'i, and to strengthen
the involvement of the peasants in decision-making agencies.
Hence one finds that the Chairman of the Revolutionary Committee of a commune is usually also Secretary of the Party,
often a P.L.A. man assigned there by the Party after the
Cultural Revolution. In a few years, most of these men will
probably be back at their Army posts, or elsewhere, and their
numbers are not now great.

Before the Cultural Revolution, the organization of the
commune consisted of a Management Committee elected by
the Commune Congress annually, itself an elected body whose
members, as in the 'electoral college' system, then elected the
Management Committee. The Management Committee (now
replaced by the Revolutionary Committees since the Cultural
Revolution) was itself supervised by the Supervisory Committee composed only of Communist Party members, whose
job it was to see that the Management Committee carried out
the policy of the Party.

The new Revolutionary Committees in the communes are
composed of three different elements: the so-called 'three-in-
one' principle of organization. Just what these three elements
are varies widely, in fact, according to whether the institution
is a school, a commune or a factory. The 'three' elements,
indeed, often seem to be so different as only to share that
number in common. They may be teachers, students and
cadres in a school; peasants, cadres, and P.L.A. 'appointees' in
the commune; workers, cadres, militiamen in a factory; and so
forth. The basic division seems to be between representatives
of the 'masses' (whether peasants, workers, or students);
representatives of the administration (cadres); and a political
element (P.L.A., militia, etc.). One has to remember that the
Army is singularly politicized in Chinese society. Leading
cadres, too, are political men, and include many Party members,
who are further to be found amongst the representatives of the
'masses'.

In some ways, this omnipresence of the Party, and the

interwoven structure of Party and Government are reminiscent of Eastern Europe. But a tremendous jolt was given to those cadres who were becoming petty local bosses and bureaucrats, sometimes unwittingly, by the Cultural Revolution, and the involvement of the rank-and-file in the taking of decisions has grown enormously.

In one not untypical case there was a meeting every three days at the beginning of the Cultural Revolution, at which cadres were criticized and they criticized themselves.

Every single person in the entire brigade spoke up ... Many times over. No one in the whole brigade remained silent. To begin with there were many who were unused to speaking. They had never spoken in public before.

But as the Cultural Revolution went on, they all plucked up courage and expressed their views at the meetings ... Since everyone had by now expressed his opinions, the number of meetings had been reduced. First, to one meeting every five days, then to one every ten days ...

What has happened is right. Previously, even if all were formally directed by the Party, there were many parallel organizations. Now there is only the Revolutionary Committee. It is a unified leadership. It requires less administration. The masses can check up on the administration. The people have more power now. Today the masses speak their minds openly and have more to say about how things should be run than they did before. This is Chairman Mao's line. (Kao Pin-ying, a Brigade Treasurer, in Jan Myrdal and Gun Kessle, *China: the Revolution Continued*.)

The commune, today, has to be distinguished in two major aspects: as a unit of local government (the very name of the Paris 'Commune' itself was, of course, simply the French term for 'municipality', nothing to do with communism), and as a unit of agricultural production. The next administrative unit upwards is the county, and, beyond the county, the province. There used to be regional groupings of provinces, but these have been scrapped as they threatened in the fifties to become 'satrapies' of powerful regional bosses, notoriously T'ao Chu in Canton and Li Ching-Ch'üan in Szechwan.

As an *agricultural* unit, the commune is part of a different chain of authority. Originally, it came under the Department of People's Commune Affairs in the Ministry of Agriculture for planning purposes: the incorporation of the development plans drawn up by the local communes within the overall agricultural development programme of the country. For the everyday work of growing crops, it came under the Bureau of Commune Management of the same Ministry, and for research and 'extension' purposes was serviced by a section of the Academy of Sciences. Even then, the Academy had 15,000 of its 21,000 technical experts posted out in various parts of the country. But since the Cultural Revolution, they have streamlined this structure and intensified the policy of getting the civil servants off their bottoms and out into the fields (better still, abolishing them).

The communes were first established back in 1958, during the Great Leap Forward. In retrospect, the grandiose claims made by the Chinese that their formation was a world-historic turning point begin to look more and more justified. But at the time, journalists in the West had a field-day filling their columns with amusing (and sad) tales of the things that went wrong and the zanier things that were done at the time, principally the over-enthusiastic rush to industrialize – symbolized in the mushrooming of thousands of 'backyard' steel furnaces; the preoccupation with sheer size as an ideal in setting up communes; and ultra-communistic excesses of a social kind, notably melting down family pots and pans in the furnaces, and setting up communal dining-rooms so as to live as communistically as possible. They certainly did all these things, and they cost a lot to unscramble. But they were often not just the outcome of *communist* ideological enthusiasm: they represented an attempt to fulfil the millennial peasant dream of a free, secure and abundant supply of food.

Before the Great Leap Forward, the Communists had moved very cautiously, because they were on more familiar ground, and were, for long periods of time, at war. Bold as their land reforms were after Liberation, when they distributed land to those who had dreamed of owning enough to live off as bygone generations had dreamed, the multiplication of millions of tiny pocket-handkerchief farms (a scale of agriculture so small that anthropologists often prefer the label 'horticulture') was clearly no basis for technological and social advance towards a socialist form of life. It was necessary to link all these holdings together, and this was done in two stages: firstly, by setting up 'mutual aid teams' in which peasants loaned their equipment to each other – buffaloes, implements, carts, etc. – for use on their still-private parcels of land, and received some modest return for so doing. This phase lasted from 1949 to 1952, when, gradually, the exploitative role of the intermediary private grain-buyer was also brought to an end, and agricultural production now came to market via a national system of purchase-points.

The solidarity of these early 'mutual aid' teams, however, was limited, because of the persistence of private property, for peasants owning such equipment still expected special priority in its use on their own land, and received special income from loaning it. The next stage, therefore, was to move to the 'lower' or 'semi-socialist' phase of co-operativization. Here production was still carried out on privately-owned land, but it was coordinated by the whole membership, who worked the lands together, even though those with more land received more income still; those with only their labour to contribute, less. Economies of scale, however, now became possible which would have been beyond the capacity of any individual peasant household, for the co-operative brought together on average thirty-two households, which could, notably, undertake waterworks. Nevertheless, the persistence of private parcels inhibited both mechanization and equalization. Hence leading co-operatives now moved into the 'advanced' or 'socialist' stage, in which all land was pooled, and reward was calculated, not on the basis of how much land or equipment an individual had contributed, but on how much work he did. The famous system of work-points (surely influenced by Soviet collective-farm models – which the Chinese neglect to mention today) now came into existence, and at the same time, a new unit, the Brigade, composed of about five existing co-ops and uniting about 168 households, came into being. By 1957, most of China's villages had been organized into these Advanced Agricultural Producers' Co-operatives – only three years after the campaign for co-operativization had begun. Traditional village particularism and inter-village hostilities still persisted: David and Isobel Crook describe reactions to an inter-village water-conservancy irrigation project mooted in Hopei in 1956:

> The response was far from whole-hearted. The people in the villages upstream were not interested, because they had their own water and those far downstream swore the water would never reach them. One man in Bailin [village] said 'If a drop of water ever flows here from Little Yetao [another village], I'll crawl between your legs three times'. Only the villages in the middle reaches favoured the project, but they lacked the resources to undertake it alone.

This kind of co-operative differs from the rural co-ops found in capitalist society in that both production and ownership were now collective. In Third World countries (as in nine-teenth-century Britain), for instance, co-operatives often get smashed by landlord thugs or financially broken by private middlemen. Under capitalist conditions of agriculture, farmers nevertheless sometimes succeed in establishing viable producer co-operatives, particularly when there is a friendly state to support them (e.g., by favourable legislation, protection against violence, etc.). Producer co-ops enable the con-stituent members to sell their crops jointly and thus bargain for higher prices than they could hope to get were every tiny producer to try to negotiate separately: in unity is strength. The 'producer' co-ops also have their 'consumer' side, for farmers combine to bulk-purchase petrol, chemical fertilizers, etc., direct, thus cutting out middlemen's profit margins. They also make no profit out of sales to their members. Hence members get the goods cheaper. Rural people also set up 'consumer co-ops' proper, which deal principally in household goods of everyday consumption, similar to the co-ops of the cities of England. The collective benefits are passed onto members in the form of lower prices, or dividends, or im-proved services. Finally, there are credit co-ops, which similarly encourage people to save, not with capitalist banks, but with socialist 'credit unions', which they can draw on, at minimal rates of interest, in proportion to the savings they have invested. All three forms of co-operative had long been tried in China. Rewi Alley, the great New Zealander who has devoted his life to China and still lives there, played a leading role in the formation of the 'Chinese Industrial Co-operative' movement in the 1930s.

But there are limits, and Alley's co-ops encountered them, too. There is the opposition of landlords, merchants, and political organizations to cope with. But the co-op is not so much a socialist solution as a socialist defence against the wider capitalist society. It does not equalize, for each member retains what he owns, and benefits in proportion. There remain richer and poorer members, and these inequalities, as I have seen in Canada, and as John Saul has shown for Africa, often *increase* as a result of co-operative organization. Notably, they do not eliminate private property in land or capital equipment. The co-op, then, is a compromise between private ownership or consumption, and collectivism; it is not a collectivization of the means or mode of production, nor does it equalize. Co-ops remain federations of small producers, some of whom are 'big men', who, because of their material assets and social skills in running meetings, keeping accounts, etc., usually dominate the co-ops. Budding entrepreneurs in Africa have made their start as capitalist farmers by taking advantage, often illegal advantage, of the facilities which co-ops provide for their members, e.g., they have had the greatest use of tractors owned by the co-ops, whereas the smaller men have been elbowed aside or simply operate on too small a scale to make this kind of cultivation worthwhile. And though economies of scale can be achieved in purchasing and sharing, the private ownership of wealth – land, capital, equipment – sets limits upon what can be jointly achieved. To step beyond these limits requires bringing society's assets into common ownership. Moreover, had the Communists not pushed forward to new socialist forms of organization they would have found themselves faced by a massive population of smallholders, each out for himself. A new mass capitalism in the countryside would have emerged within no time at all.

The setting up of co-operatives was a transitional strategy, appropriate to the period, and, in particular, to the level of peasant consensus. It was not a compromise of principle, nor a substitution of what Max Weber called 'formal rationality' (the policies cold-blooded analysis indicated) by 'substantive rationality' (a 'realistic' taking-into-account of what was possible). It was a policy which involved no renunciation of long-term goals at all, nor were short-term policies any deviation away from socialism. Rather, short-term policies were steps on the road to the ultimate goal. From the very beginning, the mutual aid teams, and then the co-operatives, brought peasants together into ever-larger groupings. Then, they became no longer simply associations of individual producers, but units of collective production, actually doing the farming together, pooling equipment, and often working on consolidated lands jointly, rather than on each separate parcel in turn. By this time, private ownership was becoming an anomaly, for agriculture was more and more (with enormous variations) becoming a jointly-run enterprise on plots still legally private and separate, but *de facto* worked collectively. Relations of production had become socialized, and even forms of ownership themselves largely or partly joint.

The time being ripe, in 1958 the Communists crossed the

Rubicon. They abolished private ownership of land. In its place, they put the communes.

Within an amazingly short period of time, 740,000 of the Advanced Co-ops were converted into only 24,000 People's Communes. That this could be done so quickly itself implies the 'administrative' way it was achieved, for what happened was that the leaders of the federating co-ops often arrived at the decision between themselves, albeit with mass support. Often it was done largely by county or provincial officials. They were stepping into the unknown, and mass participation was quite inadequate. Hence things that peasants knew in the marrow of their bones – where boundaries should run, in the light of geographical, economic and social factors – were often bureaucratically ignored. Hence, too, a massive reorganization had to take place, from 1959 to 1961, hard on the heels of the initial organization of the communes, for the units proved far too large, and flouted these historically-formed communities. The 24,000 communes were now in many cases broken up into smaller units, or recombined so as to form 78,000 new communes. This was accomplished by 1961–2. The enormous labour of combining, then re-dividing, assets and liabilities kept officials desperately busy constructing, then reconstructing, the whole system twice in three years. Coinciding with this was an appalling and unexpected agricultural crisis, the 'three calamitous years', when large areas of the country were flooded and others suffered drought. A Swedish businessman I met, who had been in China over twenty times since Liberation, said that the country between Peking and Canton, from the air, looked like a gigantic lake. Nature conspired to produce about as inauspicious a time as could have been picked for launching the communization of agriculture. On top of all this came the Russian withdrawal.

It is a remarkable tribute to the soundness of the underlying principles, therefore, that the communes immediately began to demonstrate the immense agricultural potential that had been locked up. In the West, the decline of agriculture between 1959 and 1961 was entirely attributed to another factor, however: the peasants' resistance to communization. It is most likely that this contributed to the problem. Though Western specialists disagree as to the actual volume of production during these (and subsequent) years, they all agree that there was a sharp decline for three years, but that an upturn began in 1962. The more ideological estimates, like Joseph Alsop's pre-

diction of a 'remorselessly descending spiral' which, if un-
reversed, 'must eventually reach some sort of breaking
point', were refuted, Alsop's in the very year it was written.
The Chinese fully acknowledge the downturn, but take the view
that not only was it not due to the formation of communes,
but that, had the communes not been formed, agricultural
production would have been a lot lower, and that the communes would have been much more successful from the
beginning had the cadres not been occupied with the problem
of feeding the deficit areas.

In the event, the effects of consolidation showed themselves
in three major ways. Firstly, in the acceleration of the rate of
mechanization of agriculture. Between 1957 and 1959, the
horse-power used in agriculture jumped by a factor of nearly
two (from ·50 million h.p. to ·90). Then came a great jump in
1960–61, when the number of pumping-stations, mobile
water-pumps, tractors, threshers, trucks, etc., suddenly shot
up, a rate of increase of 82·7 per cent in a year. To put it
another way, the number of *pieces* of machinery in use had
increased from 11m. in 1957 to 30m. in 1964, and the *size* of the
average piece likewise: in 1957 it was only ·05 h.p.; by 1964,
·23, an improvement of five times. These are only tiny units,
and a low input altogether. Even by mid-1966, only 10 per
cent of the cultivated land was farmed by machinery. But,
taken together with other simultaneous innovations, the
modernization of agriculture had been solidly begun.

The use of fertilizer was the second major application of
scientific techniques to agriculture. The rhythm of the pace of
introduction was different here, conditioned by the state of the
fertilizer industry. An industry which could only supply ·29m.
tons of fertilizer in 1954, when the amount used had reached
·80m. tons, was turning out 5·66m. tons ten years later. By
1966, 8½m. tons were being used, no less than 70 per cent of
this, however, being imported. In 1970, Chou En-Lai said that
14m. tons annually were being produced within China and
20m. tons have been claimed for 1972 by one foreign specialist.
These massive increases have been achieved both through
building large-scale, often gigantic, plants, such as the huge
Nanking urea-production plant, usually bigger than their
American or Soviet counterparts. At the same time, small
plants, which are cheaper, quicker to get into production, and
easier to run, have been widely set up. They now produce
40 per cent of China's total chemical fertilizer. In Shantung

province alone, more of these small plants were built in the
single year 1966 than in the whole period since the Great Leap
Forward of 1958. In addition to the output from the plants,
some 15m. tons of manure are utilized, mainly produced on the
communes themselves. To reach Japanese levels of fertilizer-
use, the Chinese would still have to double their output, both
of artificial and natural fertilizer. (They will also have to face
new problems of pollution, limited at present by the high
utilization of human and animal manure.)

We have already seen something of the third, and in
historical terms, the most significant development: the control
of water. Sometimes there was too much; often too little. Both
called for extensive waterworks, as Wittfogel has shown,
central to the whole Chinese imperial social order. The arrival
of communism, another strong centralized political authority,
meant a new upsurge of construction of storage and drainage
works, of dyke-building, of the digging of canals and feeder
ditches to carry the water to the fields.

This could not have been tackled without centralized
direction, and required, too, the pooling and 'socialization' of
resources. If anything symbolized ancient China it was the
designation of her great river, the Yellow River, the cradle of
Chinese civilization, as 'China's Peril'. If anything symbolized
the new China in the 1950s, it was the giant flood-control
projects like the Huai River Dam. We became used to seeing
photographs of hundreds of thousands of human beings
mobilized on these massive works, as they were mobilized to
plant trees and kill the flies, rats, mosquitoes and sparrows that
brought disease and competed with men for wheat and rice in
the fields – the campaigns against the 'five plagues and the four
pests'. We came to think of gigantism – where even a million
persons might be at work on the very largest projects – as
quintessentially communist. French journalists at this time
wrote of the *fourmis bleus* – the 'blue ants'. A knowledge of
Chinese history would not have gone amiss, for there is nothing particularly communist about massive engineering water-
works in China. Even in the earliest days of Imperial China,
two centuries before Christ, the scale on which labour was
mobilized put even pharaonic Egypt into shade: 750,000
people helped build Ch'in Shih Huang Ti's 'superpalace' and
tomb in 213 B.C.; two million *died* out of five-and-a-half
million employed on the construction of the Grand Canal at
the beginning of the seventh century A.D. Over a thousand

years later, a drawing reproduced in Joseph Needham's classic study of *Science and Civilisation in China* shows an ant-like army of peasants cutting a canal in the 1830s, as they had done for centuries, and looking for all the world, too, like some scene from the 1950s. The workers, however, were supervised by an engineer-mandarin who used work-incentives, and gave thanks to the gods.

The labour used today is no longer corvée or slave labour, nor does it benefit primarily a now non-existent landed gentry. And it is no longer 'agrarian'. Agriculture has been linked to industry, which supplies the machinery, fertilizer, better strains of seeds, and electricity from the dams which, at the same time, control inundation. It is also infused with new scientific practices: cropping patterns, closer planting, soil amelioration, the use of plant-protection material, and better management practices. The rise in production that began once the three calamitous years passed into memory was thus the result of intensification of agriculture, rather than the 'extensive' bringing of new land under cultivation. Great advances will undoubtedly be made in that direction as technical resources become available, so that whole new regions will be brought under cultivation that are, at present, agriculturally marginal. Moreover, the patchwork quilt of Chinese countryside no longer has any technical rationale. It is the legacy of hundreds of years of pocket-handkerchief ownership and land-cultivation. The job of amalgamating and re-levelling the fields will be enormous, but we can expect to see, in the not too distant future, larger fields worked by machines.

Between 1958 and 1964, quite apart from these large centrally-organized works, the communes themselves constructed one hundred reservoirs with a capacity of over 100m. cubic metres, and another one hundred medium-sized ones with capacities of between 10m. and 100m. cubic metres, plus no less than 50,000 water 'tanks' holding less than 10m. cubic metres. They also built feed-in and take-out channels more than 100,000 kilometres in length. This vast new system was worked by electric and diesel pumps producing more than twelve and a half times the total pumping power available in 1957. Hence Chinese water-control systems are not solely 'gigantic'. They 'walk on two legs'.

Since the Cultural Revolution, even greater emphasis has been laid not simply upon mechanization which depends on machinery supplied from the cities, but upon producing small machines locally for the needs of agriculture. 'Gigantism', indeed, is regarded as a Russian disease. They are encouraged to become as self-sufficient as possible. Hence, one finds mushroom growths of small workshops everywhere. In one commune factory, producing small electric generators used in water-control and irrigation-works of enormous size (built by hand labour and carrying-pole), I was told the foreman was an ex-peasant. I asked him how he had acquired his knowledge of engineering. 'I was sent on a three-months' course to a factory in Nanking,' he replied. 'So then you came back here and taught these girls how to use the lathes?' I asked. (They were operating simple machines, turning out 2·8 kilowatt and 4·5 kilowatt generators, as well as doing repair work.) 'Not exactly,' he said. 'I brought the blueprints back from the factory, and we *made* the lathes first!'

Not all their equipment is home-made. The communes buy sophisticated equipment from the city; the workshop near Nanking drew their power from two electric motors they had purchased. But the lathes were neither 'local' nor 'city-made'. They had purchased only the gears and the bearings – the precision-engineering parts. The rest – the drive-shafts, the frame, the mountings, etc. – were made on the spot. Even the metal was home-made, from a small foundry. So were the moulds, the heavy plane-milling machine, and some of the 10 ins. gears. Soon, obviously, they would be producing even more varied types of 'means of production' themselves.

One should not exaggerate what has been achieved. On the Nanking commune, 60 per cent of the cultivated land was still ploughed by buffalo-traction; 70 per cent of the transport was by carrying-pole. They are a very long way indeed from anything like the 'mechanization of agriculture', once unrealistically scheduled for 1970. During the Great Leap there was a vast mushrooming of tiny 'backyard' steel furnaces all over China. These often proved to be failures, and even where they did succeed in producing steel its quality was so poor that it could not be used. No less than 45 per cent of the industrial units set up had to be disbanded between 1959 and 1961. They also found that they had run too fast with regard to people, and that there were still those who would not bother to work as hard as their more conscientious neighbours when they knew they would get the same reward. Hence some form of individual incentive was needed.

But the record of success is striking. Up to 1972, bumper crops were recorded for nearly ten years in succession, reaching 240 million tons of grain and sweet potatoes in 1971. When I was in Peking, the temperature reached 100°F. It was hot and dusty, and the North China plain was clearly short of water. Agricultural production was not as high as in previous years, and the pattern was repeated in 1973. But they will un-doubtedly, given some kindness from Nature, begin to resume the record of continuing improvement in the future.

None of this would have been possible without the con-centration of capital and labour, and the economies of scale, which the sheer size of a commune makes possible. A com-mune can have anything from 25,000 to 60,000 people in it. There can be between five and fifteen thousand households, and between ten and twenty-five thousand able-bodied workers. It may help to bring the commune into focus if we think in capitalist terms, for it is said to be the dream of the American businessman to sell each inhabitant of China just one hamburger. If we invert that, and put it in communist terms, if one saves only a few pence or shillings per head per year, it is possible to use these savings for public services . . . and one soon begins to arrive at sizeable sums, given the size of the commune populations. The concentration and centraliza-tion of capital, which Marx saw as a feature of mature capitalism, also occurs under communist auspices for com-munist ends – the use of such savings for the common good.

These ends include much more than the production-activities on which we have so far concentrated. Work is valued, but it is not the end of life. It is a means for the achievement of a more varied and satisfying existence outside work also. The literature on communes is generally written by economists, geographers or agriculturalists who tend to emphasize agricultural activity. The Chinese, too, certainly emphasize these things, for they are a *sine qua non*. But they also point with particular pride to the schools, the clinics, dis-pensaries, hospitals, radio stations, kindergartens, and public halls, to their new houses as well as to the factories, workshops and granaries.

What communes do with their money varies a very great deal, and reflects both the localized nature of decision-making, and the localized nature of the problems they have to face. For some communes, the key problem is water-control, and this absorbs most of their capital and their work-effort during the dead season of the agricultural year. For others, with no such problems, they have gone for electrification, both of agriculture and for domestic supply to the houses. In the very rich communes, housing has been a high priority. It is enormously difficult to generalize about communes, if only because of the great diversity of agriculture practised between the cold North of Manchuria down to the tropics of Kwangtung and Hainan Island. But another reason for the difficulty of generalizing is that the communes decide on their own priorities – and who should know better than they what they need? Hence there are communes where new housing and domestic electricity have had to wait, where people still live in traditional peasant houses, with mud walls and thatched roofs – but where they are free from flooding and famine for ever (I write this as 40,000,000 are threatened with famine in Maharasthra), and where incomes have doubled in a decade. The suburban communes, like those outside Shanghai, Peking or Nanking, are likely to have electricity in all the houses, piped radio (providing news and music which can – thank God – be switched off), to have new housing, to be located on decent roads, and to have their own considerable industry.

But they are favoured: one of the results of decentralization, too, is inequality both between and within communes. Some regions are favoured naturally by virtue of soil and climate. It is for this reason that the Brigade which is held out as the model for the whole of China, Tachai, is in a stony, ill-favoured part of the country, the mountains of Eastern Shensi, and has pulled itself up by its bootstraps by building terraces of rock actually to create new land out of the steep hillsides. The Chinese did not select as a model some prosperous commune, say, in those parts of the tropical south which produce three crops a year. But between communes, at present, the richest communes accumulate as much as double the income of the poorest. Within communes, too, one can find work-teams and individuals earning twice what the poorer teams and individuals earn. Even higher disparities have been reported. A graphic illustration of these differences, in terms of consumer-goods rather than cash-income, is reported by Wertheim, an observer very sympathetic to China, who, in 1964, found an average of two bicycles per household in a wealthy suburban commune on the outskirts of Peking, and only one single bike in the whole commune in a poor part of Hopei province. The Chinese are conscious of these disparities. The present emphasis, however, is upon upgrading the backward and raising output everywhere rather than equalizing it. But they are unlikely to let such differences become too great.

Before looking at the inequalities further, however, let us first find out how communes generate the income they do distribute. Not, certainly, from renting land: land may be leased to Brigades and Teams, the next lower units, but no rent is charged. But Brigades and Teams do have to pay for the use of commune-owned tractors, threshers, trucks and pumps. A second source of commune income is from the repair and maintenance of machinery belonging to the Brigades and Teams. Thirdly, the commune's factories bring in income. Fourthly, communes often have units specializing in certain profitable lines of cash-crop production: medicinal herbs, hot-house vegetables, fruit, fish, etc.

Just as the commune is an economic unit of production, which makes income and distributes it, so each Brigade and Team is also a unit of production and distribution, and owns its own property: it produces, sells, rents equipment and pays for services, keeps accounts, and so forth. The distribution of commune income is not direct to the individual normally; it tends to take the form of the provision of collective facilities such as schools, hospitals, etc.

Anyone who has tried to make sense out of the discrepant accounts of Chinese commune organizations, as I have done, will have sweated blood, like the legendary horses of the Chinese Far West, for there are many uncertainties and many discrepancies. Some of these reflect real differences as between one commune and another over the vast and varied territory of China, and the localized nature of much decision-making. But much, too, is due to the inadequacy of the available source-materials.

Chinese accounts are able to draw on the greatest range of experience, naturally, and are often graphic and provide the basic outlines. But they are also often fragmentary, unclear, or uninformative on points where one needs crucial information. There are very few in-depth studies by foreigners; notable exceptions are David and Isobel Crook's *The First Years of Yangyi Commune*, and Jan Myrdal's *Report from a Chinese Village*, which he later briefly updated (with Gun Kessle) in *China: the Revolution Continued*. There is, of course, also the enormous industry of the China-watchers. But if we want accounts based on first-hand contact, we are dependent on a ludicrously slim set of writings, a quite inadequate base for the serious study of a fifth of humankind. One is forced back on often lively but also scrappy reports by visitors, mostly based on visits of a few hours by people who are not specialists in the field of agricultural development, nor speakers of Chinese, and who, therefore, do not always ask the relevant questions or have time to go into complex matters requiring detailed information. These reports are also lacking in observation, and are based on what is told to the visitors. For all that, they are often a lot truer and more rewarding than politically hostile scholarly tomes. One just does not recognize the China one sees from these ponderous – usually American – analyses.

The Chinese, whether in communes or factories, tend to be keen to tell you about their production achievements. It is much harder to elicit information about finance, decision-making, administration, etc., if they have not been fore-warned that you will want to explore such areas. They try hard to give off-the-cuff answers, but often the relevant cadre is absent: they are busy men. Hence reliance on such fleeting and unfocused visits as the main way of communicating what is happening amongst seven hundred million people is a quite defective policy. One of the more absurd instances occurred in 1956, when a proposal by Professor W. R. Geddes of Sydney University, to carry out a re-study of the village of K'aihsien Kung first studied in 1936 by the eminent Chinese anthropologist, Fei Hsiao-Tung, was approved. This was a handsome gesture of goodwill, as was the generous provision of assistance in the shape of a team of three Chinese research workers. But the team was limited to only four days in which to carry out this study, and it is normal for anthropologists to spend at the very least one full agricultural year in studying rural communities. In his initial study, Fei, in fact, spent two months. But in *days*, all that one can do, virtually, is to count things and to hope to get a general 'feel' of the place. The vital qualitative part – the exploration of attitudes, what the changes one can measure and count mean to the peasants – is left out. Nor is it possible to *observe* – the other crucial operation. One cannot sit in on meetings, listen to arguments, watch quarrels, see who takes initiatives and leadership roles, watch the 'sense of the meeting' emerge.

Hence I offer no apology for gaps and uncertainties, even

inconsistencies in what follows. I have tried my best; no one is more dissatisfied than I.

At present, it is the Team usually, a unit of around 150–250 people, rather than the Brigade, which is the decisive entity as far as work and individual income are concerned, what the Chinese call the 'unit of accounting', i.e., the unit which does most of the producing, selling, and distributing of income direct to its members. The way it works bears the stamp of the genesis of the communes out of the producers' co-ops of the 1950s, in particular the systems of remuneration and taxation.

Before personal income is distributed at Team level, certain things have to be set aside for collective purposes, out of the Team's joint income. Firstly, the gross income is calculated. Then that part of the past year's production costs not yet met are deducted from this. After that, agricultural tax, on average, amounts to something like 7 per cent of gross income, some-times as little as 3 per cent, and in one Chinese study of a commune obviously being held up as a model, rather than as typical, it was only 2·1 per cent.

This tax formula was originally worked out in 1953. At that time, the peasants were still in co-ops, not communes, and 10 per cent of the gross income (less for poorer co-ops) was the yardstick. The following year, this level of tax was fixed *in perpetuity*. Henceforth, co-ops would pay the *same* amount that they had paid in 1953 (with due allowance for any circumstances peculiar to that year). This meant that, as production increased, the amount of tax, remaining the same, came to constitute a *declining* proportion of total income. By 1958, it was estimated that taxation normally absorbed any-where between 7·4 per cent and 10·3 per cent of the gross income of co-ops.

In 1958, the newly-formed communes were assessed accord-ing to the amount their component – now defunct – co-ops would have paid in a normal year. Hélène Marchisio states that the rate was fixed for five years at 5·3 per cent, on average; other accounts differ. But it is universally agreed that the proportion of general income going to tax today is very much lower even than 10 per cent – somewhere between 6 and 10 is the usual estimate. One study of thirteen communes, in 1964, gave an average of only 5·4 per cent, and that is a decade ago. For the richer communes, therefore, tax becomes a smaller and smaller component of their outgoings. For the poorer, it still remains significant – perhaps 8 per cent. For both, the situation improves as production goes up, but it will be seen that the taxation system is regressive rather than progressive, insofar as it rests more heavily on the lower-income units. Stable prices ensure that greater production is not eaten up by lowered income from a greater volume of production – the phenomenon familiar, for instance, from Ghana under Nkrumah, when production of cocoa doubled but the world-price dropped by half. The work done in raising production therefore produced no sensible increase in the peasants' income.

After deducting any outstanding charges on last year's expenditures, and tax, the balance is available for the needs of the coming year, both collective and individual. Something between 6 per cent and 8 per cent, usually, is put into an 'accumulation' fund, devoted to financing new development: at least 10 per cent is the official aim, and model communes go higher. Out of this fund, at commune level, the commune will build shops and stores, workshops, storage facilities, etc., and will make loans to its constituent Teams for projects they cannot finance out of their own resources.

The proportion of the crop directly distributed usually ranges between 50 per cent and 70 per cent (the latter on poorer communes and those which have had a bad year), and averages 60 per cent. The rest is sold to the State which purchases a prearranged volume ('quota') at fixed prices (these, like the prices of basic commodities purchased by the commune from the State 'procurement agencies', have been stable or have improved to the peasants' advantage over the years).

In addition to laying aside accumulation funds for development purposes, another 2 or 3 per cent is set aside for welfare purposes, which may include relief to poorer families, school meals, meals for patients in the commune hospital, the provision of literature for reading-rooms, sports equipment, community dining-rooms and homes for aged people. All people in China are entitled to the 'five guarantees': food, clothing, housing, medical care and decent burial: the eternal dreams of the poor throughout the world. Those who actually need such help are normally the aged and the incapacitated, and those whose families are imbalanced or 'incomplete', e.g., with an adverse ratio of productive workers (and therefore earners) to non-workers (normally dependent children and old folk). 3·5 non-workers per able-bodied worker is generally reckoned to qualify a family for welfare support. In one of the less prosperous communes, in 1964, no less than 213 families out of 3,721 qualified for such assistance: about 6 per cent of the population: though this was, again, a decade ago.

So at least 50 per cent – the legal minimum – of gross income remains for general disposal after the past year's expenses have been met. Of this, about 12–14 per cent is laid aside to meet next year's production costs. The rest is available for distribution to the individual members, in accordance with work-points they have accumulated, after deduction for the value of food and other commodities the commune has advanced them over the past year. Richer communes can afford to distribute a *smaller* proportion of their remaining income to their members as individual income, often only the statutory 50 per cent they have to distribute by law. This ploughing back of capital by the richer communes would, of course, result in even higher returns in future years – and in a *widening* gap between the richer and poorer communes. Various redistribution devices exist to stop this gap widening. There is great emphasis upon assistance (usually free) from the more advanced to the less successful communes, though it does not seem at all substantial at present. Secondly, the Agricultural Bank finances development projects at differentially favourable rates for the poorer communes. Special assistance is also given them in the form of technical and scientific services. Thirdly, attention is given to developing cash-crops which command high prices. Finally, in areas of severe population-pressure, labour may be recruited for industry, though this policy has limits, since if it removes too many of the able-bodied, it becomes self-defeating.

The problem of differentiation as between communes is not satisfactorily resolved even by these policies. One obvious way of dealing with it would be by differential (progressive) taxation, which would fall harder on the richer communes than the poorer. Meanwhile, gross commune incomes have been reported as varying between 13,000,000 *yuan* (suburban Peking; 36,000 population) to only 1,320,000 *yuan* (eighty-four miles from Hangchow; population 9,316 – a commune regarded as a 'success story' because its living standards had been even lower previously). Fishing and pastoral communes were even less prosperous. Two years later, Buchanan recorded variations ranging from 17m. *yuan* (suburban Peking again) to just over 2m. *yuan* on several communes in Honan, Shensi and Kiangsu. Five of the eighteen communes he studied had incomes of over one million *pounds* sterling per annum, however (not 1m. *yuan*); one almost £2½m.; and the aggregate income of the eighteen (some income not being recorded) was larger than the G.N.P. of North Borneo or Bhutan and one-half that of Laos.

The Chinese long-range policy is that eventually the 'unit of accounting' will be no longer the Team, but the next highest unit up, the Brigade, which will then organize production, sell to the State, and receive income from sales. This income will then be distributed amongst a larger group of people in accordance with standard criteria. From there, the next stage will be ownership and distribution of income by the commune as a whole. Finally, ownership will be vested in the State, not in the individual communes, and income pooled and distributed in accordance with the general performance of agriculture across the whole country. This is clearly a long way off, but it means that the Chinese answer to contemporary inequalities is the extension of the level of public ownership, so that you end up with something like a national agricultural wage for the peasantry, which can be brought into line with industrial earnings.

It is likely that foreign visitors tend to see the more prosperous communes situated near major cities, easily accessible by road and therefore cheaper on petrol. Visitors such as Karol and Wertheim, who have been to more remote areas, report much less impressive standards of living there. Wertheim remarks: 'It is not at all unlikely that the (poorer) communes visited by me in the northern part of Hupei were much more like the majority of Chinese communes than the exceptionally prosperous ones described by most foreign authors.'

Observers like Burki (then Director of West Pakistan's Rural Works Programme) picked out the communes they wished to visit at random from a list prepared by provincial officials. (His team also visited a commune inhabited by Mongol pastoralists, on request.) It is hard to say whether one is taken to the more successful communes as an exercise in hoodwinking, or out of convenience. I believe myself that they are keen to show you their best or better, not so much to deceive you as to show off what has been achieved in some cases, which is what they are aiming at everywhere. There is distortion, then, in a statistical sense, but less so if one looks at commune development, more historically, as a process, for what is to be found on the more progressive ones today will be found on the less advanced in a few years' time. If one had visited one of the minority of a few hundred co-operativized areas in 1954 (only 15 per cent of the population) they would nevertheless have given a picture of what the whole country was to be like only two years later.

The commune, as we have seen, has its own source of income, as does the Brigade. But the unit which sells the bulk of the agricultural produce to the State, to feed the cities and supply industry with raw materials, is the Team rather than the commune. Taking distribution in kind and sales to the State together, it would appear that only somewhere between 20 per cent and 30 per cent of the crop reaches the market; three-quarters of it is consumed locally. For the peasants receive some half of their income in kind, usually in the shape of rice and other food-grains. Peasants retain memories of seasonal fluctuations of harvest, and even of famine, before 1949. I met families who had lost both children and adult relatives from starvation. So they place a high value on a full granary. Even some of the income they received in cash, until recently, might be spent on further food purchases. But my calculations suggest that today they often receive more grain than they can possibly consume, and some of this is being laid up to reserve. The State, too, and the communes, accumulate reserves against possible crises, including the danger of war. Grain reserves stood at 40m. tons in 1971. Commune and Brigade reserves alone now amount to 8 or 9 per cent of annual production, and new granaries are visible on the communes.

Having looked at how income is generated, and having taken account of collective expenditure, let us now see how the balance is distributed to the individual. The form of distribution of income used today is basically still taken over from the advanced co-ops in 1956–7. It is a system of *work-points*, in which one day's work usually counts as ten points. There have been 'super-communist' experiments, in periods of high political excitement, in the direction of equalizing income simply by standardizing it for everybody, e.g., by counting the number of days' work put in, without taking account of the quantity or quality of the work. The communist ideal, after all, is to eliminate the acquisitive and competitive striving for individual reward, which gives rise to inequalities, and to move towards something like an assured standard wage for a standard day's work. Hence the State Farm, which is more like a factory as far as remuneration is concerned, is the official long-term ideal, both in China and in the Soviet Union. In China, at present, State Farms only cover some 5 per cent of the land-area, mainly large farms in the under-populated north-east and north. On these, the workers receive a wage which is dependent more upon national rates and the health of industry as a whole rather than upon the output and profits of the particular enterprise, just as an industrial worker does, rather than the system we shall describe for the communes. This accords with the classic Marxist notion of creating 'factories in the field'.

State Farms are something for the future for China. For now it has been found necessary to retain some element of individual incentive, and wage-like experiments have given way to one or other variant of systems which do take account both of differences in the *task* and differences in its *performance*.

The first step is a kind of 'job-specification' whereby 'norms' of work are established for different kinds of task. Some agricultural jobs do not lend themselves to clear separation-out of the contribution made by a particular individual: e.g., where a team harvests fish using a large net. Again, peasants are men of many skills, not specialists in one thing, and may move from one kind of task to another in the course of the day. Hence there are problems of accounting, for time is wasted on calculating bits and pieces of tasks performed and then imputing them to individuals. This is one incentive in the direction of using standard rates for categories of skill and then calculating wages earned simply on a time basis. But most jobs can be identified with their performer and evaluated and rewarded accordingly. It is even possible to allow for differences of seasonal or other working conditions, by varying either the norm or the points. Thus a day's work carrying fertilizer to the fields and spreading it may rate ten points, whether the ground is dry or wet, but the expected norm will be lower when the ground is like brown glue: say, only 500 lb. a day as against 800. Or the points themselves can be adjusted: winter work, generally less arduous, may bring only seven points per day instead of ten in summer. If a person is limited to the lower-rated types of job, he is, of course, underprivileged, and this applies especially to women, who tend to receive seven points as against the normal ten for the male peasant.

Such a system has the advantage of tying reward closely to the actual work-task performed. It is something only the peasants themselves can work out properly: it would require an army of cadres to do the job, and they would not do it so well, and would still need to depend on the peasants' information and advice. Such a system is very flexible. But it takes a long time to iron out anomalies, and since agriculture proceeds according to the rhythms of the seasons, and not by the clock, this experience has to be sifted over several years. Each season of every six months, therefore, the whole basis of the points system is reviewed, and some kinds of work may get re-evaluated. Once the norm has been set, it becomes possible to judge whether a person is working reasonably or not.

But you cannot have too much chopping and changing. Hence certain canons are invoked which guide the Team as to those changes which are legitimate – e.g., where technological innovation makes higher output possible (new tools, seeds, etc.); where excessive rainfall or drought has affected output; where quality-standards need relaxing or tightening up; where the norms, in the light of experience, are just plain unfair. Conversely, guidelines are also used to exclude unreasonable changes: where the norms, though not perfect, are about as good an approximation to justice as one can get; where only a minority wishes to change them; where failure to achieve them is simply due to poor work; and where the reasons for change, though legitimate, do not really justify the elaborate readjustments involved.

Having established the norms, individuals are credited with work-points, in accordance with the work performed. There are innumerable variations on how this is done, all over China: another aspect of the decentralization we saw earlier. But certain principles underlie this apparent lack of uniformity: (1) equal reward for equal work; (2) skill, sheer time involved, and the nature of the work are all taken into account; (3) democratic participation of the peasants themselves in the allocation of work-points, not decision by bureaucrats.

By and large, there are two major modes of calculating the points: by task-related estimation, and on a time-basis. One variant of the latter, for instance, is used on more advanced communes where they classify each worker into one of ten classes, according to his proved record, and instead of calculating what work he has done every day, as they do in most communes, he is rewarded at the rate for his given classification for his day's work. The value of the work-points is fixed for several months in advance or even a year, in this system, rather than retrospectively, after the crop has been sold, as is usual. This is getting closer to the industrial wage-system. So far, it is rare. Even rarer is 'self-reported' estimation of work done by each worker, which occurs in politically advanced Teams. Where this has been tried, the more altruistic, at first, tended to claim less than they ought to have done, and the less conscientious more than they deserved. Such discrepancies were only sorted out after lengthy group discussion.

More normally, the points are allocated at the end of the day's work. Sometimes, they are entered in a notebook kept by each peasant; sometimes a ticket is given to him 'good for' so many points. Not many people get less than seven points for a day's work, usually, apart from children, old people, etc. Since the Cultural Revolution, too, much emphasis has been placed, not just upon the *work* done, but on attitudes towards work and on 'political consciousness'. Despite this emphasis upon 'moral incentives', upon the individual's application of the principles of Mao Tse-Tung's Thought in his daily work and his contribution to the development of others – whether by example, by giving help, or by imparting skills – factors which are given formal priority as the prime criterion according to which work-points are to be allocated, one has to agree with Wertheim that the changes are probably less fundamental than the Chinese claim them to be, and that, despite the emphasis laid on such matters, 'it is still achievement that counts'; 'to each according to his work'.

When the harvest is in, and when the State has paid for its prearranged quota and the collective deductions described above have been made, the cash-value of the entire year's income is estimated, including both the value of the agricultural product and from such ancillary sources as the sale of gravel from commune-owned quarries, dairy-farming, fish-farming, forestry, animal-rearing, and so on.

Then the accumulation fund is set aside (I am still unclear as to whether it covers only *new* development projects or constitutes a fund of 'working capital', or both). Welfare comes next: in one actual case studied, families of martyrs of the Revolution were provided for, and families in difficulty because they had men away in the Army or were otherwise 'imbalanced' – too many children or too many old people. In this case, too, peasants who had sold manure to the Team were repaid in kind (1 *yuan* of manure being taken as equivalent to 25 lb. of grain), and cash loans to the Team by members were paid back in kind, too, each *yuan* entitling the lender to 2 lb. of grain. A small amount may also be allocated to paying for work done by Team members during the 'dead' winter season, when dams, dykes, etc., are built, but the number of paid days' labour for any one person is not supposed to exceed 3 per cent of the working days in the year.

The general distribution to individuals can now be made. It takes two forms: payment in kind and payment in cash. The payment in kind provides people with a supply of food for the months to come. This may be in millet, wheat, or rice, according to the kind of crop dominant in the zone. Though each person earns and is credited with his own work-points, it seems that distribution is made to the family, presumably by aggregating the separate entitlements of the family members. Whether it is ever distributed and stored separately I do not know, but it would seem most unlikely, since they live in families, and it would be pointless and inefficient to have myriads of separate grain-stores.

Each family's score of work-points is now given a cash-value. The value of one work-point is arrived at by dividing the total cash-value of the income received by the group by the total number of work-points. One day's work (ten points) usually works out at around 10 lb. of rice or around $1\frac{1}{2}$ *yuan* in cash. It presumably depends for its value on the price the State pays for grain. In one actual case, the breakdown of total income was as follows (little was put to reserve, since every family already had a year's supply):

	lb.
Welfare support for families 'in difficulty'	918
Payments for sale of manures	8,189
Payments in respect of cash loaned	549
Reserves	170
Payments according to work-points	32,608
	42,434

The peasants in this Brigade had accumulated 25,399 work-points. Hence the value of ten work-points was $\dfrac{32,608}{25,399} \times 10 =$ 12·83 lb. This level of return in kind is more than needed for food purposes. Some peasants therefore laid up a reserve; others sold their surplus to the State for cash and further received tickets which entitled them to rationed industrial goods: cotton goods, petrol, chemical fertilizers, etc. Against the individual's entitlement according to work-points has to be set the value of food advanced during the year, and perhaps such items as cooking oil and firewood. Thus in one case, reported in 1962, a family with 3,210 points earned $\frac{3,210}{10} = 321$ day-units. This, multiplied by 1·55 *yuan* – the value imputed to a day's work – gives 497·55 *yuan*. They were also entitled to 23 *yuan* for their sales of manure, animal and human, which added to 497·55 *yuan* gave them an entitlement to income valued at 520·55 *yuan*. But they had already received 4,765 lb. of rice from the distribution in kind (made up of 4,110 lb. earned through work-points, 575 lb. from sale of manure, and 80 lb. in return for the loan of 40 *yuan* to the Team). The cash-value of this 4,765 lb. was then computed as 397·87 *yuan* (the value of one pound of grain being estimated as ·0835 *yuan*, since one day's work (ten points) was reckoned as 1·55 *yuan*, the cash equivalent of 12·8 lb. of rice). Hence 4·765 lb. is worth 4,765 × ·0853 which is 397·87 *yuan*.

The family was thus entitled to 520·55 but had 397·87 deducted, being the cash-value of the grain they had already received. This leaves a balance of 122·68 *yuan*, which is the actual *cash* they have due to them.

A second system, described by Marchisio, provides for a basic 'fixed ration' which everybody receives independently of the number of work-points they have accumulated. In the case she cites, this ration absorbed 60 per cent of all the grain distributed, after which the balance was given out according to work-points. This system obviously makes for much greater equality since you get a large ration the size of which is not determined by the amount of work you have done. It is reported for suburban communes (near Peking and Canton) and may only be typical of such areas:

Distributed as basic ration		49,735
Basic ration per person	$\frac{49,735}{177}$ persons =	281
Distributed according to work-points		33,157
Value of ten points = one day's work =	$\frac{33,157}{7,620}$ =	4·35

The distribution in kind is taken from grain retained after sales to the State. The distribution in cash occurs after the cash-value of grain distributed has been deducted from the total cash entitlement. There are wide variations in the amount of income which eventuates as cash, from about a quarter to as much as two-thirds. Food, then, is plentiful; cash, less so. Put the other way round, payment in kind can vary from three-quarters of the income received to a third. We have seen that considerable variations of income can occur between communes; they can occur between Teams within the same Brigade and Commune, but the general trend is towards the gradual reduction of the number of poorer Teams.

The Chinese do not claim to be anything other than 'poor'. But the improvement is unmistakable, both in terms of reserves held, and in terms of individual income. In Kwang-tung province, no less than a quarter of all Teams were rated as 'poor' when the communes began in 1958; only a sixth fell into that category by 1963.

*

Eighty per cent of the people of China still earn their living off the land in this way. Yet, as we have seen, thousands of tiny enterprises are springing up all over the countryside. Already they supply significant proportions of the chemical fertilizers, the cement, and the insecticides and the electricity used in the communes. Workers in the mini-factories which produce these things are no longer peasants, nor are they remunerated as peasants are, for they receive *wages* from the commune as do workers in the specialized agricultural production-units – cattle-breeding or fruit-growing, for instance – run by the commune. Such workers receive higher incomes than the peasants. On one commune they constituted 12 per cent of the labour force and received, on average, 50 per cent more than the peasants. Like industrial workers, they had some extra expenses, notably the cost of their meals at the factory canteens. But the development of specialized agriculture and the beginnings of commune industry do carry with them problems of new kinds of inequality, and not just new kinds of diversification of task.

Most foreign observers, mesmerized by the experience of the Soviet Union, where the peasants produce about a third of several key items of farm produce on their private plots (only 3 per cent of total agricultural land), assume that the same thing is bound to happen in the Chinese communes. There are various ideological assumptions implicit in their argument: that peasants will not work as hard for the collective as they will for themselves, either because they are believed to have an ingrained distaste for 'collectivism' – a sort of inherent ideological predisposition – or because they are only interested in personal profit. The experience of communes shows that, in fact, collective benefits also attract the peasants, but they have to be tangible. Public agriculture has public goals: feeding the nation, supplying raw materials to industry, and bringing in foreign earnings. The private producer has no such societal ends in mind. Private agriculture tends to concentrate on the most profitable activities (high-priced vegetables and pigs mainly). Hence, during the sixties, the income generated from one unit of work on the private plot tended to be much greater than that derived from the same amount of effort put into commune agriculture.

The growing attractiveness of the private plot soon began to turn into an economic fact of some size. What began as little allotments were, in some places, producing 20 per cent to 30 per cent of the peasants' income – more normally between 10 per cent and 25 per cent. This might have turned into a gradual slide towards the revival of small-scale peasant capitalism, but the Cultural Revolution stopped that, for the size-limits on private plots are now rigidly adhered to, and priority is given to public-sector agriculture.

Today, the private plots have nothing like the importance they had in the sixties because they are nothing like the size they were. Because China-watchers in Hong Kong had asserted that I would find private plots flourishing once more, I made a special point of measuring and photographing them. These observations confirm what other recent visitors have found: that the private plot is now reduced to what we, in England, would call an 'allotment'. Its size is miniscule, ranging from ·04 of a *mou* (·165 acres) to ·07 per person. A Team of forty families (150 persons) on Stone Well Commune near Canton had five *mou* between them (less than an acre). On Lu Kou Chiao (Marco Polo Bridge) Commune in suburban Peking, I could not distinguish the private plot belonging to a family whom I had asked to point out their private holding, for it was part of a large field of maize and other crops, farmed jointly, even if owned in private sections and the income distributed accordingly. More normally, the plots are farmed separately, though, and their function is twofold: to provide the family that works it with household vegetables, and to bring in extra cash by selling produce on the market.

Prices for the basic crops the commune produces are fixed by the State: food grains, cotton, oil seeds, and other key industrial crops. Produce destined for export, however, is purchased at a price agreed between the commune and the State trading corporations; an element of negotiation is entailed, doubtless because world prices change. Privately-produced crops are sold on local markets, held regularly on most communes, where prices depend on supply and demand. I did even see people selling at the side of the road, though this may have been a traditional 'pitch'. On the Nanking commune, some families retained their plots separately; others had amalgamated them. They also did a lot of buying and selling to each other rather than on the outside market.

But all this has to be done in a family's spare time, after a hard day's work in the commune's fields, a factor which hardly makes for massive investments of energy. Despite this, the income the Nanking family derived from its plot was 40 *yuan* a year, a not inconsiderable sum when their disposable cash – having obtained for the necessities of life (food and fuel mainly) via the system of payment in kind – amounted to only 167 *yuan* for the year. Far more important as a source of private income, I found, was income from the sale of live-stock, principally pigs, China's main meat. Thus at a suburban commune outside Shanghai, 44 per cent of the pig production was private. Most families have two or three pigs, often living in a sty in the yard at the back of the house and feeding off domestic scraps. They sell these to the State for about 60 *yuan* each, so that to sell even two a year brings in a sizeable sum. Sales of chickens, eggs, and handicrafts also add to cash income.

A strip of land about as long as a cricket pitch and a few strides wide seems a slim basis for the restoration of capitalism. But it would be an ethnocentric error to think that the private plot is no more significant to the Chinese peasant than is the produce the English town-dweller gets off his allotment. The cash the peasant derives is, to him, substantial, but, above all, it is *cash* rather than income in kind. The cash proportion of total income derived from private production, however, is now of the order of 10 per cent rather than the 20 or even 30 reported for some communes before the Cultural Revolution. As commune income goes up, too, the importance of this element will diminish.

There is little doubt that commune incomes have risen steadily throughout the sixties, often dramatically so. When one remembers that many of the older people one meets knew famine, malnutrition, indebtedness and landlessness as everyday normality, the Chinese peasant has already achieved a life which is no longer just an existence. He is on the threshold, too, of a life which will be much more appropriate to what should be possible for all men in the twentieth century. But he has not got there yet. As one walks around the more prosperous communes, one sees the old and the new side-by-side: the thatched roofs and the massive new canals; the precision tools in the workshops and the strained faces of the men weighed down by carrying-poles; on this side, the wooden plough and the children on the tread-mill; on that, the hospital, the school, and the electricity poles.

The suburban communes already exhibit a considerable degree of mechanization. A rich commune will resemble Marco Polo Bridge, which has thirty large tractors (28 and 60 h.p.), sixty-eight 'walking tractors', sixty-eight trucks, and 810 electric motors of different shapes and sizes. Ninety per cent of the people have new homes, the majority radios. There are also nineteen primary schools and five secondary schools, and a hospital with eleven full-time qualified doctors. In addition to agriculture, a variety of machinery-assembly shops and a duck farm which sends 120,000 'Peking ducks' to the city's restaurants every year.

The rapidity of these changes means that one has to be very cautious about published statistics, not only because of their paucity and inaccuracy, but because of the interval between their being gathered and their reaching the printed page. There is often a gap of nearly a decade before data which take time collecting, then processing, and then publishing, get into wider circulation abroad. Even then, they are generally mediated by researchers who spend years writing books and getting them published. Most readily-available good accounts, therefore, are often way out of date. In my terminology, they are already 'B.C.' if they refer to the period before the Cultural Revolution, if, that is, one is looking for factual material on *contemporary* China. But one sees many books which use data from before the Great Leap Forward, never mind the Cultural

Revolution, as if it referred to the China of 1973. Such material is now only of historical significance. In a communist China which has never stood still, we should be very careful to specify which period we are talking of, for the revolution is now a quarter of a century old.

Usually, figures do not stand out in the memory. People and incidents do. But one set of figures does stick with me. I recall the chairman of the commune near Nanking – where only a third of the houses, traditional thatched buildings, had electric light at all. They had other priorities. He took me to a small hill from which we could see the border of Anhwei province on one side and on the other the Yangtse. In 1954, he told me, the whole area had been flooded out. Then they had only been organized into mutual aid teams, so were incapable of organizing capital and labour to keep flooding under control. But after the formation of the commune, it became possible to undertake such works. They lost everything in 1954, and had to be fed from outside. By 1962, when the floods came again, they only lost 20 per cent of their crop, even though more of their land had been flooded. There were no further serious floods until 1969, when 600 mm. of rain fell in three days. By this time, they had built an extensive system of canals, dykes and ditches. Their labours paid off: the result, this time, was an *increased* harvest of 5,900,000 *catties* of grain. I asked him about floods in the future. 'We're not worried any more,' he said. And that is the dominant feeling one gets: that they are not worried, at least about the things that worried immemorial generations before them. Their grain reserves last year amounted to the size of the harvest of 1969. In the chairman's bucolic but poetic idiom, 'Our living-standards are blooming like the sesame flowers springing from one node after the other, each higher than the last.'

A second vivid memory is the sight of my first 'walking tractor'. I do not usually get worked up about machines, but this has a special significance in a country of buffalo-traction and human porterage. It looks rather like a powered lawn-mower, but packs a lot of power into one cylinder – 12 h.p., in fact. It eats diesel, in which China is now self-sufficient, and is probably less costly to feed than the buffalo it has displaced. It pulls carts, harrows, ploughs, threshes, and generally takes the hard work out of agriculture. Of course, the Chinese have not been the only people to think up such a machine. Harold Wilson did, in the 1960s when he was promising a 'white-hot technological revolution' for Britain. Its counterpart, as far as Britain's contribution to underdeveloped countries was concerned, was to be, he told us, not so much advanced technology as the provision of thousands of small machines, such as pumps which would 'lift water from that ditch to those fields a few hundred yards away'. Needless to say, the thousands of small machines never appeared (any more than did the white-hot technological revolution). But the Chinese did produce Mr Wilson's dream machine, though it is powered by diesel, not steam as he suggested. It can be seen all over China today, though in far from adequate numbers. They are really proud of them, and a heart-warming sight is to see them at work, replacing human brute labour. They are not even 'walking tractors' any more, for instead of walking behind holding the handles, Mark II has a seat, progress indeed.

I also remember the charming girl in the commune radio station – one of the 'educated youth' who had come from the city. She was operating 8,000 *yuan* worth of equipment belonging to the commune: the console, the various receivers, the tape-recorders and amplifiers, through which she relayed national and provincial programmes for three hours in the morning, another two and a half hours before and after the midday meal, and again for two hours in the evening. She also put out local and commune news items three times a day for twenty or thirty minutes each time. Before this equipment had been acquired, she told me, in a shocked tone of voice, the peasants had not even been able to listen to the Thought of Chairman Mao. Now they also possessed a television set in the commune hall, which showed Nanking programmes twice weekly, and a 35 mm. film-projector run by her predecessor in the radio station, a 21-year-old local lad who had gone off to University at Nanking, and was now back on the commune. She was one of many such educated young people one encounters on communes, not surprisingly, since seven million of them have 'gone to the countryside' since the Cultural Revolution, and one million are expected to go during 1973. (And this is only counting *educated* – middle school and above – emigrants from the city.) One commune I visited had no less than 329 of them. They are encouraged to immerse themselves in the lives of the peasants, to 'learn from the peasants' by working in the fields alongside them and sharing their lives in every way. But they are generally employed in some capacity appropriate to their skills, as 'barefoot doctors', as cadres, teachers, mechanics, etc. This infusion of city-educated people, imbued with Mao Tse-Tung Thought, will, of its own, have a deep effect on the villages. On the other hand, a lot of them must undoubtedly have bitterly resented being sent off to the back blocks to lead a hard life. Chinese entertainment is full of sketches on this theme: the discontented youth who thinks that his education has fitted him for a high-status existence, but who is now expected to work with his hands. That such plays exist is a measure of the problem. But this way of thinking is vigorously combated, and even the resentful learn to cope with kerosene lamps instead of electricity, and become accustomed to slogging up muddy paths instead of treading tarmacadamed streets.

Not that the peasants look upon these young people as superior beings. The whole emphasis is quite the opposite, and those with pretensions were firmly put in their place on arrival. Those sent out more as punishment than as ambassadors of new techniques often had a rough time initially. For the political level of the peasants is itself high. I have particularly vivid memories of an old swineherd in charge of the commune piggery, whom I took to be of a generation probably little affected by communist ideology. I asked him whether they crossed indigenous pigs with foreign breeds to improve the strains. 'Of course,' he replied. 'We even have some from your country, Ying-Kuo [England]. Those over there are from Bah-Kerh-Sha [Berkshire] and those, there, from Yaw-Karh-Sha [Yorkshire].' He thought I had not grasped these outlandish names, so to make it easier for me, drew the Chinese characters on his hand. 'And what's that big black one?' I asked. 'Oh, that's from Su-lien [the Soviet Union]', he replied. 'What's it called?' 'Oh, it's some long Russian name, like Kalinikov or something; I can never remember it, so I always call it after the notorious Soviet revisionist, Brezhnev.'

The communes are getting to be pretty modern places, and pretty self-reliant places. Even the food they produce they now process themselves on their own machinery, typically light-weight flour-milling machines and machines which turn it into long strips of noodle. Instead of sending grain to the city, where it is processed, then sold back as flour at increased cost owing to milling, transport charges and profit-margins, you now simply bring your own grain along and have it ground for one cent a kilo. If you need to, you can also purchase cooked food at the rude country eating-house in the main street of small shops (next door to the bookshop) where a bowl of noodles costs you 10 cents (less than 20p), a plate of meat and onions 9, and two portions of steamed bread 5 cents.

But pride of place probably goes to the commune hospitals. Not that their health-service is hospital-oriented. Each Team has its health workers, each Brigade its health centre, and it is at this quite literal grass-roots level that the famous 'barefoot doctors' work – in the fields, often, or in the homes. They attend to those complaints which, as in England, take up two-thirds of the time of a highly-trained doctor – both minor physical ailments, and those innumerable troubles which have as much to do with the patient's family troubles as with his strictly medical ones. But the 'barefoot doctors' are more likely to be handing out intra-uterine devices and condoms than Librium and Valium.

In the cities, medical services are free. On the communes, the peasants have to pay – but very little – only one or two *yuan* a year (say, 20 to 30p) – into a Co-operative Medical Scheme. Each time they attend the clinic, they also pay 5 cents, and larger items of treatment cost more. The most expensive item I heard of was 5 *yuan* (well under £1), for having an appendix taken out.

Families are closely involved when their members are hospitalized, for they bring in the food the patient wants (I saw prized tins of favourite foods in the bedside cupboards) and chat to them. The hospital attends to the cooking, but the relatives seem to do a lot of the comforting, if not the nursing. Mothers, of course, can come in with their children. The medical staff, in any case, live on the commune, and are no strangers. With such close social support, there is no need for social workers, and in the cities the neighbourhood committee takes on this role. The 'barefoot doctors' themselves are liberated for more technical medical activities, and are a counterpart to the midwife or district nurse in our system, or, much more closely, the Russian *feldshers* of the 1920s, who laid the basis for the Soviet public health service. They pass on more serious cases to the doctors proper, and themselves receive periodic upgrading and refresher courses, usually during the winter when things are slack on the commune. One woman I met had attended three such winter courses, each lasting three months.

Apart from routine injuries and internal medicine, giving inoculations, and (some) working in hospital, a major activity of the 'barefoot doctors' is family-planning work. This is mainly done at Brigade or Team level, not in the hospital. In the more advanced communes the great majority of peasants are already practising one form or another of birth-control: on one, 40 per cent were on the Pill (either 'No. 1' or 'No. 2': it sounds as though one of them must be a 'knock-out' type); 30 per cent of the women were using the intra-uterine loop; 18 per cent had had their fallopian tubes tied (last year, about 150 of them) as against 370 (1 per cent of the population) who had had the coil fitted). Only here and there could I get any clear estimate on the effects of all this on population-growth, but on two communes they thought they had got the rate of increase down to just over 2 per cent.

It was interesting, in view of the feeling that there is some-thing cold-bloodedly rationalistic, even inhuman, about vasectomy or ligature of the fallopian tubes, to find that a young couple whom I met, where the husband had had a vasectomy, were about the most 'familistic' pair I ran across. They lived next door to the husband's parents, and they and the husband's brothers and sisters seemed to be constantly in and out. Father was a joiner, and had made much of the superior furniture in the house. (I asked what *his* father had died of, and was told: 'He was worn out from a life-time of labouring as a hired hand.') On the other hand, whereas the older women usually do a lot of baby-minding, here the children went into the commune nursery while the wife was at work, for which they 'charged' by deducting eighteen work-points, the equivalent of less than two days' work.

China has claimed that the population was around 750 million in 1972, a much lower estimate than that of many foreign demographers, who continue to assert that the popula-tion problem is insuperable and out of control. The wild figures released about production during the Great Leap Forward, and later discounted, have not increased confidence in the reliability of Chinese official figures, and there have been much less dramatic variations in population figures, too. This is not surprising, for census-taking in rural areas is inherently extremely difficult, and errors which might be small in volume for any one part of the country can add up to mistakes measured in tens of millions, as can statistical errors in computing the raw data. These sources of variation seem to be more relevant than any attempt to tailor statistics to suit policy.

Observers on the ground are increasingly reporting that the usual size of a 'completed family' nowadays is between four and five, sometimes lower. Estimates that population is rising at alarming rates continue to be made in the West, but some researchers are now beginning to suggest more optimistic pictures, more consistent with what has been found on the ground. The Chinese claim that population growth has averaged only 2 per cent since Liberation, while grain output has averaged 4 per cent. These are striking figures, but downwards trends have also been reported from some parts of Asia where family-limitation programmes and propaganda, though vigorous, are nothing like as highly organized as in China. It is by no means incredible, therefore, that the Chinese may already have the problem under control. Certainly, they are very confident about their capacity to win this particular battle.

One has to remember the age-structure of the population. As in underdeveloped societies across the globe, young people make up a much greater proportion of the population than in Western societies.

In China, they have grown up entirely during the Communist era. One commune chairman, having told me about the use of contraceptive devices, then explained that late marriage was also important in keeping the number of births down. Men were encouraged not to marry before their very late twenties. People still tend to marry a year or two earlier in the countryside than in the town, and recent statements indicate that this policy has been relaxed somewhat: twenty-five for men and twenty-three for women, in the countryside at least. Even the use of contraceptive devices is not a *technical* way of dealing with population-limitation, of course, for it depends upon a complex structure of attitudes and values, upon a *decision* to limit one's family, and upon the social pressures which are brought to bear on the spouses. It is a highly social and yet an intensely personal decision.

It naturally never struck the chairman that the problem of pre-marital pregnancy was worth mentioning. Knowing how prudish they are on sexual matters, I remarked that it would be very difficult to get healthy young men and women to exercise self-restraint until they were in their late twenties in Britain. 'In our society,' he informed me calmly – as though he were making a statement which no more called for challenge than the accuracy of production figures he had just given me – 'young people always respond to the revolutionary call of the Party'! This stunned me into silence, for in Britain (I did not dare say, because he would find it embarrassing), the word 'sexy' among the young is virtually synonymous with 'good' (though more so in theory than in practice still), and the notion of sex as freedom, and certainly as unconnected with politics, is general and axiomatic.

I believe, however, that for China, the chairman's confidence was warranted, and that the Chinese will therefore overcome this problem as they have overcome famine, that other great 'fact of Nature'. Indeed, such is the confidence the Chinese exude, so well-endowed are they with natural and human resources, and so effectively organized are the efforts of 800 million people, that one begins to feel that once they set themselves even such vast tasks as the control of population that now approaches one-quarter of humanity they will succeed in what they attempt.

The treatment of illness, like their approach to birth-control, emphasizes the human and social rather than the technical; in more conventional language, 'social and preventive' rather than 'curative', hospital and doctor-based medicine. But people do fall ill, and the specialized services, both in terms of personnel and of hospitals, are impressive. In the wards in the commune hospitals, which are spacious and clean, they can deal with appendectomies, operations for hernia, urinary-tract surgery, and so forth. The theatres are fitted out with lightweight equipment, all of Chinese manufacture: lamps, anaesthesia equipment, blood- and saline-drips, etc. The X-ray machine I looked at was made in Peking in 1970: it cost 5,750 *yuan* (about £1,000). Each person had to pay his 5 cents (1p) for a check-up, and the entire population was screened every year, the children at school. Cooks, nurses, and people in similar occupations were examined more frequently. A second, more mobile X-ray machine was used in the out-lying areas and even in the fields. But by now, T.B., a classic disease of poverty, was rare. The accent, then, is on taking health to the people, and upon preventing illness. The hospital is reserved for the serious cases beyond the competence of the 'barefoot doctors'.

In the spirit of self-reliance, the hospitals also manufacture many of the drugs they use, drawing upon traditional pharma-copoeia. In the West much publicity has been given to Chinese

use of traditional acupuncture. Much less attention, however, has been paid to the massive use of another traditional resource of Chinese medicine: the pharmacopoeia of
drugs that has been the main source of medicines for thousands
of years. Today, these are used literally side-by-side with
Western drugs: through this door of the clinic, the Western
drugs; through that, the dispensing of traditional drugs. I
saw some of the raw materials growing on communes, and in
the garden of a Children's Palace. Some of them were familiar,
but not familiar friends. To me, they were weeds – dandelions
amongst them – I tried hard to eliminate from my garden.
Here they were valuable sources of *materia medica*, from which
extracts are made, in the form of powders, pills and liquids,
and packed in sanitary ampoules or tubes. The hospital thus
participates in production, and rejects the conception of its
only being a centre of treatment and of consumption of things
produced outside. It also produces the means of production of
health.

The most dramatic case of the use of these modern versions
of traditional drugs I encountered was that of a young man
in Nanking No. 1 General Hospital who had been vomiting
up blood for some weeks before being admitted to hospital.
Rather than operate, they treated him with one of the drugs.
When I saw him, he was convalescing: the haemorrhage had
stopped. Western writers have usually assumed these ancient
pharmacopoeias to be 'folk medicine', mostly inefficacious and
based on 'superstition'. Yet in China they are treated very
seriously and widely used to good effect. Scientists study
ancient recipes and treatments carefully, trying to sift out the
valuable from the rest, and to discover what it is in them that
is efficacious. Acupuncture constitutes more of a problem of
theory, however, even for the Chinese. They use it, very
successfully, without having a theory of why or how it works.
The ancient conception of the 'meridians' running up and
down the body, with certain key points at which needles are
inserted, has not been verified. A Korean doctor did claim to
have photographed cells which might have been the component material of these meridians under the electric microscope, but nobody has replicated his finding, and doctors are
dubious about the research procedures he claims to have used.
The outstanding success of practice without theory, of course,
constitutes an almost historic problem for philosophers of
science and for methodologists in both West and East.

Western ethnocentric medicine has been greatly discomfited by the Chinese breakthrough in the use of acupuncture. As one experienced Canadian medical man I met in China remarked, the whole of neurological theory has been thrown into question by our inability to explain acupunctural analgesia. Our science has been shown to have missed something vital that another scientific tradition altogether has developed over centuries. It may well involve complex processes of stimulation or inhibition of sensation that are not carried by the nervous system, but which might be produced by physico-chemical 'irritation' of localized areas of the body, 'blocking off' sensation carried via the autonomic system of the body rather than the nervous system.

Acupuncture is still predominantly used in treating internal illnesses, including the treatment of such physical conditions as deaf-mutism, where we would think acupuncture as unpromising a solution as we once thought it to be as a means of negating pain in surgery. It is even used in psychiatric treatment. It is no exotic phenomenon to the Chinese, then, in that it is both ancient and very widely used. Yet although 100,000 operations a year are now performed under acupunctural analgesia, its use in surgery only began about five years ago. The Chinese attitude towards it, therefore, is highly experimental, pragmatic and innovatory, not traditionalistic.

Equally dramatic, though not dependent on the use of acupuncture, was the sight of a young worker whose hand had been sewn back on after he had been careless enough to get it chopped off in a machine. They had pinned the bones, then attached the nerves and blood-vessels. After seven months' physiotherapy, he could give me quite a vigorous handshake with it; after seven more months, he would be back at work.

Since no account of contemporary China is complete without describing one's personal experience of acupuncture (just as, in the U.S.A., everyone has his own pet mugging story), I must recount mine.

On visiting the Nanking hospital, a large establishment which had once been a small mission-hospital and bore the date '1892' on one of the two original buildings, I had visited the wards and spoken with the doctors and nurses. I had not expected to be allowed to see an operation, and was therefore taken unawares when I was suddenly told to don theatre-garb as we were going to see a mastoidectomy. The patient was not drugged or unconscious, but had his eyes open and talked with us while the surgeon was hammering away with a mallet and what looked like the kind of metal punch I use for making holes in masonry, but which was here inserted not into a wall but the man's ear. The surgeon thumped away energetically for about forty minutes while the nurses swabbed away the blood. (They did not, as they often do, give him pieces of orange and drinks while operating.)

He had four needles in his body: two in the neck below the affected ear; two down on one flank. They were linked up to wires carrying a small current from a transistor, in lieu of the traditional manual rotation of the needles. This combination of the ancient and modern is quite typical.

When it was all over, I asked him how he felt. 'I feel as if I could run upstairs', he grinned. Then he swung his legs off the operating table, started buttoning up his shirt, and before long was walking out of the theatre on the nurse's arm. It is said that post-operative complications, pain and weakness are very much less than in those cases – also very numerous – in which Western anaesthesia is used.

The next operation involved both Western oxygen-supplying machinery and acupuncture. A team of nurses and surgeons was busily engaged in a 'hole-in-the-heart' operation. The heart was vigorously beating away in a chest held open by all kinds of clamps. To my surprise, I was allowed to take photographs, and was so busy manipulating light-meters and flash-guns that I had no time to be queasy. I was even allowed to get close-ups by stepping up onto a small platform used by the surgeons. Blood makes beautiful colour-slides.

By this time, I had developed great confidence in acupuncture. Confidence is probably an important element, and patients are prepared beforehand. They are told what it is all about, what to expect, and what they should do. They are also shown other people having their operations. The patient's co-operation and morale are therefore important. Was this something peculiar to 'the Chinese character', I wondered, as often claimed? The way to find out would be to try it. Unfortunately I was not ill, so could not tell whether pain in my ear would have been relieved by needles inserted into my hip region.

But I could at least try the needle, and my chance came on a visit to the Children's Palace in Shanghai. It was a large building formerly belonging to a racketeer, and now devoted to providing children from the city's schools with a night's access to games and recreations not available in the neighbourhoods. Some were busy with 'fun-fair' amusements, 'shooting down' plates with sideshow-type machines; others were playing with boats in a big tank, others competing in races that included some elements of military assault-courses, e.g., crawling under barbed wire.

There were also classes catering for all kinds of interest: some, such as violin classes, apparently for talented children who came more frequently. In one room, a lady in a flowered dress was showing a group of girls a diagram of the human body with the acupuncture points marked on it. I looked again, in a sort of 'double-take', and saw that she was not just pointing out the positions on the chart or on the body, but demonstrating where to put real needles in – and they were doing it. Watching the girls inserting needles into each other, I thought to myself that, if they could do it, so could I. I had expected the woman doctor to handle the guest, but she handed the needle to a girl of about fifteen, who inserted it into the back of my hand in the area at the bottom of the 'V' formed by my thumb and first finger, twisting it as it went in.

I was so busy keeping a stiff upper lip and getting myself photographed that I did not notice how far it had gone in. It felt like a tenth of an inch or so. To my surprise, the girl showed me that it had been about half an inch. It felt rather like the sensation one gets from a dentist's drill after the gum has been anaethetized (though the needle is only slowly rotated manually, unlike the high-speed drill). Having just put a staple into my hand, I know it is very painful. In comparison, under acupuncture, one can feel that there is something there but it is not painful at all.

It was a small indicator of the kind of confidence that Chinese confidence in themselves builds up in you. I would now prefer to have an operation under acupuncture than under Western anaesthesia – if the Chinese were to do it. Such specialized medicine is, of course, concentrated in city hospitals. But within a very few years, the rural areas will be covered with a network, not only of mini-factories, but also of health services that their brothers in any other Third World agrarian society would envy. To see the communes today is to see the gap between the countryside and the town being reduced before one's eyes. There is a very long way to go, but the gap is by no means the yawning chasm it is in most countries. And the sense of tremendous confidence that has been engendered has not been achieved by Welfare State handouts, foreign aid, or *de haut en bas* patronage of the villagers by the cities, but, in greatest measure, by themselves.

5

THE CITIES

Chinese cities divide into two types: colonial and Chinese. The lack of enthusiasm I initially felt for Canton was matched when I visited Shanghai, also a product of the imperialist era, as are most of the other industrial cities, such as Wuhan or Tientsin. There had been flourishing ports at these places for centuries, and in Shanghai, a cotton industry, too, but their modern industrial development dates from the era when the Europeans established themselves by force in the second half of the nineteenth century. Tientsin, for instance, had Japanese, German, British, Austro-Hungarian, Italian and Russian 'concession' areas, in which the law of those countries ran and where Chinese were subjected to Napoleonic or British law administered by foreign judges. The names of the streets were eloquent of this multiple occupation: Rue du Baron Gros, Victoria Park, Baron Czekam Strasse, Via Vittorio Emanuele, Pokotilova, Asahi Gai, and so on. The British concession area in Shanghai, the Chinese say (and 'old China hands' deny), had a notice reading: 'No dogs or Chinese allowed' at the boundary. Today, the colonial buildings are still there, but put to new uses. The Headquarters of the Shanghai Municipality was once a bank. The former Shanghai Club, for instance, at No. 3, The Bund – the great street along the waterfront, now named after Sun Yat-Sen, the founder of the Republic – is a seamen's club. On leafy Sha Mian Island at Canton, children play among the government offices which were once foreign banks and consulates, where their parents could not go without permission from the French or British authorities.

Nor do the 'red light' districts flourish any longer. Shanghai, the 'wickedest city in the East', was notorious for its gangsters and secret societies, such as the 'Greens', who had a stranglehold on the city. They also provided services for Chiang Kai-Shek's régime, notably the butchering of thousands of workers in 1927. They maintained a reign of terror thereafter, but proved to be 'paper tigers' when confronted with the Eighth Prize Company of the Liberation Army, which, in a few short months, cleaned up the Nanking Road, the 'pleasure' street of restaurants, brothels, luxury shops and bright lights, where the wealthy Chinese businessmen and the international community had been wont to disport themselves.

Most of the soldiers had never seen a city before. When they finally marched in past the luxury department stores, a French observer, Robert Guillian, compared them to 'Martians'. There was no familiar crash of boots on the pavements, for they had no boots. They wore slippers and grass-coloured sackcloth. But if low on material assets, they possessed a moral code as austere as that of Cromwell's Ironsides: the 'Three main rules of discipline and the eight points for attention', the (hardly snappy) title, now, of a very good popular tune:

1. Obey orders in all your actions
2. Don't take a single needle or piece of thread from the masses
3. Turn in everything captured

1. Speak politely
2. Pay fairly for what you buy
3. Return everything you borrow
4. Pay for anything you damage
5. Don't hit or swear at people
6. Don't damage crops
7. Don't take liberties with women
8. Don't ill-treat captives

This code of conduct, modernized since 1928, when the first 'point' read: 'Put back the doors you have taken for bed-boards', was the key to the success of the Red armies in the cities as it had been in the rural areas. The Nanking Lu today still has superb restaurants, but they are crowded with ordinary people, like the young couple I sat opposite to at the former Sunya restaurant at number 719. They were out for a dinner 'in town' that evening. It would cost them a few shillings for some of the best cuisine in the world. But I could not find the floating restaurant any longer on Canton's Sha Mian Island, because it had disappeared after the Cultural Revolution. It probably smacked too much of an era, only two generations ago, when 'little slave girls, bought from the pirates of the Western River, after rowing stoutly all day, abandoned them-selves to more dainty games at nightfall, for the profit of their owners'. A 'piquant mixture of putrefaction and precocity', was a French writer's characterization of Canton in 1916. The same term can still be applied, however, to contemporary Bangkok, or, to come nearer the Chinese heartland, to Hong Kong, where sampans, with 'companions', can be hired for the night for 30 dollars. Shanghai, too, boasted a quarter of a million girls providing every imaginable variety of obscene 'diversions' in 800 brothels. But there, they are just an historical memory, for Shanghai was also the proletarian heart of China, where the Communist Party was founded, and it has been proletarian culture that has won out over the bourgeois way of life.

The girls were given constructive work to do. There was plenty needed in post-Liberation Shanghai. Today, the colonial culture has been sinicized: on the former race-course, a canal with willow trees and a bamboo bridge stand where the home-turn and the judges' box once were. Horse racing, like all gambling, is taboo, and the clack of *mah jong* no longer resounds. The odd mock Tudor ex-bank, the occasional disused European church, some *art deco* public buildings, and a sea of poor housing are now the main visual legacy of the colonial period.

It is not only colonial culture that has gone: so has pre-Cultural Revolution 'high society'. It is astounding, today, to read Macchiochi's description, in her *Daily Life in Revolutionary China*, of the then Cathay Hotel in 1954, five years after Liberation:

The hotel salon, resplendent with crystal, silver and flowers, glitters like a great glass bell-jar ... the women of Shanghai ... are wearing their afternoon or evening clothes: long, slim, form-fitting tunics, their only hint of coquetry a slit on the side, open to the knee ... Their faces, touched with white powder ... their hair, silky and heavy ...

or of Peking:

The houses have yellow glazed ceramic-tile roofs, red architraves and columns, doors covered with yellow lattice-work and decorated with stippled ceramic panes ... Even the coffin merchants display colourful lettered signs and silk-shaded lanterns above their doors. Most unforgettable are the dentists' shop-offices whose windows are decorated with enormous paper dentures ... And everywhere there are pictures and posters showing fat Chinese men and women urging people to buy.

Today, all that has gone, every bit as vanished into the past as the 'flower girls' on the sampans. The floating population of Canton, indeed, has entirely disappeared, even if famous restaurants not so deeply symbolic of the colonial past remain, with mellifluous names like 'Listen to the Rain Falling', or 'Birds, Flowers and Music'.

'This was a consumer city,' is the first thing your Chinese guides tell you about any city in China. 'Now it is a centre of production.' Consumer goods there are in plenty in the large department stores, thronged with buyers, selling everything from kitchen equipment to *wei ch'i* chess sets and Chinese oboes. But the edge of the stairs in Shanghai's No. 1 Department Store was worn through: not only the brass-edging strip but even the stone underneath. I asked my guide why the municipality did not paint the buildings, do repairs, light up the streets better. He replied, with a certain Hegelian hauteur, 'You are only talking about appearances, not grasping the essence. The lives of the masses come first and the struggle to close the gap between town and countryside.' I eventually came to the conclusion that he was right. The places that are getting electric light – and for the first time in human history – are the villages of China. And though there is little doubt that Shanghai, now possibly the world's largest city, does have a housing problem, it is not the same situation it faced in 1949, nor the problem a very learned professor, sympathetic to China, asked me to investigate: whether there were any shanty-towns growing up on the outskirts of the cities. (He had been reading an American study of Shanghai based on satellite photographs.)

I can tell him now that there are not. There used to be. They were demolished by the People's Liberation Army in the immediate post-Liberation years. But a few have been kept, in the famous workers' district of Chapei where the great labour struggles of the twenties and thirties took place and which was later bombed flat by the Japanese. These hovels, the *kuen t'i lung*, are all that remain of those in which hundreds of thousands had once lived, and in which millions still live elsewhere in the Third World (300,000 peasants flock into South Korea's towns each year, there to work fourteen to eighteen hours a day), and which are 'home', too, for hundreds of thousands of migrant workers right in the heart of Europe. In Calcutta, millions have lived in them now for several generations. In Shanghai, half a dozen only remain as a museum. Next to them are preserved what the P.L.A. put in their place as a temporary measure: two-storey houses of stout wooden beams with plaster filling, not unlike Elizabethan buildings. This kind of building has gone, too, giving way to new workers' apartment blocks.

The old rickshaw-puller I talk to at Pumpkin Lane, one of these new workers' settlements, tells me that they cried when they moved in here because they thought only the bourgeoisie could live in places like this. 'When we came we didn't know how to work the gas-stoves; we'd never seen such things before,' he remarked. They pay 28 cents per square metre; they have 26·5 sq. m., so the rent comes to 7·42 *yuan* a month.

There were four adults and three young children in this three-generation family: the old man, the mother, their son and daughter-in-law, and three grandchildren. It was a family with a high ratio of dependants to income-earners. The old man only got a pension of 21 *yuan* a month, the mother (also retired) presumably was in receipt of a small pension (I failed to ask). The son earned 64 *yuan* as an office cadre; the daughter-in-law 46 *yuan* in a factory. It was a low-income family overall; income could not have been much more than 150 *yuan*. Rent was therefore about one-twentieth of their joint income; low compared to Britain.

They had a large enough living-room, a separate bedroom, and access to a kitchen which had three two-burner gas-stoves in it, a food cupboard, and a sink for washing clothes, with running water, for each of the three apartments which ran off the staircase, rather like an Oxbridge college. They also shared two toilets between the three families. There were thirty-five blocks of these five-storey buildings on this estate, housing 8,700 people in 1,809 households. This suggests an average family of around 4·8, which further suggests that population-control, amongst younger parents in the city at least, is becoming effective, since this was a population with only 158 retired people on the estate. Though he and his wife were retired, the old man remarked they were not retired 'ideologically'. They were deeply involved in the community life: controlling pedestrian traffic (especially the children), arranging and participating in study-groups, cleaning the surroundings, educating the children in good habits, and so on.

Over a million people had moved into estates like this; there were ten others like Pumpkin Lane, mainly bigger. The space-ration was about three times what I had seen in Hong Kong resettlement blocks, and one had only to look to see this. The estate was spacious, lined with trees, and even allowing for the able-bodied being at work there was none of that desperate press of humanity, that cramming in of bodies, that affronts the eye and offends the spirit in Hong Kong.

I was told a great deal about the horrors of life before Liberation: the *kuen t'i lung* shanties; the open drains and rubbish-tips; the daily sound of mourning as the corpses were disposed of, often just by wrapping them in mats and burying them in pits. Then, there was no running water; they ate twice daily, at best. Children polished shoes, hawked news-papers, or begged. There was one expensive school only, costing fifty kilos of rice a term. Now the estate has its own primary school, a nursery, kindergarten, shops and bank, and 40 per cent of the estate's residents were at school. The Japanese bombing and shelling had left hundreds of craters, 50,000 sq. m. of them in all. On top of all this was the rule of the local gangs and secret societies: he himself had had to pay 'protection' money. Often he had only eaten chaff as his morning meal before going off to do a day's work pulling rickshaws. Later, he turned to street-cleaning. The girls often became prostitutes; his own father had died in their shanty, with him, a young child, in his arms. They had had to borrow money to buy mats to bury him in.

The handful of *kuen t'i lung* and the specimens of P.L.A. housing from 1952 have been preserved in order to educate the younger generation. There is little likelihood of their growing up without being reminded of the past if this old man was anything to go by. The improvements, at first, had been simple, he said – but previously unimaginable: water and electricity supply, paved roads, sewage. Then the ditches and craters were filled in. They only got round to building the new blocks, however, in 1963. Two years later, they were finished. Then, there were great festivities and much buying of furniture. In the past, if they had so much as stopped on the pavement to look at buildings like these, where the rich used to live, they would have been moved on by the police. Now they were actually going to live in them.

He did not fail to draw the political moral. 'We used to think we were *fated* to be poor,' he said. 'Now we know that we were deceived by exploiters and by the Kuomintang. The real reason we were so poor was that we didn't have political power. And we owe our happiness to Chairman Mao and the Communist Party. If it wasn't for them our children would be begging today. When I came here,' he laughed, 'I had two baskets with all my worldly possessions in them. Now if I moved, I'd need two trucks!' He had had no furniture at all before 1949. Now he has two double beds, a good-sized table, two chests, a wardrobe, a treadle sewing-machine, a dresser with a mirror, etc., and he was receiving 70 per cent of his former wages as his retirement pension. 'We're fortunate,' he remarked, 'and millions like me are, but there are many in the world who still live as we used to, and it is our duty to contribute to their liberation.' The old rickshaw-puller was an eloquent spokesman and his life-story in itself pointed up the enormous improvements in the lives of ordinary people. Yet it is difficult not to feel that one has been to a showplace when one finds the same old man being interviewed twice more by visitors who have written about him on their return to this country since I was there.

Chapei is only one of Shanghai's ten districts: 5,800,000 people live in the city proper, and there are ten counties, with another five million people in them, included in the municipal area. Together with Canton, Peking and Tientsin, the Shanghai municipality is responsible directly to the central government, not to the province of Kiangsu of which it is part geographically, as lesser cities and towns would be. Each of the ten districts is divided into sub-districts. In the case of Chapei district, there are thirteen of them. Each sub-district is further sub-divided into neighbourhoods (*li lun*), usually composed of somewhere between 1,000 and 1,500 households. This estate constituted one neighbourhood unit, and was evidently bigger than the normal *il lun*, since it contained fifty-seven 'residential groups', the lowest level of administrative unit (about two to each block) – obviously because the estate constituted a natural unit. These fifty-seven groups elected twenty-five representatives to the Revolutionary Committee of the neighbourhood, of whom nine belonged to the Standing Committee. Twelve of the Revolutionary Committee were Party members, and six of the Standing Committee. This was nothing unusual, but the high representation of women was: fourteen out of the twenty-five Revolutionary Committee members, and six out of the nine Standing Committee members, were women.

They drew the conclusion that this reflected the improved situation of women. I drew the opposite conclusion. At a Nanking primary school, I had noticed that all the representatives of the Revolutionary Committee except one were women. 'Yes, we're conscious of this, too,' they replied. 'We have forty-five teachers here and forty-one of them are women.' 'Then how do you explain this?' I asked. Even the chairman (a man, of course) seemed a bit nonplussed, but then produced the ideologically correct answer: that women were valued equally in Chinese society, since they 'supported half the heavens'. True, I said, but why were the men only holding up $\frac{4}{45}$ths of the heavens here? Further uncertainty. So I proffered a Women's Lib/Marxist explanation for them. 'Yes, that's right,' they said, 'we can combine teaching with taking care of the home and children, because we leave here early in the afternoon.'

Such great gains have been made in the lives of women since the Liberation that the Chinese talk as if they have achieved complete social equality between the sexes. They are a long way from it. A quarter of a century after Liberation, few women are to be found in the higher reaches of Party and Government, and most of the key decision-makers one encounters at lower levels are men: the chairman of the Revolutionary Committee of the commune, for instance: though one or two 'token' women will grace the committee. It may well be a sign of increasing Chinese sensitivity to criticism of the persisting over-representation of men in key positions that 20 per cent of the delegates to the Tenth Party Congress held in August 1973 were women, as were

20 per cent of those elected to the Presidium, the top body. The similar percentages suggest that a deliberate policy may be being pursued, and the names of women were specially identified in the official reports. The strongly-persisting extended family, too, means a continued role for older women as child-minders while their daughters are at work, and in the urban neighbourhoods the women play a very large part because they are often at home and hence available. When one sees the crippled feet of the very old women, there is no doubt that things have changed almost unimaginably for women in China, but feminine roles are still distinctly marked and silently allocated in contemporary China. This is not a matter of policy, but of those insidious assumptions and attitudes that operate similarly in the West, which, when brought to the forefront of their attention, often surprise those who hold them. As the older women die, their daughters, though, are not at all likely to be content to become child-minders in their turn; they will want to continue working beyond the statutory age of fifty when they are entitled to retire on pension (fifty-five for clerical workers; for men, it is sixty). And if they do retire, they will certainly not be 'ideologically retired'.

Women enjoy an eight-hour working day, and free hospitalization and medical care, as workers – as workers' dependants they only have to pay 20 cents a month, as against the half of medical expenses they had to pay before the Cultural Revolution; they have fifty-six paid days off before childbirth, they are entitled to free birth-control pills, and so on. Yet differences, not very major, in wages, work-points, retirement-ages, persist, and more serious differences of occupation and occupancy of responsible 'cadre' positions also remain twenty-five years after the most radical revolution in history. The persistence of the double employment of women as mainstay of the home as well as worker outside still arouses the passion of militant Women's Liberation sisters visiting China. This is why a great deal of the local-level activity in the neighbourhood still falls on the second sex, since they are simply there, and the jobs to be done are thought of as appropriate to women. So mothers at home take care of education and health (in co-operation with full-time workers employed by the municipality), as well as participating in study-groups themselves; they watch that the children do not destroy the trees and flowers and see to the danger-spots at pedestrian crossings. Women below forty-five are increasingly likely to be in regular employment; though a 1970 study of thirty-five major industrial enterprises found that well below 10 per cent of the workforce were women. For those at home, there is group-organized 'cottage industry', usually piece-work paid at lower rates than those obtaining in the factories.

Throughout the country, there is an eight-grade wage structure in industry, workers being placed in the appropriate grade by means of collective discussions within the work-group. There is, of course, an initial training period which is generally an apprenticeship of three years' duration. There seemed to be a rough relationship between age and seniority, on the one hand, and pay levels on the other, but there must be competent workers who are young and less competent ones who are their seniors. A typical wage-grade structure, in an advanced-technology plant, is that obtaining in Shenyang No. 1 Lathe Factory: Grade 1 – 33 *yuan* per month; Grade 2 – 38·9 *yuan*; Grade 3 – 45·8 *yuan*; Grade 4 – 54 *yuan*; Grade 5 – 63·6 *yuan*; Grade 6 – 74 *yuan*; Grade 7 – 88·2 *yuan*; Grade 8 – 104 *yuan*.

Recent studies suggest that the rapid growth of the city population which post-Liberation industrialization brought about has begun to tail off. There were only 57½ million people in the cities and towns in 1949. By 1957, the year before the Great Leap, this had virtually doubled to 92 million. Most of this increase was in the major cities, seventeen of which had over a million people each by the early 1960s. But the policy of decentralization has meant a concomitant growth of the smaller interior cities also. Thus Sian, the capital of Shensi province, had grown to 1,600,000 by 1968; Lanchow, the capital of Kansu province, had reached 700,000 by 1957; Chengtu, the capital of Szechwan province, has over 1,200,000 people, and Chungking, the famous wartime Kuomintang capital, over 2,500,000 people. Smaller towns, like Kiang Men, which we described earlier, have all grown too.

Buchanan has shown how the industrial map of China began to change when the first wave of industrialization began even during the First Five-year Plan (1953–7). Sixty per cent of new industry was located in the big interior cities – Changchow, Wuhan, Sian, Loyang, Lanchow, Paotow – which experienced a new upsurge of growth. By the time of the Second Plan, it was the turn of the cities even further in the interior – towards Szechwan and Sinkiang – to begin their modernization. Even the remote 'Far West' has got its first factories: Tibet has a textile mill, at Lhasa; and Sinkiang too, the home of the descendants of the nomads who conquered China and much of the Eurasian land-mass – the Mongol, Uighur and other pastoralists of the steppelands, is now self-sufficient as far as such items as textiles, sugar and leather goods are concerned.

Hence the interior of China is gradually experiencing the growth of cities and towns, and the growth of industry. Nevertheless, the heavy industry is still concentrated in the major centres where the colonial legacy deposited urban agglomerations: Shanghai, Peking, Nanking, Tientsin, Canton, Wuhan, and the North-East – once Japanese-occupied 'Manchukuo' and now the site of very heavy industry, especially steel. Shenyang (formerly Mukden), a city which had only 580,000 inhabitants in 1937, now has about three million, for the presence of a steel industry has been the basis for the growth of heavy industry, particularly machine-industry, in the North-East: no less than a third of Chinese industry is now concentrated up here. Anshan, the second city of the North-East, is one huge complex of mines, furnaces, rolling-mills and seamless-steel tubing-mills. It has grown from 130,000 in 1949 to a million today. It produces eight million metric tons of ore from its iron mines, and turns it into four million tons of steel in ten blast-furnaces.

Today, Chinese industry has 'arrived'. Over twenty million people are employed in industry, which now contributes between a third and a half of China's national income (according to your yardstick). A former British Minister of Technology, Anthony Wedgwood Benn, has written of the 'obvious high quality' of the products of the Chinese engineering industry (*The Times*, 21 March, 1973, China Trade Supplement). China now produces jet-planes, computers, space-launchers and nuclear weapons; her cotton textile industry is now the world's largest; her steel industry three times that of India; her petroleum industry is now capable of exporting; and she has a sophisticated electronics industry and the beginnings of a ship-building industry.

Foreign, especially American, estimates of the growth in industrial production are the subject of astoundingly dis-crepant estimates: one source of the difficulty is that most such estimates go back to the 1950s, when industry was only begin-ning, and combine the output of those years with more recent figures, thus producing low rates-of-growth figures for the past two decades. Even the more cautious estimates today, however, suggest an increasing momentum of growth: one authority put the industrial growth-rate between 1963 and 1966 as somewhere between 10½ per cent and 12 per cent per annum. In the first eight months of 1971, industrial production was 18·7 per cent higher than the year before. These achievements have been possible because China has mobilized human resources which most economies leave untapped. Massive injections of capital to construct the heavy industrial base, so as to provide the basic metals, fuels and machines which, in their turn, are the source of secondary industrial development, have been a *sine qua non*, and the resources of the society have been highly focused by the planning agencies so as to provide for the key social needs. The Chinese have not been able to do everything at once, and some needs have had to wait. Housing achievements have been considerable – new residential blocks for 600,000 people in Peking alone, for example – but it only requires a walk around the side-streets of Shanghai to see that a massive rehousing programme is needed in the future, however neat and tidy the streets. China's output of electricity and cement, to take two key items, still lagged behind that of India in 1969. And some key industrial items, from computers to transport equipment, are made in insufficient quantities, and hence have to be imported. Military needs have absorbed a vast part of China's resources, including her human resources, particularly of physicists and chemists. But the formation of a corps of over a quarter of a million engineering graduates between 1953 and 1962 (a quarter of them machine-tool specialists, and another fifth in construction and city planning) has paid off.

These advanced specialists are the counterpart of another population: the tens of thousands working in the primitive mini-factories of the communes. Science and technology, too, 'walk on two legs'. Whether at the level of rocketry or of schoolyard furnaces, the same principles obtain, and the major emphasis is not upon individual effort or technical expertise alone, but upon the inculcation of a consciously egalitarian, participatory and political attitude to work. Cadres and technical experts work at the bench, just as Army officers serve in the ranks, in order to minimize 'lordism', and to sharpen their appreciation of life as it is experienced by the worker or the private soldier. The worker, too, is urged to pass on his expertise and experience to others, not to retain it as a piece of 'job-property'. Nor is this left at the level of moral exhortation. Private monopolization of skill is no longer rewarded by bonuses: instead, a man is valued for 'political consciousness', and encouraged to *'exchange* experiences' – the phrase constantly used in China. Hitting paper targets and holding meetings can be diseases in themselves, however. Hence this new culture of work aims at minimizing 'formalism' (what we generally call 'bureaucracy'), and 'perfunctoriness', and eliminating the 'four too many and the four too little', the familiar diseases of East European industry: too many meetings, too many work arrangements, too many instructions, too many duties to attend to; and their opposites: too little contact with the masses, too little participation in labour, too little inspection of work, too little ideological work. The accent is upon reducing the number of bureaucrats and the amount of time they spend in offices.

The practical outcome is visible in the dock-industry, an industry which, because of its danger, its unpredictability of schedules and variability of cargoes, its history of exploitation and the threat of new technological unemployment, has produced, in the West, a tough self-protective proletarian counter-culture of dockers' organizations, official and unofficial. Shanghai handles twenty to thirty foreign ships a day. Eighty per cent of the equipment is mechanized, and ships of 10,000 tons have been unloaded the day they arrived. One vessel, delivering 27,000 tons of fertilizer, was unloaded in $39\frac{1}{2}$ hours instead of the seventeen days specified in the contract. Such results have not been obtained simply by 'speed-up' or new machinery: they are the result of a novel kind of *socialist* rationalization which derives from quite political premises about the relationship of the individual to the group and to society and about the nature of men's motivations, that have tapped hitherto unsuspected sources of human response. The result is not higher 'output', but greater *input* – into society.

More tangible results can be seen in such a spectacular achievement as the bridge 300 feet above the Yangtse River at Nanking. This called for over 100,000 tons of steel and a million tons of cement. It is a two-decker bridge, with a four-lane motor road nearly 8 miles long (including approaches) on top, and a double-track railway, $11\frac{1}{2}$ miles (including approaches) beneath it. The section above the river proper is $2\frac{3}{4}$ miles long.

New bridges had been built earlier higher up the Yangtse

at Wuhan and Chungking. This was to be the biggest, but just after construction started in 1960, the Russians 'perfidiously' tore up the contracts to supply the steel, hoping, the Chinese said, to sabotage and disrupt the project. The workers at Anshan, in the North-East, eventually overcame that problem. Locally, Russian expertise and equipment was replaced by the hero Hou Pao-Ling who trained and led a team of divers, using ordinary equipment – all they had – for work on the rock foundations at the bottom of the river, at depths of over two hundred feet, work of which they had no previous experience. A trial concrete pier they built is still sticking up out of the water. The welders also had to learn how to join the rails together into lengths over three-quarters of a mile (480 metres) long, in order to reduce vibration. They completed the rail section of the job by China's National Day, 1 October 1968, and the road by 1 January 1969.

Today, over sixty trains a day use the bridge, instead of the former slow-moving ferry, as well as 7,000 road vehicles, and large marshalling yards are growing up around the approaches. About half a million people, too, visit the bridge every year. It was crowded with school parties when I was there; special buses take them across and back for 10 cents.

The Chinese, then have had to learn to do it themselves, cut off as they have been by capitalist embargo and Soviet-bloc withdrawal. Their economy has therefore not been able to replace everything as quickly as ideally should have been done. The aged Russian civilian planes, only now being replaced by Tridents, like the cars, often of pre-Liberation vintage, are still doing their job by virtue of meticulous maintenance and repair, but this also bears witness to the gap between the advanced military technology and 'make-do' civilian facilities. China can produce her own version of the MIG 21, but she has to import diesel locomotives from Europe, and no less than 12,000 trucks in 1970 alone.

Foreign trade is not large in proportion to the Gross National Product – only about 4 per cent. The consumption of goods commonly regarded in the West as 'consumer durables', and therefore as indices of 'development', would put China 'down among the dead men', for there are no private cars or television, and over 20,000 people per telephone, as compared to 2·4 in the U.S.A. or 851 even in India. The Chinese, however, do not wish to create a consumer society. They have not *tried* to produce cars, television or phones on a mass scale, since they do not wish to. Hopefully, the boulevards of Peking will *never* become choked with thousands of private cars (and hopefully, too, though international contact needs greatly expanding, China will never become victim of that other great consumer disease, the tourist industry). Instead, the two million bicycles, the modern, cheap buses, and the new Underground will keep the traffic flowing. No doubt luxuries like television in the home will come. At present, the bicycle and radio are China's big 'consumer durable' luxuries and there are few who would dissent from the Chinese view that public goods should take priority over luxury private consumption for a few. Indeed, the human and ecological costs of growing 'public squalor' in the schools, subways, hospitals and neighbourhoods of the U.S.A., for example, are bringing consumerist values into increasing disrepute, in the West as well as in China, and especially among the young.

Much of Chinese industry is still very backward. Where they have given high priority to a particular industry, they combine the very latest, foreign or home-devised, with a massive proliferation of the small and simple. Craftsmen who formerly specialized in traditional luxury goods like filigree jewellery now use their skills to produce tiny electronic components; plants specializing in one product have diversified, and one finds mono-crystal furnaces in textile plants; and people who have never before participated in industrial work now do so on a large scale, notably the housewives who work part-time in neighbourhood workshops and in the home itself, producing components and assembling all kinds of goods from toys to transistors.

Industry with low priority contents itself with methods and levels of production left behind in the West before World War I. Italian automobile experts from Alfa-Romeo and Fiat visited the automobile plant which produces the 'Shanghai' car, and were hard put to it to disguise their amazement when they found no more than ten per day being produced by hand 'as if they were creating a Swiss watch' (too *many* for precision craftsmanship, in fact!). The workers, they reported, had achieved miracles with 'highly heterogeneous machine tools', 'very few mechanical presses', and 'piles of materials of all types in complete disorder'. 'On the whole', the factory was 'devoid of any safety features', and the products were 'antiquated and haphazard as regards design'. Not surprisingly production costs were obviously very high. To produce the larger vehicles, many small factories specialize in components later centrally assembled – over a hundred factories are involved in producing the huge 400 h.p. diesel 32-ton dumper on display at the Shanghai Industrial Exhibition (the famous Stalinesque 'wedding-cake' Hall filled with the impressive latest products of Chinese industry).

The limits of Chinese industrial production are obvious enough. The lineaments of the future are also discernible in the advanced products on display, but as yet not emerging in great numbers. Chinese industrialization has had its ups and downs, too. There seems little doubt that at the beginning of the 1960s, in particular, industry was performing very badly indeed. Stagnation, or even retrogression, occurred, apparently due primarily to miscalculation of the problems involved in transferring men and resources from agriculture into the cities, and accentuated by the inadequacy of the transport network. Today, a stronger network of rail and air links has been created. Given the rapidity of Chinese industrialization, such troubles were to be expected, but the general direction is unambiguous – massive and sustained growth.

Industrialization has always meant urbanization hitherto. It did in China in the 1950s and 1960s when the major cities grew enormously. Not all of the city growth was from immigration, however. City populations grew rapidly by natural increase in the fifties and sixties due to the popularity of marriage, because of confidence in the future and because of better health conditions. Growth statistics are difficult to evaluate, for city boundaries have shifted, and cities are now often immense units (Tientsin alone covers an administrative area two-thirds the size of the Netherlands), for the city as a unit of administration now contains within its boundaries extensive rural areas, in line with the Chinese policy of bringing town and country together. In Shanghai's case, no less than 190 communes are included within the territory of the municipality.

To prevent the kind of development that has resulted in shanty-towns in the capitalist world, movement from country to town has been carefully controlled (you need to produce evidence that you have a job to go to, in order to get a ration card and a ticket to move to the city), but the movement of people from the city to the countryside has assumed such proportions in recent years that the flow of population, it is claimed by some, has actually been reversed, i.e., there is a net outflow from the cities to the countryside. Some recent figures purport to show a decline in the urban component of the total population, from 18·5 per cent in 1960 to 14 per cent in 1969. In dealing with China, where, to use Buchanan's graphic phrase, one is 'groping in a statistical blackout', one cannot be sure, but a very tight control is certainly being exercised to ensure that 'megapolitan' growth does not occur. Much of the growth, even within the major city municipalities, is decentralized away from the densely-settled central zones towards the surrounding countryside.

In the case of Shanghai, for instance, which has a municipal area of 6,000 square kilometres – practically the size of the Lebanon – the No. 1 Heavy Electrical Machinery Plant, the biggest in China, is now a long way out in the country. It had begun as a small back-street factory in the city. In 1952 it moved out of Shanghai, well beyond the city-limits proper, to what we would call a 'satellite' or 'new town' location. Today, the work-force, including staff, numbers over 8,000. The plant chalked up a steadily rising volume of production of ever more complex 'generations' of steam turbo-generators. Previously all such equipment had been imported. The first model was a 6,000 kilowatt machine, in 1954; a 25,000 kilowatt machine followed in 1955; then 50,000 kilowatt and 100,000 kilowatt machines. Finally, as a 'gift' for China's National Day in 1971, their pride and joy, a 300,000 kilowatt generator.

Going round the eighteen workshops one finds that a lot of the heavy machinery is East European (as we saw earlier in the small town of Kiang Men): Czech and Soviet, and also Japanese and Canadian. Of the sixteen major machines I saw in two of the workshops, no less than seven were from the U.S.S.R., one from the Skoda works, one from Japan, three smaller ones from Canada, and four were Chinese-made: one a copy of a Soviet machine, another from Harbin, another from elsewhere in China, and one made on the spot.

The first wave of industrialization, then, was clearly dependent on foreign – mainly East European – imports of machinery, a fact the Chinese do not emphasize. But I talked to engineers from Switzerland installing watch-making machinery, and to Canadian textile-importers, who both believed that within a very short time Chinese machinery would predominate (it already does in textiles) and who had no adverse criticisms of the quality of either machines or products. The Chinese themselves emphasize that though the machinery may have been supplied from abroad, they paid for every single piece. Indeed, they recall with some bitterness, they had to pay not only for industrial goods, but also for every single plane, shell and bullet from the U.S.S.R. used by Chinese forces in Korea. (The loan of $300m. granted in 1949 by the U.S.S.R. under the then Mutual Aid Pact has been described by K. S. Karol as 'derisory' in relation both to China's needs and the importance of the relationship between the two Powers.) The Central Committee of the Chinese Communist Party, in a letter to their Soviet opposite numbers in 1964, referred to the payments they had made – in goods, gold, and convertible foreign exchange – and complained of high Soviet prices for some items. 2,100m. roubles' worth of food (soya beans, rice, edible oils and meat) had also been exported, plus 1,400m. roubles' worth of mineral products (lithium, beryllium and wolfram, borax, quartz, mercury, tantalum-niobium, molybdenum, and tin: materials of special importance for the U.S.S.R.'s rocket and nuclear-weapon programmes). With exquisite irony, they offered to help out the U.S.S.R. by sending their own experts to the Soviet Union, an offer since repeated with special reference to the notorious weakest area of the Soviet economy, its agriculture, which they regard as always having tried to 'drain the pond to catch the fish'.

Rapid industrialization has its human costs anywhere. The British Industrial Revolution involved an horrific sacrifice of whole generations of stunted human beings. In China, there have been sacrifices, too, in comparison trivial, but scarcely pleasurable for those concerned. Only 40 per cent of the labour-force at the Heavy Electrical Machinery Plant, for example, were housed locally. The rest lived in dormitories of solid construction, with communal bathing, washing and toilet facilities and dining-rooms. They paid no rent, and were bussed home at weekends to their families in Shanghai. The men were accommodated at five, six and even eight to a room. The rooms I saw were about sixteen to eighteen square metres. The nearest analogy I can think of is an Army barracks. When I said this was a great hardship for families, they argued that people were willing to put up with it because of their high political consciousness, and that the fathers of families of diplomats were often separated from their families for one, two, three, or even up to six years. They put the Revolution first, as did these workers.

Many of the new city working-force are recruited from peri-urban communes which are also periodically asked to provide land for new industrial and housing sites. I visited one Shanghai commune where no less than 4,000 men had gone into factory employment. Many of them remain in their former houses on the commune lands, however, and members of their families may continue to be employed on the commune. All kinds of agricultural-industrial mixes are therefore to be found in such areas. River Gulf commune, outside Shanghai, for instance, contains ten workshops, including medicinal herb processing plants (they also grow one-fifth of the city's supply), a furniture factory, and also acts as a small market-centre for the surrounding locality.

The commune pattern of social organization, with its intimate connection between work and place of residence, can scarcely be reproduced in the city. As the armies of bicycles indicate, the journey to work alone entails a different pattern of life in the cities. Politically, the workers are organized in their factories and places of work, rather than in their neigh-bourhoods. There is not, then, the same close fit that obtains on the commune. To some degree, this can be effected, per-haps, in small towns and peripheral settlements where the factory adjoins the housing settlement, but the separation of home and work is a fact of city life that will continue to be the case for millions of urban workers. So, too, will the manage-ment of public services on a city-wide basis. Social mobility, also, will be the dominant feature of the lives of the increasing numbers of technicians, professional workers, and cadres of all kinds, and the building of new cities in the interior will call for the transfer of even greater populations than the millions who have already 'gone down to the countryside'.

China will probably hold the major cities to something like their present size by locating new industry either on the periphery of the cities or in the interior towns and cities. I, for one, will not be sorry. I have no desire to lay my bones either in Shanghai or Canton, both monuments to imperialism. (Tientsin, which I did not visit, sounds even more like a Chinese version of Sheffield or Manchester of the 1950s.) To me, Shanghai, on a wet day, has all the charm and *brio* of Oldham. True, when the sun comes out again, so do the people, and the streets and stores bustle with vitality.

The only time I ever felt in China that my hosts were not keen to meet my wishes was when I asked to be taken around

some *ordinary* housing in Shanghai. It is natural for anyone to
want to show off their newest and best, and most people
would take Chinese visitors to see new housing developments
in their own country rather than decaying slums. I had been
promised that I would see both the good and the poor, the
new and the old. In one sense, this was done: but the old
turned out to be the 'museum' of shanty-dwellings I have
described. Eventually, I simply walked off on my own for
hours around the side-streets. They were spotless (the residents are said to sweep the streets before going to work), but
patently the legacy of the colonial era. They are also overcrowded, and must eventually come down. Meanwhile, the
apartment blocks in what were once the 'smart' Western
districts are occupied by workers' families.

The rapid growth of the urban population has not been
matched, in fact, by a commensurate provision of new housing.
During the period 1949–62 the urban population doubled –
from 60 million to 120 million – but only 13 million square
metres of residential housing were built. The city of Sian, for
example, grew more than threefold during the years from 1950
to 1965, from 490,000 to 1,500,000 people, whereas the floor-
space of dwelling units only doubled. The situation has been
similar in most rapidly-expanding cities. Plainly, urban housing has not been the highest priority for China, and in view of
the far more backward state of the villages, the choice has been
well justified.

In the end, cities like Canton, Shanghai and Tientsin are
neither cities of Old China or of People's China. The splendours
of the ancient cities are still there, like Hangchow, with its
magnolias, cherry blossom, and willows, its lakes, temples and
pagodas, much as Marco Polo saw them in the thirteenth
century. He thought it 'the greatest city that may be found in
the world', for its population numbered a million when
London's hardly reached 100,000. Whole districts were given
over to taverns, restaurants, pleasure-boats, jugglers, performing animals and puppet-shows. Today it is no longer a city
where the leisured classes disport themselves. It is still a centre
of tea-production, and retains its traditional silk-weaving,
though the pictures nowadays are likely to be of Mao Tse-Tung
as a young revolutionary or of the Nanking Bridge rather than
scenes of misty mountains, bridges, islands, birds and pagodas
(though some of these are still made for export, as are
embroidered garments).

Pride of place, as both an ancient and modern city, must be given to Peking, besides which even the former Kuomintang capital, Nanking, is unimpressive. Peking's wide buildings and boulevards quite rival those of Paris, and the elegant lamps of Changan Avenue, the main East-West boulevard, remind one of that city, too. But Peking boulevards are not crowded with fashionably-dressed women and cars; instead, two million cyclists thread their way among the traffic, all of them, it seems, ringing their bells at the same time. Modern buses also ensure a fast transit system (and economy is practised by joining an extra section of bus onto the rear of the front unit, as with our railway carriages, so that one engine pulls two segments). Soon, the modern underground Metro system will ease the pressure of the streets.

The scale of the public buildings is enormous, but not gigantesque. The buildings, for all their size, seem to keep within human dimensions, and the skyline is not pierced with high blocks. And immediately off Changan are the *hutungs*, the side-streets with courtyards running off them, lined with workers' houses. On a hot evening, people are out on the pavements catching a breath of cool air; older children are playing and keeping an eye on the babies in their bamboo bassinets. It is rather as though kids from Stepney were using Piccadilly as a neighbourhood place of resort.

Yet only a few hundreds yards away is the heart of China: the huge complex of ancient and modern buildings located right in the middle of the huge boulevard. The key government offices are located in a park adjoining the Imperial Palace. Even today, the Palace covers 250 acres, but it used to be surrounded by an area six times larger, where the craftsmen and servants of the Imperial court lived amid granaries, storehouses, parks, orchards, and vegetable gardens. Here, officials and even Emperors had houses in walled enclosures, and temples – Buddhist, Taoist, Lamaist, even Roman Catholic – abounded. Many of the great cultural treasures which belong in the buildings were removed by Chiang Kai-Shek when he fell, and are on display in Taiwan. Sinologists tell me they are so numerous that many have never been uncrated. If so, it will save the Chinese a job when they are flown back to Peking.

Immediately opposite the great gate which leads into the Palace, the Tien An Men (Gate of Heavenly Peace), is the huge square where the mass demonstrations and parades of millions used to take place. The numbered paving-stones which mark each person's place are still there. Thousands of provincial visitors circulate round the square, having their photographs taken against the backdrop of the Forbidden City and the vast new Halls surrounding the square, where Marx, Engels, Lenin and Stalin look down on them, and where Mao – separated from the founding fathers – is celebrated by his own pictures and giant red posters – bearing quotations from his works.

It is a place which has witnessed many of the crucial events in modern Chinese history: the 4 May demonstration of 1919, the patriotic demonstration of 1926, the protest of 1935 which sparked off resistance to Japanese imperialism, all took place here. It was here, too, on 31 January 1945, after the city had been without electric light for some time, that the lights suddenly came on, and the bands of the People's Liberation Army could be heard as the Army marched into the square. And it was in Tien An Men Square that Mao Tse-Tung, on 1 October 1949, proclaimed the Chinese People's Republic.

CONCLUSION

In the West, people are not very concerned about what happens in most of the world: that backwards two thirds we wryly call the 'Third World'. When some event in that World becomes too large to ignore – a war, famine or revolt – the dominant reactions are, at worst (usually racist), dismissal of these miseries as all due to their own incompetence; at best, charity. They are content to leave the practical handling of relations with that World to a handful of interested people: those interests being, in the main, business and political ones. The theorizing they leave to the minority of intellectuals who engage in 'development studies'.

Within the ranks of the by no means numerous researchers in this field on the staffs of British universities is a handful of social scientists who study China, less than one for every hundred million Chinese. The pattern has been very different in the U.S.A. There, in the 1960s, twenty-five million dollars were spent by the Ford Foundation alone, in trying to find out what was going on in China. But whether China was neglected or scrutinized under the microscope in the West (and in 1967 there was a learned conference in the U.S.A. on 'The Micro-societal Study of the Chinese Political System') was not, happily, fateful for that country, because the Western Powers were in no position to affect its internal policy. In this lies the explanation of China's successful modernization, for there appears to be a negative correlation between the amount of theoretical and practical attention given by Western experts to a given country and that country's success in actually modernizing.

Two of the really striking break-throughs in transforming backward agrarian societies into modern industrialized ones, on so large a scale as to constitute a major shift in world development, have been in the Communist world: in Russia and China. But not all of them. Japan is now the number three power, and its development has been a capitalist one. The Communist world can further show the cases of North Korea, which has achieved a remarkable industrial break-through (accompanied by an astounding 'cult of the personality' focused on Kim Il Sung), and of Cuba. The Cuban record in bringing health and education to its people, and especially its formerly underprivileged rural population, is magnificent. Her successful breaking of her former 'congruent' economic and political dependence on the U.S.A. has, however, left her with a further double legacy: of economic dependence on sugar and political dependence on the U.S.S.R. Though Cuba is no Soviet satellite, her situation reflects the very different problems confronting the *small* Communist societies (and any future small Communist societies). For it is one thing to build socialism in societies massively endowed with large populations, abundant natural resources, and enormous internal markets that make possible a very high degree of independence, even near-'autarky', and quite another to do it in small-scale societies which inherit, as Cuba did, a one-crop economy in a small island off the American coast, sensitive to fluctuations in world prices controlled largely in the capitalist world. Yet Cuba, North Vietnam and North Korea have skilfully avoided becoming puppets of the great Communist powers despite their dependence on one or both of them for assistance of many kinds. The incredible ability of a tiny nation of less than two score million peasants to fight to a standstill the strongest power in world history suggests that the Vietnamese are not going to cede their independence to any Communist power either.

Development in the capitalist countries of the 'Third World' has been of a quite different kind. On the Left, some writers talk as if no development had occurred at all in the non-communist 'neo-colonial' countries. As we saw in our sketches of Hong Kong, Malaysia and Singapore, this is not so. Economic growth of a kind has occurred. It has been even more dramatic in countries like Brazil, which now has its own heavy industry, including a steel industry producing $6\frac{1}{2}$ million tons annually. But in the capitalist Third World as a whole, rates of growth, whether measured in terms of invest-ment, the establishment of industry, the modernization of agriculture, or improvements in real income, are very far from impressive, and look singularly lethargic when contrasted either with the growth of population in those countries, or when the distribution of income amongst different social classes, or the export of capital to the rich countries, are taken into account. It is particularly unimpressive when measured against the far greater rates of growth in the advanced capitalist world, and in the advanced Communist world too (even if the U.S.S.R. has to turn to the West for its advanced technology, half a century after the establishment of Com-munist power in that country).

Two kinds of contrast can be drawn: an overall contrast between the rich countries – capitalist and Communist in-cluded – and the poor. The gap between them is a yawning one. For the U.S.S.R. today, it is the 'problems' of prosperity – of providing Fiat cars for the middle and upper classes – that increasingly preoccupy their leaders. For the poor countries, the possession of a watch or a bicycle is wealth indeed. This is still the case in China; hence, their 'life-situation', to this extent, draws them to the other poor countries of the world: the 'world's countryside' as against the 'world's cities'. Yet they are not just poor; they are also Communist, and this divides them from the capitalist countries of the Third World as well as from the imperialist countries.

In the 1950s and 1960s, the notion that the countries of the Third World might steer a course which would be neither capitalist nor Communist, usually phrased as some variant of 'indigenous socialism' was widely disseminated in the rhetoric of Third World leaders of the time. The rhetoric contrasts sharply with the subsequent trajectory of that World, which, in Robin Jenkins' pithy formulation, is 'owned, run and under-developed by the imperialist nations' (*Exploitation*, Paladin).

Those few for whom 'indigenous socialism' was more than verbiage are mainly dead or in prison.

The gap between the rich and the poor is, therefore, still predominantly a gap between capitalist countries and their neo-colonial dependencies, now, for the greatest part, formally independent politically. Control is now exercised via world prices and that most disastrous of phenomena, 'aid' (of which it might truly be said: 'With friends like this, we have no need of enemies', since it shackles them to the 'donor' countries and absorbs more and more of any increased wealth they do generate), supplemented by political manipulation and overt interference when these are thought to be necessary (as in the Dominican Republic). The preservation of capitalism, in the main, is left to internal forces, as in Chile (though pressure by copper companies and the I.T.T. helped crucially in weakening the socialist government).

But there are now rich communisms (mainly those of Europe) and poor communisms (in Asia and Latin America). Hence, although the principal contradiction is undoubtedly still that between the capitalist world and the Communist world, there are very important tensions and divisions within each of those 'camps'. Writers like A. G. Frank have shown how the historical development of the capitalist countries was the outcome of the 'primary accumulation' of capital they achieved by exploiting the underdeveloped countries over which they eventually established colonial control. The ensuing decades have seen an ever-widening gap between the industrialized capitalist countries and the 'neo-colonized' ones. But this model ignores both the different kinds and levels of Communist development, and the existence, too, of a certain degree of growth, even of industrialization in some cases, in capitalist Third World countries.

We may object that 'development' is not to be equated with 'growth', that greater investment, more factories, higher consumption have different kinds of consequences in the capitalist world as compared to the Communist world, and in particular that the question of 'who gets what?' out of this growth is answered entirely differently in the two respective worlds.

Sheer material growth, for one thing, is often measured simply in *aggregate* form, and quantitatively: yet national statistics of G.N.P. or average income per head conceal the disparity between a handful of millionaires who receive half the income and the mass of the population who share the balance. Nor is the way in which this income is generated considered: Kuwait may have the 'highest per capita income in the world', but, questions of distribution apart, it is derived from one of the most lop-sided and vulnerable economies imaginable. Such statistics, too, usually completely mask the outflow of capital to America and Europe. Even where some of the wealth does filter down to ordinary people, the ethical and social implications of the word 'development' (i.e., some conception of *progress*, measured in meaningfully human terms, according to *qualitative* criteria) have to be distinguished from measurement of 'growth' solely in terms of roubles, railway-engines or rice.

Growth can occur without development, or, if we want to retain the latter word, there can be *bad* development as well as good: development can even be anti-human, rather than socially progressive. The most spectacular capitalist growth-story, of course, is that of Japan. But it is also the most depressing, since the price paid has been the creation of a society in which dedication to continually-expanding production firstly transformed the Japanese into Economic Men whose whole lives – even the schools their children went to – were determined by the firm they belonged to, and later turned them into 'total consumers'. A society in which, today, pedestrians have to insert coins into machines in order to obtain oxygen in the streets, where people fear to eat basic foods like shellfish because of contamination, and where the price of land has gone up by 2,200 per cent since 1955 and the average family's income of £193 a month buys them two good meals in a moderate Tokyo restaurant, may be said to have 'grown' but scarcely, in any human terms, to have 'developed'.

In the Communist world, a society as inegalitarian as the U.S.S.R., whose major literature is the literature of the prison-camp, is not a humane society either. Nevertheless it, too, has experienced massive economic growth, and continues to do so. One of the great advantages enjoyed by the Communist countries has been the absence of Western experts in development, who, in unending procession, go out to advise countries designated as 'developing' but which are actually '*under*-developing', i.e., relatively to the advanced Powers, they are going backwards, and many of them, in some respects, even in absolute terms. Others are experiencing what Geertz has called *in*volution, not evolution (let alone revolution): the elaboration and intensification of existing economic activity combined with an expanding population. The result is that, though no structural economic change takes place, the volume of production rises, but the outcome is still static, even degenerating, levels of 'shared poverty' as consumers.

One of the most striking aspects of China, then, to a sociologist interested in 'development', is the virtual absence both of 'development theory' and of social science as we know it. I did meet Professor Fei Hsiao-Tung, China's outstanding anthropologist in the 1940s, who returned to China after Liberation. His history is instructive, for as the Columbia-trained author of several anthropological studies, notably on rural society at village level, he is the nearest thing to a professional 'opposite number' one might find.

In the 1950s, and particularly during the 'Hundred Flowers' period, he was one of a number of people who emerged as major voices amid the flood of criticism which resulted from Chairman Mao's invitation to engage in open debate on the shape and direction of Chinese development. The direction he and his colleagues seemed to be advocating – towards a pluralistic, multi-party parliamentary-type system, with institutionalized opposition (he was a member of the Democratic League, one of the 'other' parties which still maintain a rather nominal existence in China) – proved completely unacceptable to the Communists, who associated this kind of régime with the inter-war politics of the Kuomintang period and with Western bourgeois politics. They had won power through quite a different route, the battlefield, and they had not won it in order to hand it over to bourgeois politicians. Fei was disgraced.

When I saw him, he seemed well-fleshed and jolly (he had, in fact, come through a very serious illness). He had also spent many months working with his hands in the fields. (So, too, have tens of thousands of Chinese cadres who were sent to 'May 7th schools' where they did agricultural and industrial work, and were exposed to thoroughgoing political re-education for two years. The ranks of Peking civil servants were reduced, it is claimed, by 90 per cent during this period, and whole organizations fused and streamlined.)

Fei now regards the anthropology for which he is known and respected in the West as seriously defective. He failed, he says, really to understand what the life of a peasant was like, to understand poverty, and only through working as a peasant did he come to understand what it really means. On the last point, I can accept what he says. But I do not find it acceptable, even from him, that a man who has shown such a deep insight into peasant life should assert that his work was of such little value. If he does believe what he says, it is a serious criticism of the cultural rigidity that brings him to say such things.

Today, Fei is employed at the National Minorities' Institute in Peking. There they train members of China's various nationalities in practical skills which will enable them to improve people's lives back home, as medical workers and educationalists, for the most part. What research there is seems to be principally linguistic, i.e., the production of ortho-graphies, the reduction of the many unwritten languages to written form, the writing of grammars, etc., as well as the recording of oral history. Social or cultural anthropological research as we know them appear to have ceased, and the social and cultural anthropology of the West is regarded as bourgeois ideology serving the goals of imperialism. Fei now calls his own early work 'bourgeois', and one professor who studied physical anthropology at Harvard told me he now considered that the whole mode of thinking about race in bourgeois anthropology was erroneous. The differences that were important were class differences, he argued. Race differences only became important when they became an expression of class antagonisms. If by this he meant that studying physical differences does not help us understand why and how those differences are given social meanings, and used to oppress some and glorify others, he is quite right. But bourgeois scholars have often been right, too, about very many things, big and small, and have contributed enormously in areas where the contribution of Marxism has been virtually invisible (often because of its own limitations). Hence what they have to say may be socially valuable. Had the sponsors of the commune movement during the Great Leap Forward paid attention to the bourgeois work of G. W. Skinner on Chinese marketing-areas, the waste and mess involved in having to reorganize the communes entirely, only three years after they had been set up, might have been avoided. (Nor – quite obviously – could the peasants, who know these things in the marrow of their bones, have been properly consulted in making the decisions.)

In the sphere of agriculture, again, Fei, on revisiting the village he had first studied in 1929, pointed out that incomes had only risen slowly, due to concentrating on agriculture to the exclusion of 'side-line' occupations. This brought him under violent attack – but a year later the Great Leap Forward itself constituted an admission that he had been right since it launched a massive programme of developing industry in the countryside. And attacks on those who urged population-control policies in the 1950s proved to have been wrong-headed denunciations of people who were not, as they were accused of being, 'Malthusian apologists', but honest and critical revolutionaries concerned that the revolution should survive.

China – like every society – *does* need competent and honest social scientists. Dogmatism and anti-intellectualism are by no means missing in China, and it is unpleasant to see men of Fei's stature denigrating their own work. Memories of confessions and of scandals like Lysenko immediately spring to mind.

But it would be wrong to think that research has ceased, or that debate no longer takes place. These things occur, however, in ways far removed from Western experience. The major difference is that theory and research are no longer left to specialists, but have become mass practices, and the specialist in 'development' is someone who is engaged in the practical training and education of cadres, not in theorizing and research as we know them. Since Marxism is established 'scientific socialism', a separate body of theory which purports to be a 'science of society' is unlikely to be tolerated. Important debates do take place, therefore, but they take place within Marxism, not within 'social science'. The history of Chinese Communism, indeed, is one of passionate contention and fierce struggle, a discomfiting thought for those who think of Marxism as *inherently* an intellectual straitjacket (which, of course, like any other intellectual system, it can be).

The Chinese do have their analogue of 'development theory': it is the theory of revolution, and one which had proved singularly effective and flexible. Theory, however, is not an activity left to intellectuals, for development policy in China emerges out of the collective examination of the practical activity of the whole society by the people themselves as well as the Party, in the form of the 'mass line' which Mao defined in Yenan in 1943:

In all the practical work of the Party, all correct leadership is necessarily from the masses to the masses ... This means: take ideas from the masses (scattered and unsystematic ideas) and concentrate them . . . then go to the masses and propagate and explain these ideas until the masses embrace them as their own, hold fast to them and translate them into action, and test the correctness of those ideas in such action. Then once again concentrate ideas from the masses and once again go to the masses so that the ideas are persevered in and carried through. And so on, over and over again in an endless spiral, with the idea becoming more correct, more vital and richer each time.

Given this strategy, research becomes an exercise in collective self-study addressed to real-life problems, rather than something done *to* people by experts from outside and addressed to problems *they* define (or have defined for them). A constant flow of reports moves up and down the administrative system. Centralized statistics are, of course, vital, and each province has its research agencies. But the army of specialists who man the Royal Commissions and 'think-tanks' of the West, and who turn out the books and the articles which may or may not affect governmental thinking and public opinion, is conspicuous by its absence. A very great deal of this research in the West in any case is bad and of little consequence. In the end, Ministers in Britain operate on the basis of simple aggregate information (such as statistics) and Party policy. They do not read dozens of research reports before taking decisions (though these may be mediated to them by lower-level officials who do read them). In China, fact and opinion feed into the governmental process more directly. 'No right to speak without investigation' has been a key principle, encouraging people to find out empirically rather than indulge in sheer opinionation, ever since the 1930s, when Party workers were mobilized to do 'rural surveys'.

The Chinese thus rely on the study of society by all those who live in it as an ongoing, mass collective practice. Hence they do not need to train thousands of academic specialists in the fields of the humanities and social sciences. A further factor is that, like many other underdeveloped societies, they give top priority to producing natural scientists and engineers because the transformation of the mode of production is essential if people are to have better lives. It is also a healthy corrective to the lunatic policies of countries like India and Sri Lanka that have manufactured for themselves an enormous unemployed 'intellectual proletariat'.

Chinese universities such as Tsinghua in Peking or Fu Tan

in Shanghai, like Chinese schools, emphasize 'the unity of theory and practice' in that they actually produce trucks and electronic equipment, and have very close ties with the local factories whose workers they train and whose experience they absorb.

This emphasis has been mistakenly read as an absorption with production as an end in itself. There could be no more profound mis-reading of Chinese Communist culture. Mao's Thought fiercely rejects the Western assumption that 'development' is something to be measured in terms of *things*: the volume of production, G.N.P., consumption indices, and the like. Development, rather, is a quality of relations between men. The materialistic consumerism of capitalist society and its built-in obsessional striving for an ever-greater expansion of the market are values fundamentally different from those informing Chinese development. In Mao's Thought, development, therefore, is not a unitary concept, a one-way street, at all. Rather, capitalist development and socialist development are different *kinds* of development: though Mao encourages the Chinese to 'go all out, aim high, and achieve greater, faster, better, and more economical results', it is results *in building socialism* that he stresses:

What is meant by doing a good job of production? *This in no way refers to increased output.* Rather it depends on whether or not we have developed production *according to socialist principles* . . . whether we have aroused the revolutionary activity of the masses. (Italics added.)

The notion that the crucial issue is not production *per se*, but one of values, is anathema to those in East and West alike who see development in terms of a technical operation: a combination of engineering and 'social engineering'. The improvement of people's lives certainly depends upon producing things: food, machines, houses. But the power to make decisions about which are the right kinds of things to produce, about the way they are produced, the uses to which they are put, and the people to whom they are made available: these are profoundly social – *and therefore political* – matters.

In the capitalist world, most of the experts employed in development are technical men: agriculturists, engineers, and the like. Their prime expertise is with things, not people. They are not trained to ask questions about the social implications of what they are doing. They assume that what is good engineering will be good for the nation. They see their task as a technical and socially unproblematic one: to set up machinery that will run efficiently and economically, to build dams that will not collapse, and so on. The social implications they leave to other experts, usually economists. They, in their turn, are trained within an intellectual framework that focuses on *economizing* as the crucial problem: i.e., the most 'economical' fitting of means to ends, of using scarce resources in fulfilling wants. How wants are themselves produced, or whether 'ends' are good or bad, are held to be questions of value which a scientist cannot pronounce upon, though generally wants are assumed to drive from 'human nature', and hence are the same under socialism as under capitalism. The object of the game is to make the fit between ends and means optimal. Habituated to capitalism, they extrapolate capitalist assumptions about economic functioning and human motivation as if these were universal values or imperatives. Most of them, in any case, are positively committed to capitalism and work within guidelines set by those who commission their work. Neither the engineer, then, nor the social engineer are likely to plan development which involves serious modifications to existing structures of power, whether within the given society or in external institutions such as the aid-giving agencies or the world commodity-market.

There are some 'pure' technicists who conceive of the problem of development simply as an engineering problem – one of providing some 'magic bullet', some physical thing or device which will be the answer to society's problems: food, power, or water, or better roads. But even the technicists usually appreciate that improved social functioning will be necessary for these technical innovations to come about or bear fruit, or for the fruit to reach any significant proportion of the population. Here the technicist meets up with the technocrat, for the latter believes that the introduction or increase of some *social* input will be the magic bullet which will trigger off development. Each specialism naturally tends to favour its own expertise as the required ingredient: educators believe in education, economists in capital-formation, and so on.

Both engineers and social engineers commonly assume their task to be a technical one. The job of research is to identify the 'magic bullet'; the job of government and management to introduce it. It is assumed that all reasonable men share the same goals and that the work of the expert is therefore 'value-free' and politically neutral.

Others are overtly partisan: they see themselves as committed to goals set by governments, and happily identify with policies designed to transform society in ways that promote the sectional interests of certain groups above those of others. The thinking of some of them is based on classical nineteenth-century postulates. For these people the agent of development today is the same as it was then: the *entrepreneur*, the man whose chief asset is his initiative rather than his (often exiguous) capital, and who is prepared to take risks. He is, therefore, 'progressive': he innovates and is not content, conservatively, with traditional kinds and sources of income. In agriculture, he is the richer peasant who expands his plot into a miniature capitalist farm: in industry, the craftsman who expands his workshop into a small factory. Both employ (exploit) their less successful neighbours.

A major contemporary version of this kind of classical development is the so-called 'Green Revolution', though it has had to be launched by governments 'from the top' rather than left for the 'spirit of capitalism' to take care of spontaneously. Here, the technicist and the technocrat meet, for the technicist has provided the magic bullet in the shape of high-yielding varieties of rice and other 'miracle' grains which, the technocrat hopes, will so raise food production that hunger – and hence revolution – can be averted.

The 'Green Revolution' is thus designed to pre-empt the Red one. It is not a neutral technical innovation, but a 'revolution' of the richer peasants who alone can afford the expensive ancillary practices that the new varieties require: seed-bed preparation, mechanized irrigation, threshing, reaping, etc. This kind of policy has a lengthy ancestry. In this century it goes back at least as far as Stolypin, the Tsar's great minister just before the Russian Revolution, who thought that by 'betting on the strong', i.e., building up a rich *kulak* peasantry, a new solid mass support for capitalism in the countryside – a 'sturdy yeomanry' in English terms – could be built up which would greatly widen the social basis of the régime. Since Stolypin's days, other 'modernizing autocracies' and bureaucracies, such as Egypt in the 1950s or Peru in the 1960s, have undertaken quite radical programmes of redistribution of the land and establishing co-operatives, of lowering taxes, providing credit and 'infrastructural' services of roads, power supplies, etc. – all measures once thought of as quintessentially 'Left', but designed, here, to strengthen capitalism.

The starting-point, for the modern Stolypins, is modern technology and science; to use Gertrude Steinian language, the notion that a machine is a machine is a machine. There are no capitalist lathes or communist lathes, simply lathes. For lathes to be used with optimal efficiency, not only must work be organized in certain ways, but society outside the factory gates, too. There is thus an inherent social 'logic' in industrialization *per se*. Whatever differences of political system, culture, etc., might exist at the outset, as development proceeds, all industrialized societies will come to resemble each other more and more. There is, then, only one path of development in the long run, and if we want to identify the factors leading to successful development, these can be abstracted from the historical experience of those countries which have advanced farthest along that road, i.e., the capitalist societies. Their success depended not just upon introducing machines, nor even upon new kinds of economic arrangements alone. It also required new kinds of political institutions and culture, to wit: (1) the multi-party system, institutionalized legitimate opposition, and mass electoral democracy based on underlying 'consensus': and (2) the institutionalization of mass higher education, the recruitment of the 'best' performers by meritocratic selection, and the construction of a system of differential rewards without which people would not be motivated to give of their best. Similar developments, the argument runs, are bound to occur even in Communist societies as they industrialize: they will develop liberal, pluralistic institutions and a 'mass consumption' economy like those of the capitalist world (itself already converted to economic planning under the aegis of the State). There is thus a process of 'convergence'.

These theorists operate with a definite calculus of human motivation, but one which is rarely explicit. For other development theorists, the magic bullet required is nothing so material as machines, capital, not even knowledge or novel social arrangements, but some *expressly* psychological propensity: the will to achieve or to possess. If this quality can be injected into a population, via, say, textbooks or stories with exemplary heroes as 'ego-ideals', they are home and dry. Since the richest and most industrialized country in world history is the

U.S.A., the values that underly that country's development are the ones assumed to be relevant for other countries at later times. For S. M. Lipset, for example, it was the values of *equality* and *achievement* that powered the historical growth of the 'first new nation' (the U.S.A.), and which need to be institutionalized and internalized elsewhere if development is to occur.

The chances of other nations being so lucky as the U.S.A. seem remote: they are more likely to end up with communist, particularist or 'charismatic' régimes, Lipset pessimistically concludes. And even those who postulate an evolutionary sequence do not assume that progress from stage to stage will actually occur. The nineteenth-century confidence that evolutionary laws would work themselves out in the same way in societies separated by time and space is missing. Among those theorists who still emphasize the similarity of the growth process in all societies and cultures, the quite radical *differences* of choices and values involved in Communist development strategy go unrecognized. They are not only different, but opposed: for Vietnam, the crucial obstacle to growth has been the U.S.A., which attempted to bomb that country 'back into the Stone Age', a stage of un-growth which forms no part of Professor Rostow's theoretical scheme, though he himself was a prominent architect of that bombing policy.

Since America has not been able to export her institutions successfully, much recent development theory is less liberal and more pessimistic about the 'chances for democracy' in the Third World, and expresses a new kind of 'hard-headed' mood. Failure to develop has always been blamed, in bourgeois theory, on 'traditionalism' more than anything else. 'It's not the fault of imperialism; these people just have lousy traditional institutions (chiefs, corrupt monarchies, élites, etc.), and lack the necessary get-up-and-go.' Now they add: 'They cannot be *given* democracy. They have to be *forced* to be progressive. What they need is a little dose of dictatorship.' Every frustrated bureaucrat's dream is now dressed up as 'realistic' development theory. Even a liberal like Gunnar Myrdal is affected by these moods in his discussion of the 'Asian drama'.

But some theorists, such as Reinhard Bendix, cling hard to the liberal values. They also reject not only evolutionary determinism, but economic and technological determinism into the bargain. 'The momentum of past events and the diversity of social structures,' Bendix writes, 'lead to different paths of development, even where the changes of technology are identical' (*Nation-Building and Citizenship*). Following Weber, he insists that the 'social structure' is much more than a society's economic or political institutions: it includes its heritage of legal, military and administrative institutions – and its cultural values, too – a heritage that is never the same for any two countries. Oddly, following this emphasis on cultural variety, the sole path of development that he chooses to consider is that of Western society. Far from Communist societies converging with Western ones, Communist development is only 'industrialization' *without* 'modernization', i.e., the social and political changes which accompanied industrialization in the West. In other words, Communist development is not *real* development at all.

Evolutionists and structural-functionalists, then, assume 'law-like' sequences that will repeat themselves wherever the conditions are right. Historicists think that the combination of circumstances required is so complex that such conjunctures will be rare, and that every country's history is unique, anyhow. Despite these differences, they are agreed on three things: (1) the underdeveloped countries ought to aim at following Western models; (2) they are not likely to succeed; (3) Communist development is bad or defective or not 'proper' development.

      *

Communism equally has its technicists and technocrats, its evolutionary and historical determinists and its convergence theorists. Chinese (and Cuban) Communism, however, have constituted existential refutations of all these determinisms, bourgeois and Marxist alike. Marxist determinists have insisted that revolutions cannot occur until the forces of production have 'matured' or the 'balance of class forces' has swung decisively in favour of the working class. In the earlier decades of Communism, this was interpreted to mean 'no revolutions in colonial countries'. After half a century of revolution in underdeveloped countries, the pendulum has swung the other way: 'revolutions in underdeveloped countries only'.

Judged by its own criterion – the relating of theory to practice – the absence of revolution in the West ought to have had corrosive effects upon Marxism. It has certainly affected its style: the Marxism issued from the Left Bank of the Seine is now largely only addressed to and comprehensible only to people with Ph.D.s. Marxists seem to have given up the effort to relate to ordinary people. The contrast between the simplicity of Mao's prose, and these words from a German S.D.S. leader, Hans-Jürgen Krahl, for instance, writing on the Czech events of 1968, is striking:

> In that phase of [bourgeois society's] historical dynamic, the institutionalized fiction of the autonomous, self-sufficient juridical person – embodiment of bourgeois individuality – revealed itself as a pure abstraction of the socially necessary outward appearance of commodity exchange ... This idea has been transformed in the heads of Yugoslav and Czechoslovak philosophers of reform into, at best, the mutilated form of diluted, existential, ontological or phenomenological versions of Marx's theory of alienation ...

This mandarin style reflects the isolation of revolutionary intellectuals in societies where capitalism has been able to maintain its hegemony over a non-revolutionary proletariat. The corrosion is more than a stylistic matter, however, for European Marxism began to lose its revolutionary content quite early. The huge pre-1914 German Social Democratic Party accommodated itself to the role of encapsulated opposition. Dogmatic verbal subscription to the eternal verities of Marxism by theorists like Kautsky accompanied a *de facto* practice of parliamentarism and trade unionism, rather than revolution, and ultimate capitulation in 1914. Several more decades of non-revolution produced the theory of the 'co-existence' of capitalism and Communism and the notion of achieving socialism via the ballot box (the Italian Communist Party, cynics said, at present rates of growth, should reach the necessary 51 per cent of the votes by 2001 – a jest now rendered tragic by the violent suppression of parliamentary Marxism in Chile).

Non-European revolutionaries have at times pointed to the consequences. 'For a long time now,' Fanon remarked, 'history has been made without the Left in Europe', and Nguyen Nghe, a Vietnamese critic of Fanon, agrees with him on that score at least: that the French Left, riddled with the pernicious influence of Parisian existentialism, peddled by a 'subjectivist' and individualist intelligentsia, has been unable to develop either an adequate political theory or an effective political movement since the Liberation of 1944.

Marxism has also had its share of technological determinism. It underlay the policy of forced industrialization, at whatever

Conclusion 209

human cost, in the U.S.S.R., where the regimentation of the working class and the brutal collectivization of the peasantry were the practical expression of a theory in which the maximization of production was the paramount value, sanctifying resort to force and 'administrative measures' as normal means of governing. The end-product was a society in which authoritarianism has become so deeply entrenched that it has survived beyond the end of the Stalinist era of 'primitive accumulation' – in which Man was a producer – into the era in which consumption – 'goulash communism' – has become the dominant social value.

Contemporary determinists are still 'proving' that the Chinese and Cuban Revolutions are scandals in terms of 'correct' Marxist theory, and, in practical terms, only *révolutions manquées*, not proper revolutions at all, since they were not achieved by the working class of an advanced capitalist society (a unilineal model of revolution *in perfecto et abstracto* so far remarkable for its non-correspondence with any known real life). In the industrial sphere, there was only one logic of production, no specifically *socialist* way of organizing work. A socialist factory was simply a factory with no private owners.

Yet these degenerations have not stopped Marxism spreading. It is not only the major revolutionary doctrine of our time, but the single most important of all doctrines, revolutionary or otherwise. No other world-view commands the support of millions from such a variety of cultural and historical backgrounds, and moves them to action on such a scale. It is now firmly rooted in Asia, Latin America and Europe, and, in the revolutions maturing in the 'Portuguese' colonies, authentic African variants are emerging. It is impossible to understand the twentieth century (Marxists would say *any* century) without understanding Marxism, though those who operate only within the confines of its more simplistic variants are likely to make serious mistakes and merely cut themselves off from the rest of contemporary thought, which, needless to say, includes much of value, including whole domains where Marxists have scarcely ventured. Marxism has grown and spread, however, because it is not just a body of *thought*, Marxism, but part of an ongoing 'theoretical practice', Communism, that does not seek to understand the world primarily for intellectual satisfaction – understanding 'in itself' – so much as instrumentally, as a basis for rationally working out ways of changing the world, in directions indicated by the ethical theory it contains:

the establishment of a new egalitarian, collective, co-operative, participant social democracy: communism. This has been the promise, Mannheim's 'utopia', which has attracted millions.

Between the promise and the reality, deep shadows have fallen. At times, it has spawned its opposite. We do not know in what ways revolution in advanced capitalist countries would be different, for none has occurred yet, but where communism has come to power so far, it has inherited a legacy almost the opposite to that which the father of Marxism predicated as the necessary conditions for communism: the heritage of the economic and political institutions of the most advanced capitalist countries. Instead, Communists came to power in authoritarian and archaic countries, where the struggle was ruthless, liable to engender habits of thought and organization inimical to humaneness, and conducive to over-organization, to the giving of orders and the stressing of disciplines, to *Realpolitik* and resort to sheer naked force as a means of solving problems, rather than fostering self-reliance, open discussion and grass-roots decision-making.

Communism, that is, has been a dialectical product of its opposite, anti-Communism. If State Communism, so far, has been an ideology and practice of mobilizing millions of people in backward countries, that does not mean that the Communist Party is simply some analogue of the rising bourgeoisie during the Industrial Revolution; that, to use Talcott Parsons' words, capitalist and socialist industrialisms are really only 'variants of a single fundamental type'. The very experience of struggling to develop *despite* the attempts of the capitalist Powers to keep the backward world backward ensures that any real development must take an anti-capitalist form, initially at least. Nor does it mean repeating Soviet history. Chinese development has learned from its own past revolutionary mistakes and from those of others; it has eschewed both Stalinist terror and the sacrifice of generations that laid the basis of Britain's industrialization. And far from converging with capitalism, it is developing institutions which have no counterpart in capitalist society at all: instead, as time goes on, the divergence *increases*.

Determinists, whether Marxist or non-Marxist, ignore all this. They also tend to be élitists. They assume that they alone, or some select few, can understand history and society. Other people are incapable of learning from their experiences and from those of others. Revolutions are fatally destined to repeat the mistakes of their predecessors. They are thus pessimists, too, for they have no conception of *emergence*: that new institutions and values can be brought into being; no confidence that ordinary people can think the great thoughts they think, or be educated in new ways of thought and behaviour, or learn from the past. They emphasize that men are products of their society and their times, and change as society changes, but neglect Marx's observation that it is also men who change circumstances. The notion that men are agents of history, can choose, seize the time, and 'stand up', is the 'voluntaristic' aspect of Chinese communism, a natural characteristic of a revolutionary movement which emerged in a disintegrating society that Sun Yat-Sen had described as 'a sheet of loose sand' and Mao was later to designate as 'poor' and 'blank', a 'sheet of clean paper', on which the 'newest and most beautiful' of words could be written and pictures painted. The Third World, today, the Chinese consider, is equally ripe for revolution.

But revolution does not come about without leadership and organization, education and analysis. That it is necessary to act together the right way at the right time is the other dimension of their theoretical practice. Both are Leninist notions.

Lenin was anything but a slavish adherent to orthodoxy, even revolutionary orthodoxy. He defied the authority both of Marxist theorists and the other Party leaders in his astounding claim, on his return from exile in 1917, that Russian society was ripe for socialist, not bourgeois-democratic, revolution. But it would not have been achieved had he not created a Party based on 'democratic centralism', a political instrument adapted to underground struggle and the seizure of power in armed struggle that has been imitated by other revolutionary (and many non-revolutionary) movements.

The basic principle – so vital that Lenin was to split the small Social Democratic Party into even tinier 'Bolshevik' and 'Menshevik' wings over it – was that for people to be members of the Party it was not enough to 'be' a member passively, simply to hold a Party card, not enough to theorize in Marxist study-circles. They had to be prepared to *work* politically in a co-ordinated way. They should participate in collective political education and policy discussion, but they should test and refine that theory by actively involving themselves in trade-union work, in demonstrations, in selling literature, distributing leaflets, and, when the time came, in fighting. They were accountable to their fellow-members for what they did or did not do. Communists were thus activistically committed, dedicated men and women. Their political work was not left, in 'bourgeois' fashion, to individual inclination. It was co-ordinated and directed by the collective 'will of the party'. The crucial unit was the low-level 'cell' or 'branch', the group in the locality or factory which allocated tasks and received reports on what each person had done. Guiding these activities were the authoritative directives of higher level bodies of the Party, composed of representatives elected from the lower levels.

The conditions of clandestine activity in Tsarist Russia scarcely made for the regular exercise of public and open democracy: congresses, elections, and the like; and bred habits of tight-knit control and security. Often the leadership could only meet abroad, in London or Switzerland. A tremendous tension was therefore generated within Russian Communism, inevitably intensified during the Civil War and armed inter-vention by capitalist Powers (which China did not experience), as between Lenin's 'Jacobin' centralism and the traditional Marxist stress upon democratic participation and the withering away of the State under communism, a vision Lenin himself wrote about just before the Revolution, when he looked to a society in which 'every cook would rule the State'. For a few brief years after 1917, that vision seemed to be emerging in reality, in forms ranging from the Soviets to the explosion in the arts. But it was the vision that withered, as a new kind of State grew very strong. The democratic centralist Party machinery became the vehicle of supreme power. Whoever could gain control of its General Secretaryship and the Politbureau, the topmost positions, controlled society. The man who did was Stalin.

Chinese Communism, too, developed under repressive enough conditions. Nanking alone has a memorial to one hundred thousand revolutionaries killed by the Kuomintang. It therefore had to develop an equally organized Party. But it began in the mass ferments of the 1920s, and though forced to operate underground in the cities and in rural areas controlled by the Kuomintang and the Japanese, its leadership was located in the Red bases, where a different political culture could emerge: one of mass participation and contact between leaders and rank-and-file, in which the sharing of life's dangers and its few worldly goods were the routine practices of every-day life.

There are three ways backward societies can be modernized quickly. One way is to use force: Stalin's way with the peasantry, for example. Another – the main capitalist way – is to rely on what the Chinese call 'material incentives' – inviting the energetic, ruthless and lucky to 'enrich themselves' (and not worrying too much about the rest). Or one can mobilize people by persuading them. There is no doubt that it is the last of these strategies that the Chinese have principally relied on since Liberation, and which they first evolved in the 'Red bases' before Liberation. But the Red soldiers were no Sunday school teachers. They were peasants driven by desperation to take up arms, and led by hardened revolutionaries. A revolution, Mao has written,

is not the same thing as inviting people to dinner, or painting a picture, or doing fancy needlework; it cannot be anything so restrained and magnanimous. A revolution is an uprising, an act of violence whereby one class overthrows another.

Back in 1926, he had followed Li Ta-Chao's agitational style in mocking the peasants who relied on the gods to protect them rather than the peasant associations, and had made the peasants roar with laughter. But it was not all knockabout fun about the gods; heads were cracked as well as jokes. 'To put it bluntly,' Mao remarked, 'it was necessary to bring about a reign of terror in every rural area, directed against the gentry and their creatures.'

We saw earlier how the coming of the revolution unleashed the pent-up peasant anger of generations. Jack Belden has described what happened at innumerable other 'speak bitterness' meetings, too:

In the course of the morning and afternoon, the crowd accused the landlord of many crimes, including betrayal of resistance members to the Japanese, robbing them of their grain, forcing them into labour gangs. At last he was asked if he admitted the accusations.

'All these things I have done,' he said, 'but really it was not myself who did it, but the Japanese.'

He could not have chosen worse words. Over the fields sounded an angry roar, as of the sea, and the crowd broke into a wild fury . . . Then above the tumult of the crowd came a voice louder than the rest, shouting 'Hang him up!'

The chairman of the meeting and the cadres were disregarded. For all that the crowd noticed they did not exist.

The crowd boiled round Wang, and somewhere a rope went swishing over a tree . . . (*China Shakes the World*).

But though the cadres might not be able to control the peasants, once aroused, Mao made it clear who sparked off the 'reign of terror'. Military control commissions cleared out counter-revolutionaries from positions of power and dealt with the legions of thieves, gamblers, opium addicts, pimps, vagrants and other 'anti-social' elements in ways that were often more swift and efficient than judicial. Hundreds of thousands were probably killed, and many more sentenced to long terms of 'reform through labour'. The naked use of violence on such a scale is so foreign to British experience that it is almost inconceivable – until we see, in Ulster, how rapidly both the scale and the intensity of violence can escalate and come to be regarded as quite normal. Northern Ireland, however, is a Sunday afternoon picnic compared to the Chinese Revolution, where deaths of soldiers, guerillas and civilians alike during the struggles against the Kuomintang and the Japanese were numbered in millions, not hundreds.

The period of consolidation of political control lasted until 1953. Then Mao's policy of 'killing more and not arresting most' became the watchword, and a legal system similar to that of the Soviet Union during the 1920s (with a parallel system of 'extra-judicial coercion') was introduced, involving an apparatus of courts, criminal codes, judges, etc. This came to an end in 1957, when a strong reaction occurred against those intellectuals who had advocated Western concepts of law, an 'anti-rightist' drive which was intensified during the Cultural Revolution.

I saw no courts or prisons, and a Filipino delegation was told recently that the legal organs are not for sight-seeing. Very few first-hand reports exist on penal procedures, including prisons. But the general outlines are known, and the crucial principle is that of rehabilitation through work. There is quite a lot of information as to how this operates for minor crimes, where the offender often continues to reside in the community, under the supervision of cadres and neighbours, but the contemporary operation of higher level judicial institutions remains obscure even to specialists (a control of information that is quite counter-productive, since it stimulates speculation, often motivated by hostility, which cannot be contradicted, or endorsed, for want of hard evidence).

My own 'researches' were limited to asking – once on a commune, once in a city workers' settlement – what the most serious cases were that they had had last year, and how had they handled them. The question clearly touched upon some painful memories. I was informed, on the commune, that a man had killed his wife. They had first discussed the case at length, in the light of Mao Tse-Tung Thought, but considered it beyond their competence, so had remitted it to the provincial Revolutionary Committee. The accused had then been 'suppressed', they said, in very grave tones, a sentence so serious that it had to be approved by central government institutions first. 'Suppressed?' I asked. 'Yes,' they replied, rather uncomfortably, '. . . shot.' The military heritage of the revolution is even reflected in the kind of death penalty in use.

The second serious case, in the city, was one of 'superstition'. An old man had claimed to have visions, in spirit-possession séances, and had 'exploited' people by offering his services for cash. He had, they said, been required to spend a number of sessions with cadres remoulding his ideology, and had now seen the error of his ways.

I have no idea how common the death penalty is, but I should think it very rare. Nor do I believe that there are any concentration camps. But a lot of people are put to very hard work, mainly on construction-sites, it would seem, though there are also reports of 'rehabilitative' sentences served in factories alongside ordinary workers.

The vast bulk of crime is dealt with as was the superstitious old man, and a complex set of procedures, of increasing severity, may be brought into play, from private criticism by local cadres and leading figures, through having to defend one's behaviour before one's residents' groups, with varying measures of censure, self-examination and repentance, in the most violent of which the accused may be publicly humiliated (forced to kneel, etc.).

Such sanctions became widely known in the West during the Cultural Revolution; it is very difficult to know how far the more severe were the doing of Red Guards and other groups now widely accused of 'ultra-leftism' inside China (a charge so common – no doubt often by those resistant to the Great Proletarian Cultural Revolution – that it almost seems to overlook the positive aspects of the struggle waged by the young people during that upheaval). Pressure of this kind, of course, can be every bit as hard as physical maltreatment, and occurred on a large scale.

Many thousands were demoted and sent to work in factories and villages. Their smouldering resentment must still be there and the trickle of refugees who risk the dangerous swim to Hong Kong only the tip of the iceberg. Thousands of those who were removed from universities and schools and sent to work as peasants are also doubtless far from satisfied with their fate. But it would be a mistake to assume that ideological remoulding, and genuine acceptance that one's past behaviour was deserving of criticism, do not occur. Jan Myrdal cites one such case, that of the village treasurer in the village where he had previously lived and which he revisited after the Cultural Revolution:

> When people got up at meetings and said I had not done this properly or that properly and made mistakes here and made mistakes there, and that I hadn't followed the proper line, I was most distressed. I thought it all very unjust, after all my hard work. I thought the criticism was wrong. I found it hard to stand, hearing them talking out loud about me at the meetings. But I realized I really had made mistakes. And I read Chairman Mao! After all, we're the servants of the people. We must have the courage to accept public criticism. Only in this way could I find a better style of working. And that's why I admit that, even if at first they seemed hard, these criticisms helped me. And when we'd discussed the whole matter thoroughly and I'd gone through my work and accepted being criticized and had criticized myself and realized my errors, then the masses gave me their confidence again and I was re-elected treasurer. (Jan Myrdal and Gun Kessle, *China: the Revolution Continued*.)

For the thousands of government officials, managers, teachers and other cadres who were exposed to protracted and intense examination by Red Guards and by those who normally lived and worked under their authority, and made to acknowledge their shortcomings publicly, such confrontations were painful in the extreme, and, as in all mass uprisings, not a few of the innocent suffered along with those deserving of criticism. The overall effect we have seen: an enormous revitalization, through the reassertion of the principles of equality and participation: the 'populism' without which socialism becomes élitist 'statism'.

Group discussion, using Mao Tse-Tung Thought, is not usually such a harrowing business. It is the fundamental technique, firstly, for communicating ideas and relating them to everyday life. That is by no means simply a matter of 'brainwashing' and ritual recitations from the Little Red Book (an iconic device now very little in evidence). Nor is studying Mao's Thought simply an exercise in glorifying him. There *were* those who wished to promote a cult of the personality – the 'Great Helmsman' syndrome – largely in order to reduce him to an honorific but powerless status, and Mao has said that there have been times when he, too, has made use of the cult. Mao's Thought can be reduced to ritual parroting. But it also tells people, particularly in his writings 'On Contradiction', 'On Practice' and 'On the Correct Handling of Contradictions among the People', how to do their own thinking in a rational manner: to grasp essentials, to distinguish the 'principal contradiction' from secondary ones: to do first things first, to see the relationship of the parts to the whole. It also enjoins people to distinguish honest disagreement between comrades from hostile criticism by enemies: they must never be lumped together, uncritically, as 'objectively' the same, or the critics treated as incorrigible. People need to have their mistakes explained to them: they cannot be expected to reform their ways unless they come to understand and reject the social influences that lead them to behave as they do.

Discussion sessions of this kind resemble seminars in our society, though highly focused on some text or problem and with a cadre as leader. They are also the main way of handling personal and 'social' problems, and of ensuring that they do not fester until they become so serious that they become matters for the courts or the mental health services. Minor crime, marital problems, delinquency, are sorted out in what we would call group therapy or counselling sessions, in which all the persons relevant to the issue are involved. Much of the work done by probation officers, by psychiatrists and lawyers, and by the ever-growing legion of community, psychiatric and medical social workers who try to cope with the flood of human disaster in our society is handled by these group-sessions in China.

The idea of this degree of involvement of people in each other's lives grates on the sensibilities of English people for whom the personal, the private, the independent, and the quiet life have such value. These are prime values, too, for a man like José Yglesias, who has nevertheless written out of his experience of life in Cuba that the new local Committees for the Defence of the Revolution were 'the first step towards a new cultural attitude . . . an insistence that the open life – open to the view of one's neighbours – is the natural life of man' (*In the Fist of the Revolution*).

It is not the power that grows from the barrel of a gun that is primarily used in China or Cuba, then, but the control of information and ideas. Whether you call this 'persuasion', 'political education', or 'indoctrination' depends on your values. But if people are to be moved into action by other than 'coercive' or 'remunerative' sanctions, to use Etzioni's labels, ideological mobilization is the only available alternative means. It is an omnipresent process in China: the same messages are communicated at school, in the newspapers, at the cinema, the theatre, the circus, at work, on the radio: and the sheer cumulation, repetition, and reinforcement is very compelling. The imaginative skill of the Communists is evident in the simple, memorable titles (couched in traditional idiom) given to campaigns ('the three antis') or the iconic devices which symbolize ideas and evoke them in people's minds: the face-mask during the health campaign, or the Little Red Book to bring people back to Mao's bypassed thought. Typically, the words and concepts he uses are never too elaborated: what is needed, after all, is *enough* theory, not 'theoretical overkill'. Like the language they are couched in, the messages are *focused* and the means of getting them across highly organized. The props used in theatrical performances of revolutionary operas, for instance – from landlords' moustaches to guerillas' rifles – are disseminated to amateur groups across the country, and used to stage the same popular operas, ballets, sketches and dances. The repertoire of these works is very limited, for many pre-Cultural Revolution works are no longer performed and many condemned as 'poisonous' and 'black'. There is therefore only a handful of films to see, in particular: some are new; most revised versions of earlier works, the political line of which has been 'sharpened'. The result is an extraordinarily restricted fare. The best of what there is – *The White-Haired Girl*, *The Red Detachment of Women*, *The Red Lantern*, *On the Docks*, *Taking Tiger Mountain by Strategy* – are immensely enjoyable, and people go to see them time and again (and pop out to the toilets during the less exciting passages, not so much because they have seen these same works so often, but because that is what audiences at the popular opera have done in China since time immemorial).

Not only the props, but even the details of the performances are remarkably alike, from the gestures used to the overall style of the production. This, as much as Chinese tradition, may explain the selection of the opera and the ballet as the major revolutionary forms, for the conventions of the ballet and opera lend themselves to *performance*, and can therefore be staged by people everywhere, following the models provided by the professionals, where the more naturalistic or expressive cinema cannot. Though the content is impeccably revolutionary, and the ballet conventions now include the clenched fist and the revolutionary sweep of the hand as well as the *entrechat* and the *fouetté*, this kind of cultural form, in the end, is anything but revolutionary. The place given to ballet and opera is doubtless in part, too, a Russian legacy from the 1950s, and the forms are basically classical, as constricting in their way as the forms of Chinese classical poetry which Chairman Mao writes in so well but which he discourages young people from imitating, because 'these forms would cramp their thoughts'. The music, too, is basically Western, usually with a strong Chinese flavour. The best, like that of *The White-Haired Girl*, is very attractive; much fails to rise above the level of romantic ballet music in a style more akin to Tchaikovsky or *Giselle* (and sometimes the poorer Hollywood musical). Of course, in all ages, only a little of any art is great. But there is nothing revolutionary, profound, or Chinese about the artistic mode of even the 'eight exemplary works' that are held up as post-Cultural Revolution achievements. The contrast between this policy and that of Cuba, where films are imported from all over the world, is striking. 'Public' forms of Cuban art, such as their architecture and posters, are superb. China produces many splendid posters and much good art by workers and peasants, too. But there is nothing in the modern styles freely used by Cuban poster-artists. No doubt what the Chinese are trying to do is far more difficult – not only the creation of a revolutionary art, but the creation, at the very same time, of a synthesis of Chinese, Western and other cultures which contain forms and styles as unfamiliar to them as Chinese music is to us. That is a major revolution one cannot expect to be achieved overnight. Nor does revolutionary art necessarily emerge at the heart of the political revolution. The music of Grétry or Méhul was not expressive of either the French Revolution or the wider transformation of men's minds in the Romantic era, in the way Beethoven's was.

My own feeling of cultural limitation was undoubtedly affected by my own illiteracy in Chinese. Nevertheless, judging from what is translated one still had the impression that the range and variety of available written work was very restricted, even if the volume is staggering. Time and again, I was shocked at the ignorance of my informants about important matters; their lack of knowledge of Cuba, their patent unawareness of just what nuclear warfare would entail. This kind of ignorance – politically very dangerous for, like all ignorance, it may lead people to make bad decisions – can only be attributed to the narrow range of views and of information available. Thus, on a visit to the Social Sciences section of Fu Tan University, I found no books in Western languages later than the beginning of World War II, apart from some East European volumes, such as Ulbricht's speeches, and a little literature on the Overseas Chinese (including a guide to the restaurants of San Francisco's Chinatown). When I expostulated, rather provocatively (looking for some reaction, perhaps defence), that this was not so much a library as a museum, I was told that I would find a greater variety of more up-to-date Western literature in Faculty libraries, which I had no time to verify, though colleagues who visited Tsinghua University in Peking told me they did find more modern literature in the library there.

My interpreters were surprised to hear that I saw so many films from so many countries; I think they pitied my exposure to so much bourgeois culture. It was virtually impossible to explain to them the great variety of styles and approaches to the world disguised under such labels as 'the American' film, especially since they had not seen any, or to explain the incredible volume of artistic production the consumption of which has now become a quite basic need in Western society. I was completely at a loss when asked by an English teacher to suggest some novels about life in Britain as possible works for translation. My mind whirled with the dozens I had read in the last few years. What would they possibly make of Margaret Drabble or Edna O'Brien? Sheer bourgeois decadence, no doubt. To talk of the communication of the personal, or the authenticity of responses which one might not share, would get one nowhere. For art and literature in China, as Mao's Yenan lectures on art and literature make firmly clear, are not simply 'expression' in the abstract; they are means of mobilization. 'Propaganda' is not a dirty word in China, and the lively song-and-dance performances one encounters everywhere are given by 'Mao Tse-Tung Thought Propaganda Teams'.

Yet the Chinese are undoubtedly having problems in the field of culture. They are obvious enough in the case of the film, an art-form, for them, with no great tradition behind it. But they also exist in relation to the classical heritage, which cannot be avoided or withdrawn, as 'black' works from before the Cultural Revolution can be, or developed *ab initio*, for it is an achievement that is *there*, in books and in stone. Hence it has to be revalued in the light of revolutionary concepts about Man and Society, and there are great debates when the classical novels are republished. And the texts of even Mao's writings are modified, with passages excised which do not accord with contemporary thinking. Chinese intellectuals justify this on the grounds that people would get erroneous ideas, and that what matters, historically, are those ideas which have proved to be true. What this paternalist argument neglects is the necessity of showing people what went wrong and why, and of helping them develop their own critical faculties – something they cannot adequately do without more than one version of reality to contend with. It is acknowledged that many mistakes are made in the history of Chinese Communism, but the matter tends to be dealt with in a 'Manichean' way: in a double sense, as 'all-bad' or 'all-good' policy, and as attributable to 'black' or 'red' characters respectively: the mistakes were made by people now out of power (who were never, however, physically 'liquidated' like Stalin's opponents), and the correct line was pursued by Mao Tse-Tung and his colleagues. Since Mao's contribution to the Revolution is so outstanding and has accomplished wonders in moving China towards socialism, one can understand this emphasis. But the personality cult is not just a matter of public monuments and portraits; it is, more importantly, a matter of whether the doings of *any*, however historically significant, person are open to rational evaluation, something which does not occur when the writings of Mao are treated as gospel, or have the errors removed from them, and all mistakes are (retrospectively) attributed to people like Liu Shao-Ch'i or Lin Piao. When I asked people whether they had spoken up to criticize Liu Shao-Ch'i for the crimes of which they now so freely accused him, they often said, 'No, we didn't'. And when asked why not, said that the Liuists were in powerful positions, and they were frightened to oppose them.

Attitudes towards the great 'cultural relics' of the past (as distinct from those of no great artistic or historical interest) are also quite different, in a revolutionary society, from those of either the pre-revolutionary era or in the contemporary

West. For the Chinese they are, indeed, 'relics' – an apt word –
of a past that is now remote. A well-educated girl laughed
when I asked her to identify some of the gods in paintings at
the Summer Palace. 'I can only recognize the Lord Buddha,'
she said. The historic palaces, temples, and works of art are,
today, *presented*. The great Historical Museum and the Revolutionary Museum flanking the Tien An Men Square in Peking
were closed while I was there, for the political line of the
presentation was being sharpened following the Cultural
Revolution. But one can see what that presentation will look
like when completed at places like the Tombs of the Ming
Emperors a few miles north of Peking. Here the tomb of
Emperor Wan Li and his two successive wives has been
excavated since Liberation.

Copies of the Empress's magnificent 'phoenix crowns' and
other exquisite objects of jade, gold and porcelain are displayed
in a series of cabinets in the entrance hall. They are presented
not only as aesthetic achievements, however, nor in nationalistic terms, as wonderful *Chinese* achievements. They are
presented in *class* terms. The crowds of workers from Peking
and their families are invited to admire the masterpieces, but
two lessons are drawn to their attention: (i) these magnificent
objects were not made by the Ming Emperors but by the
skilled workers and craftsmen of the time; (ii) they reflect
the unbelievable luxury which the ruling class enjoyed at
the expense of the workers and peasants they exploited. And
opposite the *objets d'art* is another row of cabinets containing
a different kind of 'cultural relics': original rent-rolls, taxation-
records, tattered patchwork clothing, whips, and modern
models of the miserable life of the peasants of the time. Over
the entrance are some statistics: building the Emperor's tomb,
they reveal, took eight million man-days of labour; building a
peasant hut at the same period, 8·54 man-days of labour. I
remembered this later at the Tutankhamun Exhibition in
London, for one got the impression there that Tutankhamun
was a rather wonderful and brilliant person. If the Chinese
had mounted that exhibition, the slaves who built the
pyramids and the craftsmen who made the death-mask would
have got their due.

This social reinterpretation of the culture of the past, and the
social orientation of their contemporary arts, have their
parallels in more direct forms of expression. I found it extraordinarily difficult to get young people to say what they wanted

to do when they left school or college, or where they wanted to go. 'Wherever I am needed to serve the people', was the stock response. They meant it. If one pressed them harder, they generally expressed a natural preference for the places they knew and where they had family and friends. Individualism, which Western society celebrates as its supreme value, is considered a bourgeois vice in China. Hence sexuality, too, is strongly de-emphasized. I had tense discussions over this several times: one interpreter criticized Chinese classical novels for their preoccupation with something for which he professed to have forgotten the English word. I am sure he was too embarrassed to pronounce it – sex. Chinese Communist puritanism I find as saddening and maddening as Western preoccupation not just with sex, but with pathological and prurient forms of sexuality. Most revolutions, conversely – once past the 'heroic' phase, at least – seem to be puritanical, and it is tempting to interpret this in Freudian terms as a gigantic exercise in sublimating sexual energy which is thereby harnessed for other ends. But the implicit theory, for China, should perhaps be couched in Marxist terms, in which 'spontaneity', whether sexual or political, is inferior to 'consciousness'. If socialized, i.e., directed to ends higher than the purely physical or the pure expression of the ego, sex becomes more enriching to the individual and to society alike. But the subject is so hedged about with taboos that this is only to put a speculative construction, consistent with Marxist categories, on sexual behaviour that is extremely orthodox in that it is restricted to sexual relations with the marriage partner. Nothing could be further removed from the many connotations (Marxist included) of 'sexual liberation' in the Western world.

Interpreting Chinese puritanism as a function of their revolutionary dedication, however, leaves out of the picture the extent to which distaste for overt sexuality is something Chinese rather than Communist, and Chinese friends assure me that (whatever the sexual unorthodoxies to be found in classical novels) they themselves feel affronted by the blatant publicization of sex that they find in Western societies. The adverts on the London Underground are profoundly shocking to many people from Third World countries (and to many Londoners, too).

It is one of the cultural shocks one receives in China, and an especially personal one, to discover just how much sexuality and ego-tripping are maximized in our culture and minimized in Chinese, and what an enormous burden we make for ourselves and carry about with us. We all know, in the abstract, that sex is no absolute need, but a want that can be culturally stimulated and supported, or de-emphasized. The loose garments of shirt and trousers worn by men and women in China do not draw attention to their physical differences, nor to the individuality of the person. After a while in China, I felt like a peacock, flaunting a succession of bright shirts and jackets, and somewhat ashamed when the Chinese were so simply dressed. Eventually, I resorted to one or two plainer shirts only (just as I found being the only long-haired man in millions was uncomfortable socially rather than physically, and had it cut – to the evident relief of my interpreter). On returning to Hong Kong, the 'normal' salience of sexuality – in dress styles and advertisements – seemed an inordinate, distasteful, and artificially-induced bombardment, and films seemed quite morbidly obsessed with nudity, sadistic violence and psychopathological behaviour.

The Chinese themselves have quite other values constantly communicated to them, both as a diffuse ongoing process and in the form of a succession of *campaigns* on specific issues in which the entire population is energized and mobilized: the health and sanitation campaign of 1950; in 1952, the 'three antis' (against corruption, waste and bureaucracy among public employees) and 'five antis' in the private sector (against bribery, tax evasion, theft of state property, cheating in government contracts and theft of information for private speculation); then the campaign to repair the dykes and the railways; to plant trees; to clean up rubbish; to eradicate the 'four pests' – flies, mosquitoes, rats and sparrows (the famous campaign that rid China of flies: I only saw four the whole time I was there). One political campaign followed another: the anti-Rightist campaign; the 'four clean-ups' (in the economy, in politics, in organization and in ideology); the 'rectification' campaigns in the Party (to weed out careerists and opportunists who jumped on the bandwagon). The Great Leap Forward of 1958, and the Great Proletarian Cultural Revolution of 1965–9 were campaigns so massive and many-sided that they shook Chinese society down to its foundations. The latter, indeed, virtually constituted a *second* Communist revolution, only a decade and a half after the first one.

There is little doubt that a second revolution was needed if socialist values were to be preserved, for élitism and reliance on 'material incentives' – values and models of organization also brought in by the 10,000 Soviet technicians who came in to set up factories in the 1950s – had become deeply rooted, and were beginning to triumph over the Maoist principles of equality, participation and 'serving the people'.

The Chinese describe the Soviet system as 'social imperialism', a label which refers primarily to the foreign policies of the U.S.S.R. and does not spell out too precisely just what the internal system of that society is considered to be. A second common label, not much more precise, designates Soviet society as being on a 'capitalist road'. The Chinese presumably do not imagine that private ownership of the means of production will actually be restored in the U.S.S.R. What they seem to imply is what critics of Marxism, from Weber and Pareto to Djilas and Dahrendorf, have long said: that the increased power of the State under socialism could or would give rise to new, perhaps greater domination, not by an 'ownership class' but by those who controlled the State machinery in a monocentric society.

This, in sophisticated and less sophisticated variants, has always been the conservative message. ('The Gestapo,' Churchill said in an unsophisticated version in 1945.) More academically, philosophers like Popper have attacked the very notion that society can be rationally organized as a whole, since society is very complex, and human subjectivity gives rise to such shifts and combinations of circumstances that, in the nature of things, life is unpredictable and therefore cannot be planned, except in a Procrustean way. Better to go slow, to change little things in a piecemeal fashion, rather than to make mistakes on a large scale.

Such criticisms were ignored by Marxists when they came from the 'class enemy'. They took more notice when what Communists love to call 'life itself' – life, this time, within the Communist world – caught up with them, firstly, with Khrushchev's 'revelations' after the death of Stalin, and later, after Hungary and Czechoslovakia. They then began to look for an interpretation of what had gone wrong, using Marxist, not bourgeois categories.

The Chinese are so far removed from capitalism now that when I told the chairman of a commune (who had asked about incomes in Britain), having explained the range of earnings of working people, that I also had to point out that one or two per cent of the population owned about a third of the wealth, he replied, gravely, 'I am greatly shocked.'

One has to remember that anyone under thirty-five was less than ten years old at the time of the Liberation and has lived his entire conscious life under Communism. Hence there are Museums of the Class Struggle, displaying the brutal conditions of life for the masses before 1949. In the film, *On the Docks*, a young man with good education who wants the exciting life of a seaman, not the toil of being a docker, is taken round such a museum and reminded, by an old docker, what his life would have been like under capitalism, and how he ought to be glad to serve others by performing socially necessary labour (neither of these ploys convinces him, by the way).

Capitalism, in China, is something they learn about in museums. They know even less about capitalism as it still exists, and though they know it to be exploitative and inegalitarian, in the abstract, they find it shocking to learn that in Britain only two in a hundred children from homes where the father is an unskilled or semi-skilled worker will get to university, whereas one in three of those whose fathers are professionals or managers will. To find this occurring in the U.S.S.R., where eight out of ten of the city intelligentsia's children will go on to tertiary-level education, but only one in ten of the children of agricultural workers, is far *more* shocking to the Chinese, however, because this claims to be a socialist society.

It is this parallelism the Chinese are talking about when they speak of the 'capitalist road'. The emergence of a similar pattern of stratification *inside China* was disturbing in the extreme. There is no doubt that, before the Cultural Revolution, China was coming to look more and more like the U.S.S.R. In the educational field, for instance – and education is the high road to important social positions – an urban-oriented and élitist approach had so far triumphed over the Maoist strategy of 'half work – half study' that the 'three bad years' of 1959–61 were used as an excuse to step up attacks on the policy of providing education for peasants. In 1962, according to 'incomplete figures released during the Cultural Revolution', the number of agricultural middle schools is said to have declined from 22,600 schools with 2·3 million pupils to 3,715 schools with 260,000 pupils, and the number of students at Peking University from worker and peasant backgrounds to have fallen from nearly 67 per cent in 1958 to only

38 per cent in 1962, while the number of students from 'exploiting class' backgrounds nearly doubled. These are astounding figures, and it seems that the reduction of the population of the agricultural middle schools by two millions 'at one stroke', as the official account has it, would have brought about mass protest and dislocation (possibly not, if the two million were split into 'penny packets' all over China). Nevertheless, there seems to be ample ground for accepting that meritocratic competition was working in favour of those from higher-status homes: some 5,000 students of worker, peasant or soldier class background were said to have been expelled from higher schools in Peking alone, and another 5,000 forced to repeat a grade. The rationale for all this was, of course, 'standards of excellence'. For the 'high flyers', a 'three-stage rocket' system to train an élite of super-scientists, on the lines of the Soviet think-tank at Novisibirsk – where the intellectual cream of the new generation, selected and re-selected from the whole population, is concentrated – was talked of for Tsinghua University in Peking. The privileged life of the cadres, too, was reviving the age-old Confucian dream of every family: to have a son who was an official.

The Cultural Revolution called a halt to this creeping élitism. Millions of workers' and peasants' children had found themselves increasingly blocked off from educational opportunity in a society where status differences were becoming ever more accentuated. The contrast between the lip-service paid to Communist ideals, and the *de facto* priority of 'expertness' over 'redness', was the source of the pent-up frustrations which exploded during the Cultural Revolution and included not a little 'ultra-left' persecution of individuals as 'bourgeois' on superficial or trivial grounds, and the (largely symbolic) destruction of things from the past.

The Maoist strategy of 'positive discrimination' – of deliberately favouring the poorest (and politically most radical) – of encouraging 'all-round' development of the many rather than the production of a super-élite, the shortening rather than the protraction of education (now, in the West, taking an advanced graduate into his late twenties, after which he probably still stays in the academy), and the linking of study with practical work – triumphed only with the most bitter struggle. It was, indeed, a revolution, at times breaking into physical violence.

The current attacks on 'ultra-leftism', and the complaint of would-be students who have been loyally working in the countryside or in the factories that they have not had the opportunity to prepare themselves for entrance examinations, which have been partly reintroduced, show that the conflict between 'redness' and 'expertness' has not ended. Nevertheless, since the Cultural Revolution, two cardinal virtues have been reasserted: equality and participation. Of these, the most visible and striking is equality. The spread of incomes, firstly, has been reduced. A young industrial apprentice will start at about only 15–18 *yuan* a month. Once trained he starts on a salary of at least 35 *yuan*. (For comparison, students at Kwangtung Teachers' Training College get 21 *yuan* a month; at Fu Tan University in Shanghai, 19·50 *yuan*.) The maximum for a worker varies between 104 *yuan* and 128 *yuan* in different factories. Wages, then, are not absolutely standardized according to national scales, if only because it costs somewhat more to live in the larger cities, and more in Shanghai, where winters are cold, than in Canton.

There are still people who earn much more than the workers: an experienced senior consultant at a top hospital could get 260 *yuan* or more a month, and salaries of 345 *yuan* a month have been reported for some Peking University professors. Most professors there, however, were receiving only 50–60 *yuan*. These scales were being revised, and it was claimed that the higher paid professors were pressing harder than anyone else to have their salaries reduced! At Kwangtung Teachers' College staff salary scales ran from 61·5 *yuan* to 320 *yuan* maximum. The average was 80 *yuan*. In Nanking No. 1 General Hospital, the starting salary for a newly-graduated doctor was 52 *yuan*. The administrative staff salary scale ran from 40 to 130 *yuan* a month; service personnel from around 35 to only 75; and senior nurses from 40 to just over 130. In a commune hospital, medical staff (not doctors) began as apprentices on 30 *yuan* and, once trained, were on a scale from between 50–60 *yuan* a month, but rising no higher than 80–90 *yuan*. At No. 1 Heavy Electrical Machinery Works, the workers were, as elsewhere, classified into eight skill-grades, starting at 42 *yuan* and ending at 123 *yuan*; the average wage of workers with ten years' service was 65 *yuan*. The highest individual wages I actually encountered amongst industrial workers were 87 *yuan* (a man with twenty years' service in a key plant), and 78 *yuan* (a store manager of 51 with fourteen years' service in a sizeable small-town factory).

The dispersion of the range of incomes recorded is, at its very highest, around 10:1. In the U.S.A., less than 2 per cent of the population owns over a quarter of all personally-owned wealth and a half of all personally-owned business assets, plus 80 per cent of the corporate stock and virtually all state and local government bonds.

The vast majority of city incomes for men in China fall within a range of no more than four to one, and if trainees are excluded, three to one. By any standards, this is an extraordinarily narrow spread. Peasant incomes, as we have seen, are still generally lower, in disposable cash terms. Money wages have been going up: between 1952 and 1970 by about 50 per cent. Nearly all observers concur that prices for everyday consumer goods have been extremely stable ever since the immediate post-Liberation reconstruction, and scarcely vary more than a cent or two across the country. I gave up taking down detailed prices after a while for this reason. Many consumer 'durables' have been reduced in price, some by 20 per cent to 30 per cent over this period.

In our society, too, food is the single major component of family budgets, on average one-quarter, and the poorer you are the greater the proportion of your income it takes. It would seem to be equally true in China. In Britain, accommodation is the next major call on earnings; in China it absorbs no more than 4–7 per cent of income. One third major 'outgoing', personal taxation, does not exist in China.

Equality is not just a matter of income, however. Social status is also differentially evaluated and allocated in our society. In China, differences are de-emphasized about as far as can be imagined. The incredible bears repeating: officers in the army really do serve as privates for several weeks of the year; managers return to the bench, and government cadres and intellectuals go to the countryside or the factories. Differences of 'position' – the term the Chinese reluctantly use – are virtually invisible. Just as sex is de-emphasized in clothing, so is social status. Officers wear no badges of rank (they have extra pockets!), nor are medals worn. A man might be a manager or a clerk, a worker or a professor; it is hard to guess by looking.

This massive reduction of class and status differences is not the end of the road for the Chinese Communists: it is only the beginning. It was all foreshadowed long ago, in the writings of Marx. They have eliminated capitalist private property. Now

they intend to eliminate the 'Three Great Differences' Marx
identified as so deep and ancient that they go back, beyond
capitalism, to the beginnings of class society: the division
between town and country, the division between industry and
agriculture, and the division between mental and manual
labour. Development elsewhere accentuates these. Peasants
flock to the shanty-towns of the city; young men crowd the
universities and find no jobs when they come out (the recent
uprising in Sri Lanka (Ceylon) was precisely a rising of this
alienated population); and those who are fortunate enough to
join the neo-colonial élites fear, scorn, exploit and repress
those less fortunate than they.

'Alienation', in radical-chic usage, is a term borrowed from
Marxism, but defused. For Marx, alienation was a function of
class society, its source the exploitation of classes of men by
other classes of men. It was not a 'non-economic' phenomenon,
or a synonym for inhumanity, even less some existentialist
notion of the eternal tragedy of the 'human condition'. Class
society, Marx wrote, poisoned not only men's working lives,
but their non-work interpersonal relations, too, dehumanized
them, and turned them into 'fragmented' rather than 'whole'
personalities. Later writers were to rephrase these themes as
the 'lonely crowd', the 'organization man', or 'the divided
self'. Alienation, for Marx, then, was a social condition, and
remediable. It was certainly not synonymous simply with
'disaffection' or 'unhappiness', as in radical-chic usage: if
this is Marxism, we are all Marxists. For Marx, the *happy*
worker was a victim of 'false consciousness', if there ever was
one, in that he failed to understand that there was no such
thing as a 'fair day's wage' under capitalism – *all* labour was
exploited labour. Since Marx hated crystal-ball gazing and (*pace*
Popper, he insisted that the future would be worked out by
the men who made the revolution, under circumstances
impossible to predict) he only gave very general indications of
what the ending of alienation would entail. He 'begged the
pardon' of people who thought his 'historical sketch' of
capitalism in Western Europe was an 'historico-philosophical
theory of the general path every people is fated to tread,
whatever the historical circumstances in which it finds itself'.

The Chinese have always stuck closely to Marx's thesis that
ownership of the means of production is the basis of class
power. But they have seen capitalism as a total configuration,
too, stamping its values – or trying to – on all who live under

it, and that what is often taken to be human nature is simply the habits men have developed and live by in *class* society: possessiveness, competitiveness, individualism; and that these will have to be replaced by their opposites: co-operation, comradeliness, mutual aid, and service to others. For this to occur, these values have to be both institutionalized in society and internalized within men.

Marx never thought this could happen overnight. There would be a transitional stage, after the seizure of power, before the liberation of human creativity and the rational organization of 'the productive powers of social labour' would make possible that abundance from which human wants – not just elemental *needs* or commercially-induced wants – could be met. The Chinese have not interpreted this to mean that production comes first, and socialism later. Rather socialist values have to be the very premises of development, built into it from the beginning so that the re-socialization of men starts now. Thus the mutual aid teams, co-operatives and communes were stages in re-socializing peasants whose historic dream had been to own the land they now had, not to collectivize it.

In Western political theory, mass participation in politics is represented as a bad or impossible thing, for democracy, it is held, cannot work except where the uninformed are prepared to leave politics to politically cultured minorities who control the parties which compete for the votes of the masses, but who share a basic consensus, and where the loser, therefore, operates as a loyal opposition. If the apolitical intervene in politics, it is for the worse. The politician who seeks to appeal directly to the masses and establish contact with them is a dangerous 'populist'. 'Populism' is the enemy of 'true' democracy.

It is precisely this involvement that Chinese Communism seeks, though it aims through education at raising mass political consciousness, not simply reflecting it. Like all socialists, they see the classical bourgeois ideals of Liberty, Equality and Fraternity as formal and incomplete in societies based on 'possessive individualism'. For true fraternity requires the ending of exploitation, and, in class society, there can only be the fraternity of the exploiters, on the one hand, and the fraternity of the exploited on the other. Any sense of identity between the two is spurious, whether it be an 'other-worldly' equality in the sight of God, or a 'this-worldly' sense of common interests (chauvinism, racism) vis-à-vis other nations and groups. Equality before the law or in front of the ballot-box is negated by economic and social inequality which gives a few men enormous power over the persons and minds of millions of others, or the power to buy themselves a privileged freedom from constraints others labour under. Sir Gerald Nabarro put it in a nutshell: 'If a man can afford to pay for justice, he will secure it. A man who cannot afford to pay will rarely secure it.'

Socialism, for the Chinese, had to reverse this pattern. The most crucial agency, the Party, is today a force of twenty-eight million people, roughly one in thirty, compared to one in ninety-five in 1951. It is scarcely a tiny 'vanguard' élite in size; in terms of composition, two-thirds of the delegates to the tenth Party Congress in 1973 were workers, peasants or soldiers. Nor is the daily involvement of millions in the work-ing-out of the mass line phoney participation (indeed, people complain of too many meetings). 'From the top down and the bottom up' is a slogan that reflects this mass process.

This attempt to bring ordinary people back into decision-making, and the decentralization of government, attracts many people in the West for whom the ever-growing power of impersonal and centralized organizations means an 'eclipse of community' and the loss of a sense of identity and attachment. It underlies the exodus of tens of thousands of young people in the U.S.A. to join communes and has driven others to engage in 'community action'.

Many of them adhere to classical anarchist ideals (though few are conscious 'anarchists'), believing that the individual is and should be the decider of his own fate, free to choose to enter into association with others or not, but preferably only where he can 'be himself' and play a direct part, rather than being governed or even 'represented' by others. Hence anarchists have rarely sought or been able to bring into being or sustain organizations larger in scale than the self-governing guild, municipality, *pueblo*, factory or co-operative. The State was their enemy. This ideal, which formerly appealed to petty craftsmen and farmers threatened by capitalism, today attracts all those opposed to 'bigness' – Big Business, big armies, mass parties, machine politics and a society which seeks to com-mercialize the very symbols of dissociation, from hippie clothes to rock festivals.

The categories of Left and Right scarcely capture the com-plexity of these moods. Traditional anarchists were of the

Left, against the powers-that-be: the rich and the 'tall poppies', their parties and their State. They were equally hostile to centralization and organization when they found it on the Left. There have also been right-wing populisms, which have appealed to 'little men' and 'silent majorities' from the American mid-West to the villages of France, terrified of organized Labour and revolution as much as Big Business.

Labels like Left and Right, however, scarcely capture the complexity of these moods, nor do contrast-pairs of terms like 'passive' or 'active', 'retreatist' or 'escapist', since these neglect the active rejection of the material values represented by the primitive communism of the Diggers, or that affirmation of life symbolized by the girls who offered flowers or bared their breasts to the troopers with their rifles. Hippie language, Stuart Hall has pointed out, has typically a 'prepositional flavour' and is located in the continuous-present: from 'where it's at' or 'love-in', to 'turning on' and 'dropping out': forms of language which emphasize the existential and the situational, and express the urge to move 'right out of this world' altogether into mystical or hallucinatory experience, or into some private oasis where they can concentrate on the most personal of human relations most intensively: love and sex.

Yet the wider society is never far away, and it is a counterculture always conscious of what it stands against. As Hall remarks, the hippie slogan, 'Zap them with Love' is the counterpart of the brutal game of the Vietnam War, 'Zapping the Cong' – picking off guerillas from the air. Flight from society can lead underground, but guerillas live underground, too, and the American underground has been no friend of the establishment. Yet, in the last analysis, the Californian commune stands at the opposite pole from the Chinese, which seeks to enlarge the range of human belonging. Chinese communes, Mao has said, are 'big and public', not worldrenouncing or parasitic monasteries. They are highly organized, and closely integrated with the life of the whole society. Little wonder that my interpreter was horrified at a brochure a young American had sent him showing life on an American commune: naked people and wooden knives and forks were not his idea of the progressive life.

The involvement of ordinary peasants and workers in decision-making at the grass-roots is too well-attested and visible for it to be doubted that it takes place to an extent quite unfamiliar in Britain, where people leave local government to others unless a crisis occurs, and where self-government at the place of work is only a theory or a mystification. Yet there is little evidence that the ordinary citizenry in China exercise much influence over what goes on at higher levels. National policy, domestic or foreign, is the outcome of decisions inevitably taken at the top and then transmitted downwards. There is much involvement in implementing, discussing, and modifying them, but little in their creation. Paradoxically, even the Cultural Revolution was launched from the top, and initially an urban phenomenon, later carried to the villages. Nevertheless, that extraordinary convulsion which gripped Chinese society is something no government in the West would contemplate unleashing.

That the 'mass line' is not a *product* of the masses seems scarcely contestable. Nor is there much tangible evidence of open debate over policy at Party congresses (though enormous debates must occur out of sight). Even official reports merely give the 'guideline' speeches and the results of elections to office. One index of the persistence of a stable top leadership is the age of its members. For such a revolutionary society, power has remained in the hands of a small body of men for a very long time, now one of the oldest leaderships of any major Power. The election of Wang Hung-wen as Vice-Chairman of the Party (among four other Vice-Chairmen) is a welcome sign that thought is being given to the question not only of 'succession' to Chairman Mao, but also to the introduction of younger cadres into top policy-making circles. The older men have earned their positions, and what they have achieved has been the emancipation of 750 million people who have been put on the road to socialism. So great was the role of young people during the Cultural Revolution, that observers sometimes write as if there was a 'cult of youth' in China, and that the youth were inevitably more revolutionary than their elders. In one sense, this may be true, but the Chinese have always sought to maintain a balance of maturity and youth, of experience and readiness to throw off the old, that expresses itself in the 'three in one' composition of committees: not a monopoly by any of the age-groups in the population, but a blend of the young, the middle-aged, and those with lengthy experience. But, at the highest levels of society, there is an obvious imbalance of age, and it is the centralizing aspect of 'democratic centralism' that is dominant, rather than the democratic or mass-participatory. The tension between the two elements – democracy and centralization – is, in part, a difference of levels of decision-making, for as we have seen participation is a reality at grass-roots, and countries the size of China cannot be run by mass meetings. Yet much of the institutionalization of strong, centralized government is a function of the severe pressures China finds herself under, as she has been ever since Liberation and in the years of armed struggle before then. As long as the necessity remains for high mobilization, in a society pressing hard to lift itself by its own bootstraps in a hostile world, so will the need for a strong State.

The attempted seizure of power by Lin Piao is therefore worrying. It is also worrying that the Chinese people knew nothing about it for a year, except insofar as he suddenly dropped from public view, while the outside world did. It shows that the danger that such a powerful instrument might get into the wrong hands is no abstract fancy. And it demonstrates that mass involvement, at this level, is largely symbolic. That it did not succeed is indeed heartening, but there is no assurance that other attempts might not. Nor has there been any serious explanation of how the man designated as Mao's successor and 'comrade-in-arms', right through the Cultural Revolution, could so suddenly turn into a 'bourgeois careerist, conspirator, counter-revolutionary, double-dealer, renegade and traitor', or his comrade, Chen Po-ta into an 'anti-Party, anti-communist Kuomintang element, Trotskyite renegade, enemy agent and revisionist', terms so absolutely incredible that one can only treat them as vituperation and not as epithets with exact meaning. Whatever the mistakes, perhaps even crimes, of Lin and Chen, these words are not justified. Far more serious is that there has been no serious analysis of how these 'degenerations' could happen, of what social forces these men represented, or what shortcomings in Party or Government organization or political culture they point to.

The Western reaction to this kind of crisis at the top is to look for *structural* insurances and defences against their recurrence – checks and balances, institutionalized criticism, opposition, independent trade unions and the like. The Chinese, it has been said, do not rely so much on passing laws, they launch *movements*. And it is this strategy that they have recourse to in their thinking about any future danger from non-accountable and irresponsible leaders and bureaucrats or from attempted coups. They are resolved that 'monsters and demons' will 'jump out' every seven or eight years, i.e., that there will be periodic Cultural Revolutions. The accent, then, is not so much on structural arrangements, nor on legal devices, but on the unleashing of mass action. What is left unexplained is how such movements are to be initiated.

One crucial factor is that the men who launched the last Cultural Revolution are in positions of power. One of them was Wang Hung-wen. Very many of those who opposed that Revolution are also back in office, though they have received a profound jolt and undergone a lengthy political re-education. Hence, though forces tending to routine, and the perhaps eternal necessity to be vigilant for the emergence of new forms of inequality, are problems for China as for any society, the forces opposed to such tendencies are also very strong.

China is a huge and complex country. Though power is centralized, it is also devolved in other ways, so that the seizure of power is a lot more problematic an operation than it would be in countries where it mainly involves grabbing the airport and the radio station. For Lin Piao at least it seemed by no means inconceivable.

The only ultimate insurance is to develop the other element in the phrase 'democratic centralism' even further – to increase the participation and politicization of the mass of the people to such an extent that any perversion of the revolution would meet with mass resistance – and this would mean providing them with the means by which, in the worst eventuality, this could be ensured – by the use of arms. In this respect, the militias of China and Cuba demonstrate a degree of confidence in the relationship between Government, Party and people that few Western governments would be prepared to imitate. Raúl Castro has described how the Cubans dealt with 179 C.I.A. bands dropped into that country up to 1967. It was very simple, he said, we armed 50,000 workers and 50,000 peasants. 'All you have to do to destroy guerilla bands,' he advised reactionary governments, 'is the same.'

The other alternative – or complement – is to look for ways of institutionalizing criticism, for these things cannot be safely left to leaders to initiate, since they may not do so, and, since they experience life differently from the way the ordinary citizen does, may have different interests and think some criticisms illegitimate. They also have the power to label some criticisms as justified and others as illegitimate. Many ideas have been canvassed to cope with these problems, even within the Communist world, some by Lenin, when he realized that the centralized machine he had built up and his elimination of opposition had given birth to a monster. Hence at the end of his life, he began throwing up ideas about rotating leadership, direct membership by peasants and workers of leading committees, the acceptance of legitimate factions within the Party, open debate and the open dissemination of information and of competing policy-documents, etc., etc.

The Chinese have gone a good way towards building the principle of criticism into the Party Constitution: leading bodies at all levels have to report regularly on their work to congresses or general membership meetings, and constantly to listen to the masses. Party members have the right to criticize organizations and leading members at all levels and to make proposals to them. If they hold different views, they have the right to reserve them and to bypass the immediate leadership and report to higher levels, up to and including the Chairman of the Central Committee. 'It is absolutely impermissible to suppress criticism and to retaliate,' the Constitution now runs. 'It is essential to create a political situation in which there are both centralism and democracy, both discipline and freedom, both unity of will and personal ease of mind and liveliness.' All this has been summed up in the slogan 'Going against the tide is a Marxist-Leninist principle'.

At the same time, the classical principles of democratic centralism are reasserted: the individual is subordinate to the organization, the minority is subordinate to the majority, the lower level to the higher level, and the entire Party to the Central Committee.

These are classical principles, as is that of election to all committees, even in bourgeois democracy, though the rights of those who dissent from majority opinion, or from official policy, *as groups*, are often more strongly stated in bourgeois principle (however little observed in practice). All depends on whether and how such principles are operated, by whom and for what ends.

The Chinese way of doing things has been so unprecedented that it has discomfited those who looked only at laws and structures. Whether revolutions as thoroughgoing as the Cultural Revolution will come about again we cannot know. The Chinese say they will, and they have already done it once, on a scale that was truly world-historic. For my part, I hope that the next Cultural Revolution will be by and about women's place in society, for their status still falls far short of what it ought to be in a Communist society that is now a quarter of a century and two revolutions away from capitalism. Improved as the lot of women is out of all recognition (and a look at the deformed feet of the older women is a salutary reminder of that), the new generation of women is not going to be content with lower wages than men, or to be childminders, or to carry the main burden of the home in addition to their job outside, or to have a still unequal share of the key positions in society.

The relevance of China's peasant-based revolution for underdeveloped countries, especially such agrarian societies as India, Indonesia or the Philippines, is obvious enough. But it can scarcely serve as a model for revolution in such an urbanized continent as Latin America, or in those other parts of the Third World where the ever-growing city populations are made up of ex-peasant sub-proletarians (or 'proto-proletarians') and only contain small proletarian populations. Hence future movements of liberation will, almost by definition, be made up from elements which are not predominantly peasant.

The relevance of the post-Liberation Chinese model of development, e.g., the sequence of aid team, co-operative, and commune, the policy of 'agriculture as the foundation and industry as the leading sector', the strategy of 'walking on two legs', will prove to be of immense significance for the future development of other countries, once they, too, have abolished capitalism.

China's growing economic and political power, which has already restored her to her major place in the United Nations, will also enable her to assist liberation movements and to provide much more aid of the kind she has spectacularly given to Tanzania and Zambia in building their railway. The contrast between Chinese aid and capitalist aid makes the former very much more attractive, based as it is on the 'Eight Noes': (1) no restriction of aid to the production of primary products (readiness to help industrialize), (2) no special status or conditions as a consequence of giving aid (e.g., no requests for military bases or insistence on certain kinds of repayment), (3) no interest, and repayment only as it becomes possible, (4) no 'tying' of the two economies; encouragement of local self-sufficiency and continuity of projects once established, (5) short or medium term investment (to avoid tying up scarce capital, and to speed up return on capital), (6) provision of only top quality goods, (7) the training of local people to take over aid projects, (8) local living-standards for the Chinese technicians and workers on the aid projects.

There is a comfortable tendency in the West, in the present era of *rapprochement*, to admire the Chinese development as something patently good for them, and of interest to under-developed countries, but quite irrelevant for advanced econo-mies. It is a euphoria likely to be dissipated, as Edgar Snow warned, when the capitalist world realizes that China's Communists still look to world Communism.

At one level, a great deal of the specifics of China's experience are obviously inapplicable to advanced industrial societies. As I tried to explain to commune members, who always asked me about grain production in England, we have a very different kind of economy, let alone polity, culture and history. More-over, we live in a non-revolutionary situation. Nevertheless, it would seem unlikely in the extreme that the inevitable detachment of more and more Third World countries from the capitalist sector of the world economic and political system will not have profound repercussions, over time, even in those richer countries whose stability seems unproblematic now. Nor is there any reason to believe, especially after May 1968, that the West is completely immune to revolution or that, in that event, the Army would not be called upon to deal with it.

The Chinese perspective on the future of the world is one of unbounded confidence in a revolutionary future. Though China's impact on other countries has hitherto not been very impressive, her support and example were crucial and historic in enabling Vietnam to win what was, in effect, a victory over the world's greatest super-power. Certainly, Mao looks at world history with a truly Chinese sweep of vision, not from year to year. In 1957, contemplating the danger of a third world war, he warned the capitalist world that the First World War had brought about the birth of the Soviet Union, with two hundred million people, and the Second World War the formation of a socialist camp with nine hundred million people in it. A third world war would be the end of capitalism, and one of the few countries likely to survive nuclear devastation would be China.

China has carefully avoided getting entangled in military confrontation, even on a sub-nuclear level, unless driven to it by external threat. Yet she has been driven to it on occasion. On the Right, the enemies of China have been alarmed by her intervention in Korea, and her support for North Vietnam and the N.L.F. They rarely stopped to reflect that if China had sent troops to Alaska, and penetrated through Canada up to the U.S. border, wrecking everything *en route*, and then sent troops to Mexico and bombed the villages and towns of that country flat, right up to the borders of California, Arizona, New Mexico and Texas, they would have had reason to be worried. Yet these are the analogues of what has been done, not by China, but by the U.S.A. in Korea and Vietnam. Had the Chinese not been patient, World War Three would have been over long ago, and those of us who had survived the nuclear explosions and the fall-out would now be scratching for food in the fields, sheltering among the rubble and ashes, and fighting for survival against packs of spear-armed looters.

The other 'evidence' of Chinese aggressiveness that worries the Right is the Sino-Indian border war of 1962, a war described now, even in the West, as *'India's China War'*, the title of the authoritative study by Neville Maxwell, the London *Times'* South Asia correspondent in New Delhi at the time. What was extraordinary about the war was that, having pushed back the grossly ineffective Indian Army, and with nothing between them and Calcutta, the Chinese proceeded to *withdraw*. The same correspondent has now reported from the Ussuri (Wu-su-li) River border with the Soviet Union, where clashes occurred with Soviet forces. Since the Chinese took him to Chenpao Island, which the Soviet claimed to have thrown them out of four years ago (London *Sunday Times*, 23 September 1973), it seems clear that Russian versions have all the veracity of the explanations they produced to justify their invasions of Hungary and Czechoslovakia.

Mao's nuclear calculations are extremely chilling ones to have to make, like all 'thinking the unthinkable'. The Chinese have also repeatedly stated that they would never be the first to use the bomb, and have a limited capacity to do so, as well as an interest in avoiding getting sucked into an arms-race which has already absorbed very scarce capital, skills and industrial output. They have said that they have developed nuclear weapons to balance the threat represented both by the super-powers' own bombs and by the American land forces, and now the third of the Soviet Red Army on her northern border. They know that 'hawks' in the Kremlin have advocated a quick knock-out of China's main cities as a means of equalizing the enormous Chinese superiority in manpower. It is quite clear that they expect to be the attacked rather than the attacker, not only in words but in practice, for the Peking workers have built miles of fully-equipped shelters in their spare time. The slogan used is important: 'Dig tunnels, store grain, *and never seek hegemony.*' There can be few calls to arms so explicitly defensive in contemporary geo-politics. Nor are the Chinese armed forces designed for offence. The army contains less than three million men, a far lower proportion of men under arms, relative to the population, than either the U.S.A. or the U.S.S.R. (so much for the Western stereotypes of numberless yellow – or red – hordes): the air force is almost derisory for any power with aggressive intentions; and the naval forces are only slightly more credible.

But the Chinese are prepared to defend themselves. School children's races include jumping over ropes with bags of 'explosive' which 'go off' if they fail to clear the rope. Tens of millions in the villages, men and women, train regularly and carry out manoeuvres with live ammunition. They live in a society which has grown out of war, and they are ready to use their experience in defending what they have built up so painfully.

Mao made his remarks about the bomb being a 'paper tiger' because there were those who argued that revolutionary challenges to imperialism were no longer possible in the nuclear era, as any local war would lead to the extinction of human civilization. The cynic might well argue that as China's present low level of industrialization is left behind, so she might become less worried about devoting more plentiful resources to nuclear weaponry, and might therefore become herself a well-heeled nuclear power. I was, myself, infuriated with people who parroted Mao's words about nuclear weapons being only 'paper tigers' without having, apparently, any real knowledge at all of the power of modern thermo-nuclear weapons. They were still thinking in terms of Hiroshima. (Equally, their ignorance of the U.S.S.R. was breathtaking: income-differentials had been much less marked under Stalin, they asserted; they had widened under the revisionist Krushchev: the exact opposite of the truth.)

The last of these military confrontations on China's frontiers, that in Tibet, has been the one that has aroused most hostility and apprehension in the West. The picture presented by the media has been a simple one: Tibet was, it is claimed, *de facto* an independent country until the Communists came to power. They then proceeded to invade Tibet, which provoked a massive popular resistance which the Chinese overcame by ruthless military repression, including the mass murder of civilians and the wholesale destruction of monasteries.

Not surprisingly, the Chinese version of these events is very different indeed. For many in the West and particularly many young people, Tibet was a 'Shangri La' oasis of peace, where monks were solely preoccupied with transcendental meditation. It is an image of Tibet which leaves out those aspects of traditional Tibetan culture emphasized in an exhibition in the National Minorities' Institute in Peking: the drinking-vessels used in lamaist rituals, made of human skulls, and the bugles made from the thigh-bones of young virgins. On display also were whips, instruments of torture, and photographs of mutilated people with their noses, ears, fingers and feet cut off for having offended against the laws of a society in which the 'church' was the biggest land-owner and serfdom was widespread.

I raised the question of the discrepancy between Western and Chinese versions of Tibetan culture later with a European long resident in Peking, since foreign residents often express the Chinese viewpoint more sharply than the Chinese do themselves (for this reason they are often pejoratively dubbed 'two hundred percenters' by Westerners who feel they have gone over to the 'enemy'). The violent emotionality of the reaction showed that I had touched on a sensitive issue (and probably especially so for one who could understand Western attitudes more readily). 'Try to imagine what life was like in medieval Europe for a serf,' I was told, with some heat, 'then multiply it by a thousand and you'll have some idea of what life was like in Tibet before Liberation.'

What happened in the 1950s and 1960s becomes every day more and more a matter of historical interest only. Even to the Chinese, it is the contemporary development of communes and factories, schools and hospitals, that matters. But insofar as the record still needs straightening out, there is growing recognition, even amongst Western students of Asia, that the version we were presented with at the time is suspect. Firstly, the Communists did not simply invade Tibet. Rather, they stayed on the borders for two years and negotiated. Then the agreement was signed with the Dalai Lama's court, in 1951, which accepted Chinese suzerainty. The Chinese did, indeed, attempt to stimulate some of the traditional notables into becoming agents of modernization, whilst leaving the formal structure of government virtually unchanged. But the resistance of traditionalist elements at court, and of the regional dissidence in the eastern marches proved too strong for them. Yet, far from leading an armed national opposition, the Dalai Lama at this stage went to Peking, and lived there, even writing poems in honour of Mao Tse-Tung. The initial resistance to the Chinese came from a very different quarter – the Khamba tribesmen of eastern Tibet who certainly resented the Chinese, as they always had done. They had also always resented the other claim to legitimate suzerainty over them: that of the government in Lhasa, the capital. Their revolt was therefore a double-edged one, as subsequent events were to show.

At first, the People's Liberation Army was, even according to pro-Tibetan sources, welcomed as an 'army of Buddhas' because of their good behaviour. Their envoys, however, were killed by the Khambas, and armed clashes broke out. Now the Chinese were faced with having to assert their claim to Tibet in the face of armed opposition. By 1958 the Khambas were in full revolt; by 1959 they were attempting to extend further their resistance to the Chinese and to the Dalai Lama's policy of co-operation with the Chinese – by staging an uprising in the capital itself. The Chinese reacted vigorously, and suppressed it. The rebels then fled the country, taking the Dalai Lama with them. The C.I.A. provided air cover with American aircraft which flew for hundreds of miles inside Tibet, parachuting supplies, radios and money, and strafing Chinese positions. Colour films of this operation have been viewed by several sources in the U.S.

The C.I.A. had long dabbled in Tibetan affairs, with little response at first. One interesting exhibit in the Peking exhibition is a letter from Lowell Thomas dated 10 May 1950, addressed to the Dalai Lama, proposing to supply him with arms, and suggesting sending Max Thornburg, who had formerly worked for the State Department and had considerable experience of 'keeping communism out of the Near East' (he had helped the C.I.A. to unseat Premier Mossadegh of Iran), but who might best enter Tibet, Thomas suggested, not as a government official, but 'merely as another traveller'.

In 1950, since relations with China were still positive, the C.I.A.'s overtures evoked little response from the Lhasa authorities. But, by the later 1950s, especially after the unsuccessful *coup* in Lhasa in 1959, arms and supplies began to flow in via India and Taiwan, making a protracted armed struggle inevitable. (Armed parties were also dropped into China's Yunnan province from C.I.A. bases in Laos, Burma and Thailand.) Accounts of vengeful brutality on the part of the P.L.A. now began to flood the Western Press. But years later, Robert Ford, the British radio operator in Lhasa who was arrested and imprisoned by the Chinese for five years, declared that there was no sacking of monasteries.

From the Chinese point of view they were merely reasserting rights over a frontier region of China that no Chinese government had been able to administer since 1912, when the Manchu garrison had been driven from Lhasa. No Chinese government since that time has ever conceded its right to govern Tibet. Ironically, though Taiwan assisted the rebels in their resistance to Peking, the Nationalists have always insisted, no less than the Communist government in Peking, that Tibet is part of China.

Despite these traumatic events, the Chinese continued to regard the Dalai Lama as the spiritual leader of Tibet and as chairman of the committee to prepare a modern system of government for Tibet, five years after his departure. In retrospect, he appears a tragic figure – a young man swayed by whosoever exercised effective power immediately around him: the feudal élite, the Khamba rebels, the Chinese, the C.I.A., or the Indian government. Whatever his personal role, however, China's assertion of control over this vast eastern border territory, in the era of growing hostility with the U.S.S.R. and with India, was inevitable. But armed conflict, and the removal of the Dalai Lama, were not inevitable; they were brought about by the intransigence of the feudal circles around the Dalai Lama and through the manoeuvres of the C.I.A. Yet, if the revolt failed, the C.I.A. must be credited with a moral victory in the cold war, for their version has gone virtually unchallenged for two decades.

The Left have a quite different set of worries about Chinese foreign policy from those of the Right. The first of these is Chinese support for Pakistan, especially during the phase of brutal suppression of West Pakistan under Yahya Khan which led to the Bangla Desh War. The main justifications adduced by the Chinese are that they regard the resistance of the Bangladeshis as eminently just, but that this was becoming a movement so powerful and so socially radical that it threatened to turn into a People's War under left-wing leadership. The people of Bangla Desh, they say, could have coped with Yahya Khan. But India feared such a radical development so close to Calcutta, and therefore stepped in, not so much to liberate Bangla Desh as to make sure that the new State was well under their thumb, and the radical armed forces disbanded and its leaders imprisoned. Nevertheless, Chinese respect for the principle of non-interference in other country's affairs has not, in the past, prevented her from fierce denunciation of unfavoured régimes, and she did not say, loud and clear, as she should have done, that she did not support Yahya Khan's policy of genocide, including the murder of the intelligentsia of Bangla Desh. Marxist exegeses apart, it is difficult not to see the situation in the much simpler terms of the balance of power in areas of Asia close to China's borders. One is reminded, indeed, of the Arab proverb, 'The enemy of my enemy is my friend', since, in China's view, India is the principal rival in Asia (apart from Japan), a country with which she has already been at war, and which she now sees as having fallen under Soviet influence, and that she wishes to counter-balance by supporting India's enemy, Pakistan (who provides China, too, with an important communications outlet onto the Indian Ocean). It may well be that even a country so crucially guided by Communist principle as China cannot always sustain this as her sole consideration in developing policies for relations with other States whom she has also to look upon in terms of their role in a world system of balances of power (which at times forces some strange bedfellows together).

On the question of Sri Lanka, however, I confess myself unable to proffer any rational explanation for the astounding language used by Chou En-Lai in congratulating Mrs Bandaranaike on her success in suppressing the rising of the young revolutionaries of the J.V.P. (Janata Vimukhti Peramuna) who died in thousands, and were arrested in even larger numbers. In a letter to the Sri Lanka Prime Minister, Chou wrote:

The Chinese people have all along opposed ultra-'left' and right opportunism in their protracted revolutionary struggles. We are glad to see that thanks to the efforts of your Excellency and the Ceylon Government, the chaotic situation created by a handful of persons who style themselves 'Guevarists' and into whose ranks foreign spies have sneaked has been brought under control . . .

The Chinese regarded the rising as 'adventurism' rather than a 'people's war' led by a mass Marxist-Leninist Party, as they would have preferred. But that does not excuse the condoning of the wholesale massacre of young revolutionaries nor the support for a reactionary government addressed in such unnecessarily fulsome terms. More fundamentally, such an attitude runs counter to the principle, often repeated by the Chinese, of not trying to impose their revolutionary models on other movements. Here, the J.V.P. was condemned for trying to run a revolution their own (mistaken) way. The duty of revolutionaries should have been, rather, to support revolutionaries. Finally, the language used ('chaotic situation') is reminiscent of that condemned by Mao Tse-Tung back in 1926, when he attacked those revolutionaries who said the peasants were 'going too far' and committing 'excesses':

To right a wrong it is necessary to exceed the proper limits ... The opinion that the peasants are 'going too far' is on the surface different from the opinion that the peasant movement is 'an awful mess', but in essence it adheres to the same viewpoint, and is likewise a theory of the landlords which supports the interests of the privileged classes.

Finally, China has offended many on the Left in Europe by endorsing the integration of Europe, which its opponents see as an economic and political strengthening of capitalism at the expense of the separate Labour movements. She is understandably seriously concerned at the Soviet menace on her borders. She is also preoccupied with the very real domination of the world by the two super-powers. Yet the major contradiction is still that between capitalism and communism, and there is too much emphasis in Chinese analysis on the collusion between the super-powers and a relative underplaying of their very real and continuing hostility. The national and particular interests of the Chinese in the survival of China as a State naturally leads them to emphases in their analysis of relations between States that differ from the classic internationalism of Marxist theory. Thus it is true that China categorizes the Market as first and foremost a move by the capitalist countries to step up exploitation of Europe's workers, but this theme is only lightly emphasized, whereas the hope that Europe could become a third super-power, disturbing the two 'contending and colluding' super-powers' 'collusion' to parcel out the world, is at the root of Chinese support for the Market. Nor has Chinese analysis of the causes of 'social imperialism' – which is the label used to describe Soviet society – gone much further than identifying bureaucratization, élitism and inequality as possibilities in Communist societies. To go further would require severe modifications of basic Marxist postulates about the central importance of relationships of ownership and production. Such theoretical problems are therefore not seriously confronted.

I found their ignorance of Cuba – which one man described as a 'bourgeois' revolution – equally disturbing. That particular judgement (though wrong) is perhaps comprehensible in view of China's deep suspicion of any State which identifies closely with the U.S.S.R. But it reflects – at the lowest level – a lack of information that is worrying. It is natural enough for the Chinese to be principally concerned with those countries which affect them most closely: Japan, the countries of Eastern and South-East Asia, the U.S.S.R., the U.S.A., etc. In comparison, Europe is rather remote. But the principal revolutionary country in Latin America should be an object of great concern and interest.

These may be aberrations of Chinese policy. There are also those who see them, however, as symptoms of a deeper disease: that of co-operating with 'national bourgeoisies' of Third World countries, against imperialism and 'social imperialism' (i.e., the U.S.S.R.) to such an extent that criticism of the policies of those governments towards their own people is muted, and exploitation silently tolerated. The temptation is also always there to attempt to make alliances with 'progressive' elements in those governments, rather than relying upon the mobilization of the masses for revolution. In Indonesia the largest pro-Peking Communist Party in the world was butchered through relying on the populist alliance with Sukarno. Too late, they began arming the peasants.

China thus confronts extremely difficult problems, as any revolutionary State must, in knife-edging her way between support for the exploited peoples of the world and necessary co-operation with the very governments that exploit those people when they resist the pressures of the super-powers. It is a situation in which they are bound to make mistakes and to alienate revolutionaries abroad. But there is no reason to assume that China has abandoned her commitment to world socialist revolution.

China's own emergence as a world power (she strongly rejects the use of the label 'super-power' because of the 'big stick' politics that term implies) will, in itself, transform the world. What she has already achieved is extraordinary, and since that achievement includes the evident happiness of her people, the achievement, out of a country steeped in decades of misery, is the more remarkable.

But China's emergence onto the world scene will be accompanied by the growth of other hitherto minor countries. It cannot be long before countries as diverse as Brazil and Australia begin to count for very much more than they have done hitherto, and the translation of the sheer human numbers represented by the populations of India and Indonesia into terms of world political power and influence only awaits the political emancipation of those countries. The era of high imperialism is already receding into the history books, and it did not last long. The next twenty-five years will see an even more rapid transformation of the world.

Anthropology used to be a subject which extended the range of human vision by requiring of us that we look at our own culture as only one of a number of possibilities, primarily by studying tribal societies. Today, the tribes have not long to go. But what was thought of in the Cold War as one enormous monolith – the Communist world dominated by Stalinist orthodoxy and control – has since disintegrated into a set of 'polycentric' Communisms, still importantly influenced by what Moscow thinks and wants, but by no means so automatically or obediently as in the 1950s. In this situation, the moral challenge posed by China both to capitalism and to existing forms of Communist culture is a growing one, and one very different from the experience of Eastern Europe, where Communism arrived with the Red Army. The vision the Russian Revolution represented for an earlier generation has faded in Europe, and we have not yet recovered from the damage that loss wrought to the human spirit. But the vision of an 'alternative reality', which for earlier generations was communicated via the writing of utopias about imaginary socialist worlds, is today embodied in actual societies. The most crucial and gigantic of these actual experiments is that going on in China. Hence it is important to look carefully at it, not to be frightened off by habits induced by lifetimes of cynicism about Communism, and, if it looks good, not to be afraid to say so. Equally important, it is essential for the

Chinese revolution's health to say where it looks less than satisfactory. For me, it has demonstrated that things can indeed be otherwise, that man can be re-socialized, and that the future of the world is by no means necessarily a capitalist one. But it is not inevitably a Communist one either. The world is inevitably nothing; it is only what people make it.

What we might make of revolution in advanced industrialized societies would be something very different from what has happened in China. It is no chauvinist thought, but one that Marx insisted on, that the optimal conditions for socialism were those in the advanced capitalist countries. They would now have to learn from countries which have pioneered socialism like China. But our needs would be very different: not mobilization to raise production by forced-draught methods. Higher production is not the problem in the West: it is one of distributing more equitably the wealth that already exists, and of asserting human scales of value, not those of profit or conspicuous and wasteful consumption. The radical movements of the last decade have shown how quite different kinds of issues preoccupy the West: of the 'quality of life', concern with natural resources, with personal self-expression and variety. These are not simply bourgeois weaknesses, but assets, parts of a cultural heritage that have had to be fought for and defended, lest they be abolished or perverted. Thus the puritanism of revolution in underdeveloped countries, for instance, might never appear at all, and the radical emphasis in Western thought (including Marxist) has been upon sexual emancipation and not upon constraint. Whether such concerns would survive the stress and strain of a truly revolutionary era, which would inevitably be tougher and more polarized than anything we have experienced, one cannot guess. It would be a very different kind of revolutionary culture, and it would not be a revolution of peasants. The lessons to be learnt from China would be at a higher level of abstraction: about principles of organization, about strategy, tactics and theory, and about principles of living, too: above all, about equality, of which we know so little.

*

I had had moments of frustration and not a little irritation. One is not easily moved by impersonal things, even by seeing a whole society in revolution. But 'revolution' and 'society' are abstract labels for the actions of people, and as I crossed the bridge back, it was the memories of people which raced through my mind: the old rickshaw-puller, the young girl who had lost her superstition, the swineherd with a pig named Brezhnev. This time, as the *Internationale* played, because it symbolized them, all the hard work they had done and the friendliness that was everybody's, I could not stop my eyes filling with tears as I walked across the bridge.

I soon knew I was home, for Hong Kong is part of the capitalist world. When a ten-year-old girl badgered me with her tray of chewing-gum, whisky, and Hong Kong newspapers, I thought to myself 'Young lady, two hundred yards away you'd be at school'. It was only after she had gone that I noticed she had cheated me of twenty cents.

APPENDIX

Prices of Some Everyday Goods

Translating the prices of Chinese goods from *yuan* and *fen* ('dollars' and 'cents') into pounds and pence is a misleading procedure. It results, in general, in an *over*-favourable impression of the cost of living in China, for Chinese goods then sound extremely cheap to us. Thus, in terms of international exchange-rates, a country where you can buy a pound of rice for about one penny would sound like heaven to the peasants of Asia. Such basic items, of course, are kept very cheap. An item like meat, on the other hand, is a luxury food in Chinese terms, though to the European 13p for a pound of mutton or pork sounds equally heavenly.

What such equivalents conceal, of course, is that they only tell you what it would cost *us* to buy these items if we had access to the shops of China and could change our money into Chinese money. We generally assume, too, in making that kind of comparison, that we would have our European incomes. But calculations of this sort give no idea of what such prices mean to the citizens of China. It is, to use a Chinese expression, a 'left-wing deviation' simply to translate prices in this way, for it puts a ludicrously positive construction on Chinese prices.

A more 'neutral' way of presenting prices is simply to give them in Chinese money-terms. Table I, for the record (and the possible interest of economists), gives some comparative prices. Note the small variations between one part of the country and another, for basic commodities. We have already commented on the stability of prices over time, since these have not seriously altered for well over a decade: an amazing achievement in the light of current inflation-rates here. The prices given are all for *rural* areas, though, to my surprise, they correspond extremely closely with prices recorded in Peking in December, 1965.

Some of the blanks in Table I were due to local seasonal or other variations in supply; sometimes owing to the incomparability of items locally produced and therefore varying in size, quality, material, etc., and partly because I was single-handed. One becomes fairly adept at converting 'catties per mou' into 'lb. per acre' after a while, Chinese weights and measures being basically metric, whatever the strange names used. (Even such bizarre questions – in response to my asking the price of chickens – as 'with or without feathers?' cease to throw one after a while, for the work involved in 'dressing' chicken, as we would say, is considerable, and the difference in weight also significant.)

Such neutral prices, however, don't tell you what they mean to the Chinese consumer. A more right-wing construction can be put upon prices if one relates them to typical *earnings* of the Chinese worker or peasant, for what may sound like trivial price-differentials to us are serious to someone earning 50–70 *yuan* a month in a factory, or only 300 *yuan* in cash a year in the countryside. Overall, however, food costs in the city for adults probably absorb no more than 15% of income (housing, as we saw, about 4–5%). With basic grains and other produce distributed in kind by the commune, the peasant's limited cash income need only be called upon for other kinds of foods or consumer goods, or may even be saved.

Though being alone was normally a great advantage, it did restrict the volume of information I could record single-handed on occasions. But an eight-man delegation of the Amalgamated Union of Engineering Workers, led by Mr Hugh Scanlon, the union's president, which visited China two months after I did, was able collectively to compile fuller and more systematic price-lists, reproduced here as Table II, and, being trade unionists, made an invaluable 'Comparison of Costs and Time Utilization'. My thanks are due to Mr Scanlon and the Union for permission to reproduce their calculations, and to Mr Victor Spencer of Preston, a member of the delegation, who drew my attention to the Appendix of the Delegation's Report from which the comparisons contained in the table are drawn. (The full report, in instalments, was published in the Union journal in 1973.)

The table is based on estimates of the amount of time a Chinese *skilled engineering* worker needs to work in order to earn enough to buy the items shown, in comparison to his British counterpart, whereas the prices shown in Table I were those obtaining in *rural* areas. British prices, of course, have risen sharply in the meantime. Nevertheless the comparison still bears out the Chinese insistence that, however much the living-standards of the ordinary people of China have improved, China is still a poor country when measured against the West.

I. COMPARATIVE PRICES FOR FOUR COMMUNES

Food Items (per kilo)	Nanking Commune (Tung Jing) yuan cents	Canton Commune (Sha Chao) yuan cents	Shanghai Commune (Tang Wan) yuan cents	Peking Commune (Lu Kou Chiao) yuan cents
rice (top quality)	30	40		43
rice (bottom quality)	26	33	30	30
flour ('good' quality)	48	44	44	37 (one quality only)
flour (medium quality)		34	34	
hens' eggs	1 38	1 60		1 80
sugar		1 40		
groundnut oil	1 28*	1 70		1 70
,, (unrationed)		3 00		
fish		1 80		
chicken		1 68		1 30
duck	2 28	2 40		1 70
mutton		1 42		1 42
pork	1 48			
beef		1 50		1 54
cabbage	04	09		04
apples ,, (top quality		1 40		94
,, (lower ,, quality)		1 00		76

*monthly ration
250 grams @
32 cents

I. COMPARATIVE PRICES FOR FOUR COMMUNES

Non-Food Items	Nanking *yuan cents*	Canton *yuan cents*	Shanghai *yuan cents*	Peking *yuan cents*
1 m. cotton material				
(top quality)	2 82	1 80	2 40	2 28
(bottom quality)	1 40	1 50	2 00	1 27
1 m. silk	4 47		1 50	
1 m. rayon	3 84 (none in stock)		1 78	1 43–1 54
1 m. dacron (top quality)	2 12		1 55 (one quality only)	3 84
(lower quality)	1 89			
1 galvanized bucket			4 07	3 15 (smaller size)
1 pair plastic sandals	2 67–3 76 (according to size)		3 28	3 00
1 pair pumps	4 05–4 53		4 01	4 00–4 50
1 kilo kerosene		76		92 (little used)
1 straw hat		70–1 70 (according to size)		45–65

II. COMPARISON OF COSTS AND TIME UTILIZATION

China

Chinese Worker: 70 yuan per month (1 yuan = 100 cents) 840 yuan
  per year
16 yuan 20 cents per 48-hour week – 34 cents per hour – 0·6 cents
  per minute

Commodity		Price yuan cents		Time worked hours minutes	
Flour	1 lb.		15		25
Tea	,,		91	2	31
Sugar	,,		82	2	22
Salt	,,		10		17
Rice	,,		18		30
Jam (cheap)	,,		36	1	
Jam (dear)	,,		91	2	31
Potatoes	,,		17		28
Carrots	,,		9		15
Cabbage	,,		10		17
Lettuce	,,		9		15
Cauliflower	,,		17		28
Cucumber	,,		8		13
Tomatoes	,,		16		27
Apples	,,		30		50
Chicken	,,	1	47	4	5
Women's Clothes					
Sandals (Canvas)		7		19	26
Shoes		7	13	19	48
Trousers (Cotton)		7		19	26
Jacket (Cotton)		7		19	26
Trousers (Woollen)		25		69	26
Blouse (Cotton)		6		16	36
Men's Clothes					
Sandals (Canvas)		7		19	26
Shoes (Leather)		8/19		22–12/50–54	
Jacket (Cotton)		7		19	26
Trousers (Cotton)		7		19	26
Shirt (Cotton)		7		19	26
Shirt (Silk)		15	90	44	
Singlet		4		11	6
Underpants		2		5	33
Hand Towels (Pair)		6	50	18	
Double Blanket (Standard)		21		58	20

II. COMPARISON OF COSTS AND TIME UTILIZATION

Britain

British Worker: £30 per 40-hour week
75p per hour – 1¼p per minute

Commodity		Price £ p	Time worked hours minutes
Flour	1 lb.	5½	4
Tea	,,	34	27
Sugar	,,	4½	4
Salt	,,	2	2
Rice	,,	6	5
Jam (cheap)	,,	10	8
Jam (dear)	,,	13	10
Potatoes	,,	3	2
Carrots	,,	5	4
Cabbage	,,	5	4
Lettuce	,,	21	17
Cauliflower	,,	10	8
Cucumber	,,	16	13
Tomatoes	,,	15	12
Apples	,,	10	8
Chicken	,,	19	15
Women's Clothes			
Sandals (Canvas)		1 20	1 36
Shoes		6	8
Trousere (Cotton)		3 25	4 20
Jacket (Cotton)		5 50	7 20
Trousers (Woollen)		4	5 20
Blouse (Cotton)		2 99	4
Men's Clothes			
Sandals (Canvas)		1 20	1 36
Shoes (Leather)		6	8
Jacket (Cotton)		4 50	6
Trousers (Cotton)		2 90	3 52
Shirt (Cotton)		1 35	1 48
Shirt (Silk)		11	14 40
Singlet		60	48
Underpants		60	48
Hand Towels (Pair)		1 20	1 36
Double Blanket (Standard)		5 60	7 28

continuation

II. COMPARISON OF COSTS AND TIME UTILIZATION

China

Commodity	Price		Time worked	
	yuan	*cents*	*hours*	*minutes*
Beer (1 pt. bottle)		30	1	23
Brandy ,,	4	50	12	30
Wine (cheap) ,,	1		2	46
Wine (dear) ,,	2	27	6	18
Soft Drink (Schweppes size)		15		25
Cigarettes (20)		15–30		25–50
Tobacco (1 oz.)		20–27		33–45
Boiled Sweets	1	5	2	55
Caramel	2	55	7	5
Ice Lolly (Standard)		4		7
Bicycle	141		339	
Sewing Machine	175		486	6
Transistor Radio	from 60 to 145		from 166 40 to 402 46	
Cycle Licence	2		5	32
Coal (cwt.)	3		8	20
Haircut		35		58
ENTERTAINMENT				
Opera		50	1	23
Cinema		20		33
RENTS				
One Room Flat	5 (per month)		13	20
Peasant Hut	3 (per month)		8	20
Canteen Meal (three course)		20		33
Taxation (man, wife and two children under 16 years of age)	Nil		Nil	
National Insurance Stamp (employee's contribution)	Nil		Nil	

II. COMPARISON OF COSTS AND TIME UTILIZATION

Britain

Commodity	Price		Time worked	
	£	p	hours	minutes
Beer (1 pt. bottle)		12		10
Brandy ,,	3	55	4	44
Wine (cheap) ,,		55		44
Wine (dear) ,,	1	50	2	
Soft Drink (Schweppes size)		10		8
Cigarettes (20)	tipped/plain 20½/31½			16/25
Tobacco (1 oz.)	St Bruno 40½			32
Boiled Sweets		30/35		24/28
Caramel		40		32
Ice Lolly (Standard)		3		2
Bicycle	28	50	38	
Sewing Machine	31	95	42	16
Transistor Radio	from 9 to 30		from 12 to 40	
Cycle Licence	Nil			
Coal (cwt.)	coalite 1	43	1	54
Haircut		30		24

ENTERTAINMENT

Opera	average 1	70	2	36
Cinema	,,	60		48

RENTS

One Room Flat	20	60	27	28
Peasant Hut	(per month inc. of rates)			
Canteen Meal (three course)		25		20
Taxation (man, wife and two children under 16 years of age)	Nil		Nil	
National Insurance Stamp (employee's contribution)	Nil		Nil	

Income – wage £30 per week. Family Allowance – 90p per week. Total Annual Amount – £1,606·80. Total Annual Amount of Tax – £115·48 appoximately.

Employee's weekly flat rate contribution, 88p. In addition, if he has not contracted out of the State Pension Scheme, 4·75% of that amount of his weekly pay which lies between £9 and £48.

For an employee earning £30 a week the contribution to the Pension Scheme is £1·02. This, added to the flat rate contribution of 88p, equals a weekly payment of £1·95, and 2 hours 32 minutes in time worked.

SUGGESTIONS FOR FURTHER READING

Edgar Snow's *Red Star Over China*, written in 1937, still conveys the spirit of the Chinese Revolution better than anything else. The elaborate notes added to the revised Pelican edition of 1972 enhance its value as an historical source. It is compulsive reading, and readability has been a major criterion in selecting the following books. This means that the enormous scholarly literature, especially from the U.S.A., is underrepresented. Accessibility has been a second criterion, and I have preferred, too, accounts based on direct experience of China. Whatever their prejudices, they are free from the distortions bred of rancour and of sheer distance from the subject-matter which vitiate so much of the work of professional China-watchers, and have been selected because they communicate in various ways, not only analysis, but also something of what I, at least, consider to be the 'feel' of the Chinese revolution.

The best general introduction to Chinese history and culture is the first volume of Joseph Needham's *Science and Civilization in China* (Cambridge University Press, 1954), though it naturally stresses Chinese science and technology as heavily as C. P. Fitzgerald's *China: A Short Cultural History* (revised paperback edition, Cresset Press, 1961) emphasizes the arts. An excellent economic history is Mark Elvin's *The Pattern of the Chinese Past* (Eyre Methuen, 1973). We still await a really good general history, though there is a good short account of *Modern China*, by John Robottom (Longman, 1969), written for use in schools.

For the flavour of the culture of the ruling classes in imperial China, the magnificent novel, *The Story of the Stone* (also known as *The Dream of the Red Chamber*), has no equal (Penguin, 1973, first volume only so far). John Gittings' *A Chinese View of China* (B.B.C., 1973) contains excellently-selected passages, including many original texts, particularly on China's relationships with the outside world and the development of revolution. Its 'Facts, Figures and Further Reading', pictures and maps, enhance its value.

Jean Chesneaux's *Peasant Revolts in China, 1840–1949* (Thames and Hudson paperback, 1973) and his equally fascinating *Secret Societies in China in the mid-19th and 20th Centuries* (Heinemann Educational Books, paperback, 1971) show that Confucianism was by no means passively accepted in imperial times (the latter contains excerpts from original documents).

Any self-respecting public library ought to have a copy of the *Encyclopaedia-Guide* to China published by Nagel (Geneva, 1968) in English, even though its one and a half thousand pages don't cover every Chinese city. It also has an authoritative introduction by a team of French scholars on geography, languages, history, religion and philosophy, literature and art, and on contemporary institutions and culture – including cooking. The sixty pages of truly 'practical information', and the sixteen maps and city-plans, are vital for any-one visiting China.

William Hinton's *Fanshen: a Documentary of Revolution in a Chinese Village* (Pelican, 1966) is a classic account, comparable with Snow in first-hand authenticity and vividness, but, in contrast, focused on one village only. Jack Belden's *China Shakes the World* (Pelican, 1973) takes up where Snow left off, and follows the course of the revolution up to Liberation in 1949. Jan Myrdal's *Report From a Chinese Village* (Pelican, 1953) gives a lively and detailed account of one village in the early years of the communes. Keith Buchanan's *The Transformation of the Chinese Earth* (Bell, 1970), by a geographer, is the best single overview of the scope of Chinese development, rural and urban, since 1949. E. L. Wheelwright and Bruce Macfarlane, both economists, examine planning, the role of ideology, and the 'human factor' in development, in *The Chinese Road to Socialism* (Pelican, 1973). Mao's thinking and policy on economic questions, so radically different from both 'bourgeois' and orthodox Communist development theory, is ably expounded in Jack Gray's contribution, 'Mao Tse-Tung's Strategy for the Collectivization of Chinese Agriculture', in E. de Kadt and G. Williams (eds.), *Sociology and Development* (Tavistock Publications, 1974, pp. 39–65). For the 'hard politics' of the Chinese revolution, K. S. Karol's *China: the Other Communism* (Hill and Wang, New York, 1968), written from the point of view of a left-wing journalist brought up in Eastern Europe, is particularly good on the Sino-Soviet ideological controversies lying behind the present confrontation. Han Suyin provides a useful, though totally uncritical, account of how the Chinese see their society, their achievements, and the future, in *China in the Year 2001* (Pelican, 1967).

Anything like a definitive study of the Cultural Revolution has yet to emerge, but valuable insights are provided by William Hinton's *Hundred Days' War: the Cultural Revolution at Tsinghua University* (Monthly Review Press, 1972), though it only deals with one Peking university and leaves many questions unanswered. The general background to this first-hand account of the struggle at its height is presented in John Gardner's 'Educated Youth and Urban-Rural Inequalities, 1958–66', in *The City in Communist China*, ed. John Wilson Lewis (Stanford University Press, 1971, pp. 235–286). Jan Myrdal revisited the village he first lived in in 1963 seven years later to see what the effects of the Cultural Revolution had been there. His report, *China: The Revolution Continued* (Pelican, 1970), contains many splendid photographs by his wife, Gun Kessle. Life in a less 'advanced' village (where marriages are still arranged, for example) is described in a highly personal way by Jack Chen in *A Year in Upper Felicity* (Harrap, 1973). There are, alas, no comparable accounts of post-Cultural Revolution urban/industrial life.

The thought of Mao Tse-Tung is a *sine qua non* for any understanding of the Chinese revolution, whether in the form of his *Selected Works* (4 vols., Foreign Languages Press, Peking), or in the selection by Stuart R. Schram, *The Political Thought of Mao Tse-Tung*, (Pelican, 1969), who also indicates bits omitted or changed in subsequent Chinese editions. (The 'Report of an Investigation into the Peasant Movement in Hunan', which I discuss in Chapter 3, is in vol. 1 of the *Selected Works.*) Finally, the work of a highly-esteemed poet and calligrapher, reflecting his early upbringing at the beginning of this century: *The Poems of Mao Tse-Tung* (Barrie and Jenkins, 1972). The monthly journal, *China Now*, and other publications of the Society for Anglo-Chinese Understanding (24 Warren Street, London WIP 5DG), provide up-to-date information about China, particularly accounts of recent visits.

INDEX

Acupuncture, 67–8, 166–9

Administration, 65, 69–70, 86–7, 130–32, 177–8

Afforestation, 59, 77

Agrarian Reform Law (1947), 122

Agricultural Bank, 147

Agriculture, 67, 72, 74 (*see also* Land reform; Peasants; State Farms)
    capitalist, 134, 204–5
    communes, 73–5, 131–2, 136–7, 141–2, 156–60
    co-operatives, 133–4
    modernization, 137–40, 158–60
    private sector, 75, 132–3, 135, 155–8
    under Empire, 86–7, 96

Aid, Chinese and capitalist, 238–9 (*see also* Soviet Union)

Aircraft industry, 184

Alcohol production, 79

Alienation, 230

Alley, Rewi, 134

Alsop, Joseph, 136–7

Americanization, 41, 43

Amethyst, H.M.S., 30

Anarchists, 232–3

Anshan, 181, 184

Anthropology, Western, 198–9

Apprentices, 228

Art, 61–4, 219

Automobile industry, 184–6

Autumn Harvest Uprising, 115

Balance of power, 245

Ballet, 218–19

Bangkok, 35, 173

Bangla Desh, 17, 244–5

Belden, Jack, 213

Bendix, Reinhard, 206–7

Benn, Anthony Wedgwood, 181

Bianco, Lucien, 97

Bicycles, 75, 185, 191

Boxer Rebellion, 101

Brazil, 195

Bridge-building, 183–4

Britain, 12–13, 30–32, 35–8, 46, 50, 225–6, 229, 233–4, 256–9

Buchanan, Keith, 147–8, 180

Buddhism, 39–41, 87

Buildings, style of, 61

Bureaucracy, 183

Cambodia, 35
Canals, 86, 138–9
Canteens, factory, 82
Cantlie, Dr James, 102
Canton, 59–61, 72, 115, 173–4
Capitalism, 33–4, 91, 226, 230–31
  agriculture under, 134, 204–5
  development under, 195–7, 202–7
  co-operatives and, 134–5
  under-developed countries, 34–9,
    43–7, 50–51, 195–6
Capitalist attitudes in China, 69
Capitalist embargo, 184
Capitalist world, China's impact on,
  239, 249
Caste, 41–2
Castro, Raúl, 236
Cement production, 182
Cemeteries, 77
Centralization, 234–7
Ceylon, see Sri Lanka
Chang Kuo-t'ao, 118
Changsha, 115
Chemical production, 79, 81
Chen Ping, 36
Chen Po-ta, 235
Ch'en Tu-Hsiu, 115
Cheng Ho, 39–40
Chengtu, 180
Chiang Kai-shek, 28, 30, 105, 117, 121,
  172, 191
Chi'en Lung, Emperor, 88
Children's Palace (Shanghai), 168–9
Chile, 196, 208
Ch'in Shih Huang Ti, 85–86, 138
Chou En-Lai, 18, 105, 118, 245
Christianity, 98–9
Chu Teh, 114
Chungking, 180
Cinema, 220–21, 226
Cities, 171–92
  administration, 177–9, 186
  communications, 184–5, 191
  concessions, 101, 171
  construction work, 183–4, 191
  housing, 174–7, 182, 188–90
  industry, 180–83, 185–9
  population, 180, 190
Class system, 16–17, 65–6, 226–7,
  229–31
Co-existence, 18
Cold War, 28–30
Colonialism, 18, 35–9, 41, 43–6, 50,
  60, 171, 195–6
Communes, 125–8, 132, 136, 141
  administration, 130–32, 136
  agriculture in, 73–5, 131–2, 136–7,
    141–2, 156–60

Cultural Revolution in, 130–32, 156
  educated people in, 160–61
  education in, 76, 77, 158, 160–61
  engineering in, 140, 158
  equipment, 160–62
  housing, 77, 142
  incomes, 141–2, 143–55, 158
  industry, 72–5, 155, 182, 189
  inequalities between, 142–3, 147–9
  medical services, 162, 165, 169
  nurseries, 163
  prices in, 252–9
  reorganization of, 199
  size and numbers, 75, 127, 136, 141
  taxation, 145–6
Communism, world, 239, 248
Communist Manifesto, 104
Communist Party, Chinese, 17, 30,
  104, 232
  alliance with Kuomintang, 105–6,
    121
  decision-making, 115–17 (see also
    Mass participation)
  government and, 130–31
  peasants and, 97–8, 110–14, 119–21
Concessions, foreign, 101, 171
Confucianism, 41, 88, 90, 93
Contraception, 163–4
Cooking, 77, 83
Co-operatives, 133–6
Cottage industry, 180, 185
Counter-revolutionaries, 214
Craftsmen, 185
Crime
  China, 214–15, 217
  Hong Kong, 51–2
  Singapore, 42
Criticism, 237
  and reinstatement, 78–9, 216, 236
Crook, D. and I., 133, 143
Cuba, 194, 209, 217–18, 219, 236, 247
Cultural Revolution, 17, 52, 56, 76, 79,
  214–15, 224, 226–7, 234, 236–7
  communes, 130–32, 156
  education, 65
Culture, 40–41
  overseas Chinese, 39–40, 41–2, 44
  past, 75–6, 86–7, 93–5, 221
  revolutionary, 173, 218–22
Customs, 56
Czechoslovakia, 81, 187, 225, 240

Dalai Lama, 242–4
Dances, 62
Deaf-muteness, 167
Debray, Régis, 111–12
Decentralization, 142, 232

Decision-making, 115–17, 200–1, 232, 234–6
Defence, 239–41
Democracy, 231
Democratic centralism, 16–17, 234–7
Democratic League, 198
Denmark, 34
Development
  capitalist world, 195–7, 202–7
  China, 31–3, 38–9, 200, 202, 210
  Communist world, 197–8, 207–9
  Third World, 22, 193–7, 206, 210, 238–9, 248
Diversification, industrial, 79–80
Dockers, 183
Doctors, 'barefoot', 161–3
Dream of the Red Chamber, 78, 91, 93
Dress, 60–61, 224
Drugs, 47, 167–8

East European machinery in China, 81, 187
Economic reconstruction, 56–7
Economic zones, 87
Educated people in countryside, 160–61, 198, 228
Education, 65–8, 92–3, 110, 201–2, 226–8 (*see also* Teachers)
  communes, 76, 77, 158, 160–61
  political, 76, 78, 198, 218, 220, 222, 231, 236
Electricity, 73, 77, 142, 174, 182, 187
Electronics, 79, 181, 185
Elgin, Lord, 99
Elitism, 225, 226–7
Empire, Chinese, 85–102
Engels, F., 128
Engineering, 181, 182
  communes, 140, 158
  'do-it-yourself', 81, 140
English, teaching of, 68–9
Entertainments, 62, 78, 218–19
Epstein, Israel, 114
Equality, 120, 228–9, 232 (*see also* Communes, inequalities between)
Ethnic divisiveness, 40–41
European culture, 33
European Economic Community, 12, 246–7
Exhibitions, 62–4
Expeditions abroad, 39–40, 89

Factories, 72–5, 78–82, 187–9 (*see also* Industry)
  managers of, 78
  multi-purpose, 79

Families
  incomes, 153–4, 157, 175
  size, 76, 82, 164
Family-planning, 163–4
Fei Hsiao-Tung, 144, 198–200
Fertilizers, 137–8
Feudalism, 86, 90–91
Fish-farming, 73–4
'Five guarantees', 146
Five-Year Plans, 180
Food, 86
  prices, 83, 157, 229, 252–9
Ford, Robert, 244
Foreign policy, 238–9, 244–9
Foreign trade, 45–6, 88–9, 187–8
Foshan, 72
France, 16–17, 208
Frank, A. G., 196
Furniture, 82–3, 177

Gangsters, 51
Geddes, W. R., 144
George III, 88
Gordon, General, 99
Gouldner, Alvin, 19
Grain reserves, 149, 159
Great Leap Forward, 57, 66, 73, 132, 140, 200, 224
Great Wall, 85–6
Green Revolution, 204
Group discussion, 216–17
Guerilla warfare, 111–12, 114–15
Guevara, Che, 111
Guides, 61
Guillain, Robert, 172

Hail, W. J., 100
Hair styles, 60–61
Hall, Stuart, 233
Han dynasty, 86
Hangchow, 190
Heart operations, 168
Heroes of the Marshes (*Water Margin, All Men Are Brothers*), 90, 94
Hierarchy, 88, 90–91
Hinduism, 40–41
Hinton, William, 121
Hippies, 233
History, teaching of, 71
Holidays, 71
Honesty, 72
Hong Kong, 39, 43–54, 173, 176, 224, 250
  return to China, 46, 52–3
Hospitals, 158, 162, 165–8, 228

Housing, 190
  communes, 77, 142
  factory, 82, 188–9
  Hong Kong, 47–50, 176
  Shanghai, 174–7, 182, 188–90
'Hundred Flowers' period, 198
Hung Hsiu-Chüan, 98
Hungary, 225, 240

Imperial City, 88
Imperialism, 32–3, 39, 59–60, 248
Incentives, 63–4, 74, 140, 150, 152, 225
Incomes (see also Salaries; Wages)
  communes, 141–2, 143–55, 158
  family, 153–4, 157, 175
India, 33, 175, 201, 244–5, 247–8
  1962 war with China, 240
Individualism, 223–4, 231
Indonesia, 247–8
Industry, 62–4, 180–89 (see also
  Factories)
  in communes, 72–5, 155, 182, 189
Interest, bank, 77
Interpreters, 21, 56, 62
Irrigation, 73, 86, 138–9
Isolationism, 27–8, 40, 88–9
Italy, 208

Japan
  economic affairs, 39, 45, 187, 194, 197
  occupation of China, 44–5, 72–3, 100, 121, 212, 214
  occupation of Hong Kong, 44, 52
Jenkins, Robin, 195
Johnson, Chalmers, 119
Judicial system, 214

Kao Pin-ying, 131
Karol, K. S., 148, 188
Khamba tribe, 243
Khrushchev, N., 128, 225
Kiang Men, 77–83
Kiangsi, 115
Kindergarten, 76
Korea
  North, 94
  South, 38, 175
  War, 30, 57, 239–40
Krahl, Hans-Jürgen, 208
Kuala Lumpur, 35–6, 38
Kuomintang, 97, 104–5
  allied with Communists, 105–6, 121
  campaign against Communists, 117–18, 121, 212, 214
Kuwait, 197

Kwangtung, 58, 76, 155
  Teachers' Training Institute, 64–71, 228

Labour Party, British, 13
Lanchow, 180
Land reform, 119–20, 122, 132, 136
Landlords, 119–20, 121–2
Laos, 35
Lattimore, Owen, 14, 28
Leadership, 234–6
Lenin, V. I., 211–12, 236–7
Leninism, 17
Li Ta-Chao, 103–104, 105, 213
Lin Piao, 21, 118, 121, 235, 236
Lin Tse-Hsu, 59
Lipset, S. M., 206
Literature, 78, 90, 219–20
Liu Shao-Ch'i, 66, 74, 76, 130, 221
Living standards, 64
Loans, 77, 147
Locomotives, 184
Long March, 37, 118–19

Macao, 52
Macartney, Lord, 88, 95
Macchiochi, M. A., 173–4
Machinery, 80–81, 137, 140, 159–60, 187
Malaysia, 35–9
Manchu dynasty, 98–100
Mao Tse-Tung, 28, 90, 102–4, 114–15, 118, 120, 127–8, 192, 218, 221, 239–41
  succession problem, 234–5
  writings of, 103–4, 106–10, 200–2, 213, 217, 219, 246
Maosim, 18, 63–4
Marchisio, Hélène, 145, 154
Marketing zones, 127, 199
Marx, Karl, 128–9, 230–231
Marxism, 17–18, 103, 207–12, 225, 230
Mass participation, 200–1, 232, 234–6
Maugham, Somerset, 35–6
Maxwell, Neville, 240
May 4th Movement, 104
Medical services, 162, 165–9
Medicines, manufacture of, 73
Middle Kingdom, 88
Military intervention abroad, 239–43
Militia, 236, 241
Ming dynasty, 39–40, 89
Ming tombs, excavation of, 222
Minorities, 62, 87, 100, 181, 199, 242
Missions abroad, 89
Modernization, 193–4
  agricultural, 137–40, 158–60

Morocco, 34
Museums, 61, 175, 222, 226
Music, 219
Myrdal, Gunnar, 206
Myrdal, Jan, 143, 216

Nabarro, Sir Gerald, 232
Nagel: *Encyclopaedia-Guide*, 27–8
Nanking, 99, 183, 191
National Minorities Institute, 199
Nationalism, 38, 41
Natural disasters, 57–8, 136, 159
Needham, Joseph, 139
Nghe, Nguyen, 208
Nixon, Richard, 23
Nomadic invasions, 87
North China, 86–7
Nuclear war, 239–41
Nurseries, 163

Officials, imperial, 90, 92–4
Opera, 62, 218–19
Opium, 59
Overseas Chinese, 36–9, 41–3, 53

Pakistan, 17, 244, 245
Paper production, 79, 80
Paris Commune, 127–8
Peasants, 103–4 (*see also* Agriculture; Communes; Land reform)
    classification, 69, 107–8
    communism and, 97–8, 110–14, 119–21
    discontent, 87, 111
    incomes, 148–58
    Mao on, 106–13
    revolts by, 87, 95–102, 106, 122
Peking, 89, 101, 147, 174, 182, 191–2
Penal sanctions, 214–15
P'eng Teh-huai, 118
People's Liberation Army (P.L.A.), 172–3, 175 (*see also* Red Army)
Personality cult, 221
Petroleum, 181
Photography, restrictions on, 58
Pig production, 157, 161
Polish equipment in China, 81
Political
    campaigns, 57–8, 224, 236
    consciousness, 69, 182–3, 188, 231
    education, 76, 78, 198, 218, 220, 222, 231, 236
    reorganization, 57
    textbooks, 71
Politics
    socialist, 116–17
    teaching and, 68–9

Pollution control, 61–2
Polo, Marco, 190
Population, 87, 96, 163–4, 180–81, 190
Populism, 231, 233
Powell, Enoch, 12
Power generators, 81
Praxis, 115, 117
Pregnancy, premarital, 164–5
Prices, 253–60
Production Brigades, 73, 75, 133, 143, 148
Production Teams, 73, 145, 149, 155
Prostitution, 15, 35, 41–2, 51–2, 172–3
Pu Yi, Emperor, 100
Puritanism, Chinese, 223

Radio, 82
Rahman, Tengku Abdul, 38
Railways, 58, 184
Red Army, 111–112, 114–15, 117–19 (*see also* People's Liberation Army)
Red Guards, 215–16
Red Spears secret society, 104
Refugees in Hong Kong, 44–5, 216
Rehabilitation, 78–9, 214–16, 236
Religions of China, 41, 103–4, 213
Rents, 83, 175, 229, 258–9
Research, 199–201
Retirement, 179
Revisionism, 66, 74, 76
Revolts, 87, 90, 95–6, 98–102
Revolution, 16, 71, 207, 210–12, 249
    capitalist world, 249
    Chinese, 18–20, 22, 31–3, 57, 101–102, 114–15, 209, 211, 212–14, 248–9 (*see also* Cultural Revolution)
    peasants and, 97–8, 110–14, 119–22
    Russian, 16–18, 32, 211–12, 248
    under-developed countries, 20, 125–6, 207, 211, 238
Ricci, Matteo, 40
Rich and poor countries, 195–6
Right opportunism, 245
River control, 86, 138, 159
Road transport, 60, 72, 83, 184–5, 191
Romance of the Three Kingdoms, 87, 90
Rostow, Walt, 206

Salaries, 70, 228–9
Sanitation, 83
Savings, 77
Science, teaching of, 65–8
Scientists, 182
Seasonal labour, 79–80
Secret societies, 95–6, 104, 172
Sex 223–4

Sha Chao Commune, 72–7
Shanghai, 171–7, 183, 186–7, 189–90
Shensi, 118, 119
Shenyang, 181
Shops, 60, 75, 162, 174
Sian, 180, 190
Silk production, 74–5
Singapore, 38–9, 41–3, 46, 48, 52
Sinkiang, 181
Skinner, G. W., 126–7, 199
Snow, Edgar, 22, 111, 239
Social inventions, 125
Social mobility, 189
Social status, 229
Social system, imperial, 88, 90–91
Social values, 65–6, 129–30, 229–31
Social welfare, 217
  communes, 146–7, 152–3
  Hong Kong, 47
  women and, 179
Socialism, 125, 128–9, 231–2
Socialist realism, 61, 63
South China, 86–7
Soviet Union, 15–17, 20, 195, 197,
    208–209, 226–7, 240–41, 244, 247
  aid to China, 105, 161, 187–8, 225
  withdrawal of, 58, 136, 184
  Communist Party, 211–12
Spiritism, 215
Sports, 62
Sri Lanka, 17, 41, 201, 245
Stalin, 17, 212–13
Starvation, pre-Liberation, 82
State Farms, 150
Statistics, 158–9, 163
Steel industry, 181
Sterling area, 46
Sugar, 78–82
Sun Yat-Sen, 101–2, 104–5
Surgery, 167–8
Szechwan, 87

Tachai, 142
Taiping Rebellion, 98–100
Taiwan, 30, 38, 100, 244
  recovery by China, 52
Tamils in Malaysia, 37–8, 40
Taoism, 41, 87
Tawney, R. H., 95
Taxation, 92, 119–20, 145–7
Teachers' training, 64–71, 228
Technicians, 182
Telephones, 184
Television, 184–5
Textile industry, 181, 187
Thailand, 34–5, 41

Thomas, Lowell, 243
Thornburg, Max, 243
Tibet, 181, 241–4
Tientsin, 186, 189
Tractor, walking, 159–60
Trotsky, Leon, 16
Tz'u Hsi, Empress, 100–1

Ultra-leftism, 18, 227–8, 245
Under-developed countries
  co-operatives, 134–5
  development, 20, 22, 193–7, 206,
    210, 238–9, 248
  revolution, 20, 125–6, 207, 211, 238
United States of America, 28, 30, 35,
    45, 185, 206, 229, 232–3, 240
    243–4
Universities, 201–2, 220, 227–8
Urbanization, 186–7, 189–90

Vietnam, 113, 194
  War, 35, 43, 58, 206, 233, 239–40
Village forts, 59, 76
Villages, 75, 126–7, 133

Wages, 70, 74, 76–7, 82, 155, 175, 180,
    228–9
  in agriculture, 75, 148–55
  in kind, 149, 153–5
Waley, Arthur, 29
Wang Hung-wen, 234, 236
Waste raw materials, utilization of,
    79–80
Weber, Max, 135
Western attitudes to China, 12–15,
    17–19, 29–30, 98–101, 126, 132
Westernization, 41, 43, 53, 100
Wilson, Harold, 159–60
Wolf, Eric, 126
Women's status, 178–80, 237–8
Working standards, 58, 70
World War II, 30
World War III, 239–40

Yahya Khan, 244–5
Yangtse Valley, 87, 159, 183
Yeast production, 81
Yellow River, 138
Yenan, 121
Yglesias, José, 217
'Young Marshal', 117, 121
Yuan, 55
Yuan Shih-K'ai, 105
Yung Lo, Emperor, 89
Yunnan, 87, 244

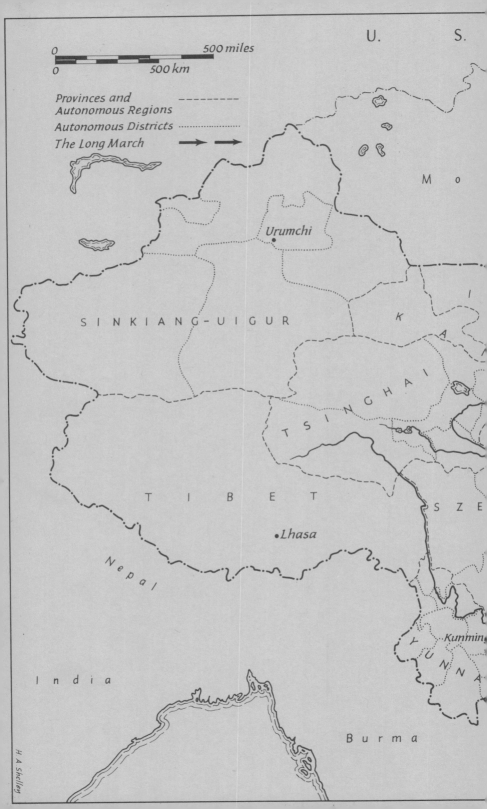